Margaret Fell and the End of Time

# Margaret Fell and the End of Time
The Theology of the Mother of Quakerism

*Sally Bruyneel*

BAYLOR UNIVERSITY PRESS

© 2010 by Baylor University Press
Waco, Texas 76798-7363

*All Rights Reserved.* No part of this publication may be reproduced, stored in a retrieval system, or transmitted, in any form or by any means, electronic, mechanical, photocopying, recording or otherwise, without the prior permission in writing of Baylor University Press.

*Cover Design* by Pamela Poll
*Cover image*: *The Peaceable Kingdom, c.* 1840–1845 (see also 480) by Hicks, Edward (1780–1849) Brooklyn Museum of Art, New York, USA / The Bridgeman Art Library. Nationality / copyright status: American / out of copyright

BX
7795
.F425
B78
2010

Library of Congress Cataloging-in-Publication Data

Bruyneel, Sally.
 Margaret Fell and the end of time : the theology of the mother of Quakerism / Sally Bruyneel.
   p. cm.
 Includes bibliographical references and index.
 ISBN 978-1-60258-062-6 (cloth : alk. paper)
 1. Fell, Margaret, 1614-1702. 2. Society of Friends--Doctrines. 3. Eschatology. I. Title.
 BX7795.F425B78 2009
 289.6092--dc22
                                        2009027658

Printed in the United States of America on acid-free paper.

To my husband, Alan

Because . . .

# Contents

| | | |
|---|---|---|
| Abbreviations | | ix |
| Acknowledgments | | xi |
| Introduction | | 1 |
| 1 | Margaret Fell: An Overview of Her Life and Work | 21 |
| 2 | A Measure of the Times | 57 |
| 3 | The Kingdom of Light: Margaret Fell's Theology and Eschatology | 77 |
| 4 | A Salutation to the Seed of Abraham: Margaret Fell, Quaker Evangelism, and the Jews | 119 |
| 5 | Living in the Last Days: Women's Equality and Peace Testimony | 141 |
| Concluding Remarks | | 163 |
| Notes | | 169 |
| Bibliography | | 199 |
| Scripture Index | | 209 |
| Index of Names | | 210 |
| Index of Doctrine | | 214 |

# Abbreviations

| | |
|---|---|
| Letters | *Undaunted Zeal: The Letters of Margaret Fell*, ed. Glines |
| *Spence MSS* | Spence manuscripts |
| Wallace | Margaret Fell, *A Sincere and Constant Love*, ed. Wallace |
| Works | Margaret Fell, *A Brief Collection of Remarkable Passages* . . . (1710) |

Full citations for these and all works cited herein are found in the bibliography.

# Acknowledgments

This work would have been impossible without the support of the theology department at the University of Durham, its excellent library, and especially my esteemed supervisor Professor Ann Loads (now emerita). Several libraries in England and North America kindly allowed me access to manuscript materials, including the Friends House Library, London, and Woodbrooke College in the United Kingdom, as well as the Friends Center of Azusa Pacific University, Swarthmore College, Haverford College, and Pendle Hill in the United States. I am grateful to these institutions and their friendly staff who made my time there pleasant as well as fruitful. I am also very grateful to David Brown and Ben Pink Dandelion for reading this entire work, making several suggestions for improvement and encouraging me to publish it. Though many in the wider circle of Friends have helped me learn the language of Quakerism and make it my own, there are some whose help with reading, support, and ideas have been essential to this particular project finding the light of day. Included in this group are Elsa F. Glines, whose own work on original Fell manuscripts has energized scholarship, and Douglas Gwyn, Ben Pink Dandelion, Gayle Beebe, Jane Orion Smith, Raquel Wood, Friends Meetings in Saint Paul (Minnesota), Donna Martinson, Ashanti Austin, my father (and diligent proofreader) Roy Bruyneel, and my beloved husband Alan Padgett. He is the model of scholarship to which I aspire. Finally, it is always good to work with quality people, and the editorial staff at Baylor University Press is excellent. Carey Newman in particular has been very supportive of this project, for which I am ever grateful. Any shortcomings that remain are my own.

# Introduction

For those who savor history, early Quakers provide a dynamic challenge to the palette. This Christian movement, later to be known as the Religious Society of Friends, was a passionate wrestling between the rigors of religious self-discipline and the onus of apocalyptic prophecy. At the center of this often ecstatic tension was Margaret Askew Fell Fox (1614–1702), a woman destined to light fires of indignation in the religious establishment of her day. Known generally as Margaret Fell, she was equal parts warhorse and workhorse, and her home at Swarthmoor Hall in northern England became the center of gravity for Quakerism in its infancy. There she came into the fullness of her power during a time of intense social upheaval, working as organizer, leader, and lay theologian as the country descended into civil war and then regicide. The deposition and beheading of Charles I, in turn, beckoned the Interregnum and the social experiment represented by Oliver Cromwell and the period of the English Protectorate. Against this backdrop, where political tide turned on tide, the religious and political fortunes of Quakers experienced their own ebbs and flows. One of the original adherents to the nascent movement, Margaret Fell was numbered among the "First Generation of Friends" who experienced the inward revelation that fired and fueled early Quakerism. At the core were the "valiant sixty" who coalesced in leadership around founding member George Fox and proclaimed a unique millenarian vision for Christ's triumphant returning in the flesh. For this they paid dearly in loss of liberty, property, and life under some of the most appalling circumstances imaginable.

Of these first soldiers in what they called "the Lamb's War," George Fox and his early protégée Margaret Fell were remarkable in their very survival.

The fervor with which Quakers proclaimed their often apocalyptic and antinomian gospel frightened, alarmed, and angered many, and within a decade the early leadership of this religious movement would be decimated by England and her people. This ecclesial tragedy secured the historical precedence of Fox and Fell in the story of Quakerism, and theirs became the dominant voice in the rescue and reorganization of the battered Society of Friends.[1] In a regrettable twist, the role of Margaret Fell and her material and intellectual contributions to the survival of the Friends would itself quickly be eclipsed by the mythology of George Fox as sole founder of the movement. The scarce representation she would later receive in print was attached to her eventual marriage to a lionized George Fox and drew upon the comforting image of a matron who offered spiritual encouragement and a warm hearth to the much put-upon first generation of Friends. But when attended to, archival information presents a different and much more dynamic portrait of Fell and her influence upon their fate and direction.

Current scholarly inquiry takes place at a time when older hagiographic and one-dimensional portraits of Margaret Fell are falling by the wayside. The thumbnail sketch of Margaret as protecting mother of the Quaker hearth and wife to founder George Fox has been replaced by a newer, more socially and historically conscious model. She is no longer just an historical footnote to the halcyon days of early Quakerism, but an increasingly valued part of the Friends' religious heritage. Equally significant for the present moment in scholarship, contemporary work in areas such as women's studies has explored her ample catalog of extant writings. This has provided a wealth of information as well as a sense of historical solidity that must come as a relief to scholars charged with integrating "herstory" and history. Margaret Fell's status is squarely conferred by her historic and sizeable contribution to Friends' theology and polity and she is as worthy of reverence as any iconic figure in the English Reformation. This claim is solemnized by the fact that in her position as the wife of a judge, as well as a land-owning minor aristocrat in her own right, she was uniquely poised to lose more than others in the Society of Friends. Fortunately for us, her true importance as a religious reformer and theologian is now being recovered by the current generation of scholars, as is that of her contemporaries such as James Nayler and even George Fox himself.

Although her importance has been underappreciated by succeeding generations, those who crossed paths with Fell in her own time were left with no doubt that she was a force to be reckoned with. Her commitment to Quaker beliefs and their expression in her religious convictions provoked some to wild fury, and there is no doubt she suffered for being caught in a defining moment of religious history. Her firebrand ways made her the subject of disapproval and castigation by her fellow aristocrats and cost her the love and loyalty of her only son. But she was swept up by a higher power into the heart of a religious movement pulsing with raw energy and a new vision for humanity. Her hope in a risen Christ now poised to return in emerging glory led her to pursue God's kingdom with unvarnished commitment. From the outset of her "convincement" (the preferred Friends term for conversion to a Quaker understanding of salvation), Margaret was committed to living out the egalitarian model established on the idea of Christ's presence in the conscience of each individual. As Fox's most illustrious early convert, her humility and deference to Friends of lower social and political status were sources of discussion and generated either dismay or affirmation depending on one's opinion of Quakers.

Although Fell's behavior was altered by her convincement experience with George Fox, she already possessed a theologically adept, mature, and reflective mind before she ever encountered the man and his teachings. Certainly the Jesus of the Gospels was already a model for action. In the same way, many of her theological views developed in the context of the Christian Old and New Testaments and preceded her first meeting with Fox. Her conversance with Scripture had already been established and shaped by her years as a devoutly spiritual woman who spent her free time questioning religious dogma. What can be said is that she spent her own troubled times in spiritual wilderness where questions about the church had pushed her to inward seeking, even though she continued to attend local worship in her role as wife of Thomas Fell, Lord of Ulverston Manor. Likewise it is certain that once she heard the message of George Fox she considered herself to have found some definitive and transformative truth about Christ. Her first encounter with Fox's preaching made her willing to use her personal authority and social resources to protect the Quakers from their enemies. From that point onward, Fell willingly poured herself out as a sacrifice for others in the cause of the Inward Light that is Christ. Fell's social status also gave her access to court and royalty, which she exploited to dizzying fullness in service to Quakerism.

### Existing Work on Margaret Fell

In the face of her influence it is important to bear in mind that Margaret Fell paid a steadily increasing personal cost for her views. To the extent that she both shaped history as a Quaker and made history as a woman, her various religious and political efforts are worth the good intentions already extended her by capable scholars. Likewise she continues to merit the closest examination possible. A first-year student of mine once commented, "How do historians manage to keep so busy when most of the people they write about have been dead for a very long time? They're dead. It's not like they've done something new lately." In the case of Margaret Fell the problem is not that she has died, but that historians generally have taken no notice of the fact that she ever lived. That time of relative neglect has permanently been put to rest, thanks to modern scholarly efforts within the academy and in print. The richness and diversity that began to accumulate in the twentieth century is a cause to rejoice and presents a model of irenic creativity. At the same time, the wealth of new contributions also brings its own uneven biases, and these in turn challenge us with the question of how best to honor her historical legacy? This is a natural, transitory, and healthy state of affairs appropriately addressed by the continued critical study of her work. It is vastly superior to the earlier malnourishment. At the time of my initial research nearly twenty years ago, there was little in print on Fell outside of a few standard works on Friends history and a biography which was exemplary though dated. Even more perplexing was the fact that Quaker communities showed little awareness of her in even the most general sense.

In what was largely a biographical undertaking, this work began with an attempt to produce a more accurate and nuanced portrait of the so-called "nursing mother of Quakerism." However, early in a research effort on Margaret Fell it became clear that this unplowed field in scholarship had a larger importance. Older secondary resources gave her only occasional mention, and in newer works her contribution was noted and generally remarked upon, but the task of producing more concentrated scholarship was left to later writers. With regard to primary sources, there was little beyond the work of Isabel Ross and earlier undernourished discussions of Mother Fell. Though it was frustrating at the time, it proved a blessing of an unwelcome but beneficial sort. It became necessary in a real sense to spend a great deal of time delving into her own writings, many of which were unpublished or in rare-book collections scattered across the United Kingdom and the United States. Thus my conception of her sprang largely from reading her own communications, both public and private. Time spent with nothing but this woman's own words definitely forced many of the preconceptions I had into the rubbish.

By the time publications by scholars such as Christine Trevett, Bonnelyn Kunze, Kate Peters, and Phyllis Mack began appearing, much of my initial effort in biography was unnecessary. At the same time, there were still areas of Margaret's life and thought that even these fine efforts had not had the opportunity to address, with the result that the research now before you was undertaken in earnest. In the long run, what remains most lacking in the overall presentation on Margaret Fell is more theological study of her work, and in particular the connection between her eschatological beliefs and her larger life and ministry. Equally, although it seems counterintuitive from the perspective of biography, her work with the Society of Friends drew nearly as much from her marriage to Thomas Fell as it did from her life with Quaker founder George Fox. Given what is known of Margaret's own writings, by the time she met Fox she was a mature and middle-aged adult fully in command of her social environment. Though she had doubts of a spiritual nature at the time of her convincement, she was soon writing a great deal on behalf of early Friends and their views. Her first works indicate a strong will and an independent, forceful confidence in her ability to express and defend Quaker beliefs along theological lines. But whatever her natural inclination toward religious reflection and introspection might have been, she was only a young woman of eighteen at the time of her first marriage.

Margaret was a recent widow nearing fifty by the time she reached her zenith in terms of personal freedom and religious activity. It would be longer still until she married George. It therefore seems highly unlikely that nearly thirty years of marriage to Thomas—a highly respected barrister, judge, and Member of Parliament—would have had no influence on how she conceptualized her symbolic universe. Because of observations along these lines, this book will look to Margaret Fell's eschatological beliefs as they influenced her overall theology. This will move forward with an eye toward social location where it enriches or expands our reading of her religious writings. The example of Margaret Fell and her first marriage to Judge Fell is instructive as an indication of how such an emphasis can be useful. By attending more closely to their relationship, the reader will gain insight into several aspects of Margaret's life and work. Thus illumined, it is possible to more accurately assess her value and significance to early Quakerism by recognizing the high social status and prerogative that was hers both by birth and by marriage. Correspondingly, this assists in accounting for the familiarity with legal writs and processes evidenced in Margaret's letters to Friends and to those in positions of secular authority. For example, in her letters to the Lord Protector, the King, judges, magistrates, and Members of

Parliament, she made regular reference to the abuses of local authorities in their improper use of warrants, search, seizure, arrest, and imprisonment against Quakers. It is plain that she understood what was due under the law and that she viewed this evidence of their disregard for the rights and liberties due English citizens as an indictment of their character. This illustration is one of many in which the study of Margaret Fell as an organizer, leader, and lay theologian benefits from evaluating her contributions within a personal context.

This appreciation for both biography and theology contributes to the unfolding body of information about Fell by treating her seriously as a person as well as a theologian and religious activist. Coming alongside important newer explorations of Friends history and theology, such as H. Larry Ingle's *First Among Friends: George Fox and the Creation of Quakerism*, emphasis will be placed on the origins of the Society of Friends. While it is valuable in any study of her life and thought to place Margaret Fell in her social and historical context, it is desirable to give her work careful theological consideration. It is advantageous and at times essential to think in both historical and theological terms when sifting through the Christian history. At the same time, my own formative spiritual upbringing did not occur within the Society of Friends. To address this, I have spent a good deal of time absorbing the work and methodology of contemporary Quaker scholars whose efforts reflect a passion for excellence and a respect for theological and historical nuance. Of these, Douglas Gwyn has emerged as an example of all a scholar should be, and his written contributions are always remarkable in some way or another. Here I would cite his *Seekers Found: Atonement in Early Quaker Experience*. This was supplemented recently with Elsa F. Glines' miracle of research, *Undaunted Zeal: The Letters of Margaret Fell*.

Through this combination of lenses, Margaret Fell and the early Friends come into focus. Because her written efforts were often prompted by particular instances of religious or political threat against Quakers, her work can appear simultaneously disjointed and repetitive. Consistently though, and regardless of content, Margaret wrote from a Quaker perspective at a time when the social, political, and religious threads of English life constituted one inseparable cord. Upon closer inspection, it is apparent that underlying theological commitments do in fact flow through her work, and these coalesce around a Christ-centered eschatology that is essential to understanding and interpreting her religious thought and action. When viewed through the lens of her realized eschatology, one in which Christ had already returned in the Spirit to the hearts and minds of his true followers and was thus "realized" in the flesh, we see an underlying unity to her efforts in apologetics and evangelization. This then provides a further key to her work for freedom of conscience in worship, the equality of women, the mission to the Jews, and her peace testimony.

Though not all efforts to convey Margaret Fell's contribution to religious history are equally effective, they all have value wherever they kept her name alive. At the very least they have acted as placeholders, keeping her name in the historical record when others had long forgotten. For the historian, even an artifact which represents an intentional misrepresentation has value in attempting to understand an event or person. With that in mind, it is useful to note that prior publications on Fell generally sort themselves into one of three camps. First, there are works that treat of her as "the Mother of Quakerism" and the wife of George Fox. These texts are appreciative and at times affectionate works by Quakers which employ only the most rudimentary documentation or bibliography and oftentimes border on hagiography. However, due to the limited number of publications that focus directly upon Fell, they still remain significant. In *The Life of Margaret Fox*, American Quakers published a short treatment of Margaret Fell owing to the fact that "her works having long been out of print, and almost unknown in this country."[2] The biography reconstructs the story of Margaret Fell from sources including her own epistles and autobiographical materials, as well as the journal of George Fox and correspondence from others in the Society of Friends. Maria Webb published a study of the Fell family in which she loosely moored Fell in her historical, genealogical, and social context. In what became a pattern for other works on the subject, she did this by providing an overview of Fell's life, ministry, and relationship with Fox.[3]

Still treating Fell as one who assisted and encouraged the founders of Quakerism and as the wife of Fox, Helen G. Crosfield published *Margaret Fox of Swarthmoor Hall* in 1913. This book focuses more specifically upon Margaret, but still shows keen interest in Swarthmoor Hall itself as the physical home of early Quaker organization and mission.[4] As mentioned elsewhere, these works are significant in a scholarly sense primarily because there is so little written about Mother Fell over the long term. Each effort is sincere and helpful, but relies primarily upon the biographical information available in Fell's own brief autobiographical recollections and material found in the journals of George Fox. Although these works kept the name of Margaret Fell alive in Quaker memory, they also served to embed the received perception of her as nurturer of Friends and helpmate to Fox. The best of the Quaker books in this genre is the most recent one *Margaret Fell: Mother of Quakerism* by Isabel Ross. This is the first of the modern scholarly works about our subject. A distant descendant of Margaret, Ross also lived for five years in Swarthmoor Hall, the longtime home of Margaret Fell and center of Quaker activities in the north of England throughout much of the seventeenth century.

Given the dismal state of research on Fell at the time, Ross' work is an extremely conscientious piece of scholarship, and the treatment is a bridge between the earlier hagiographic material on Fell and later, more critical studies of her contributions. In a manner similar to Crosfield's, Ross affirms and embraces the older view of Quakerism "founded and nurtured by a man and a woman in sympathetic partnership." She too devotes study to the Swarthmoor Hall account books for insights into the economic and social conditions in which Margaret Fell and the Quakers went about their work in northern England. In many ways the work of Ross, like that of Helen Crosfield before her, seems empowered by the solid physical and meta-physical "weight" of Swarthmoor evidenced in the account books. Both women seem to have encountered there the forgotten dynamo, Margaret Fell, who walked the very real Swarthmoor Hall. There is no doubt that Isabel Ross demonstrates a discernable appreciation, bordering on affection, in her approach to Margaret Fell. In light of material previously available on the "nursing mother of Quakerism," the Ross work organizes and contributes significantly to the body of information about Margaret Fell.

Read against the backdrop of other Quaker histories published prior to this, Ross' work represents an evolutionary step forward in Fell scholarship. Ross approaches the life of Margaret Fell topically, working within each topic chronologically. She sets the stage for her work with introductory material on Swarthmoor Hall as it was during Fell's residence there. As with Crosfield, this includes a recitation of the scant information obtainable on Margaret's early life, as well as the oft-rehearsed account of George Fox's first visit to the Fell household. Fortunately, Ross' appreciation for her subject pushes her beyond the well-traveled stories of early Quakerism to Fell's extended family and life in and around Swarthmoor Hall. From her unlimited access to the Swarthmoor household account books of Sarah Fell, Ross brings scholarly inspiration and insight to the study of the social context of her subject. Ross includes the seven Fell daughters in her discussion of their mother's life, work, and contribution, "not only because the seven daughters were themselves women of character and achievements on their own account, but also because of their illuminating relationship with their mother."[5]

Perhaps because of her residence in the Hall during her writing, Ross manages to convey the vibrant, sometimes hectic level of activity common to a manor the size of Swarthmoor. This adds to the development of Fell scholarship, in part because it conveys the dynamic nature of early Quakerism and Margaret's central position of power and authority in the north. However, her scholarship never sheds its haloed perspective on the Fell women, and it is through this lens that she approaches early Quaker history. For this reason, Ross' treatment of significant events such as the imprisonments of Margaret Fell and of the disgraced Quaker James Nayler do nothing to challenge the received tradition of the early Society of Friends. For example, she portrays Nayler as the much-loved man of promise taken to the bosom of early Friends, who is nonetheless swayed by the praise of a few sycophants, leading him to abandon truth and bring shame and suffering on the Quakers. This caricature of the "Nayler affair" goes unchallenged and unexplored by Ross. Despite this, she does manage to introduce a sense of historical and social context into her narrative of these events. She likewise invigorates her scholarship with broad appeal to published and unpublished correspondence between the early Friends. This is a part of the evolution previously mentioned.

A second type of scholarship about Margaret Fell comes from the broad intellectual interest in women's history. In this approach, the authors look at Fell's social activity and radical ideas, and they focus on the sociopolitical dimensions of her life. A good example of this kind of work is the recent book by Rebecca Larson, *Daughters of Light: Quaker Women Preaching and Prophesying in the Colonies and Abroad 1700–1775*, which begins its study of women in Quakerism with a chapter on Fell. What such works provide is an important perspective from which to view Fell's life and work, one unconfined by denominational concerns or prejudices. Here, Margaret Fell is not merely an inspirational minor player within the larger story of the establishment of the Society of Friends. Placed in a different meta-narrative—one more concerned with understanding and recovering the power and presence of women in history—Fell's life and story take on new depth and meaning. These works present a more complex, less beatific woman whose humanity makes her more understandable but no less remarkable. Of these, the most important contribution of this type is the published dissertation by Bonnelyn Young Kunze.

Kunze's fine work *Margaret Fell and the Rise of Quakerism* is a bellwether in the field. She draws upon the same sources as earlier writers along with a few new additions, but musters more contemporary scholarly methods in her examination of Fell material. For example, Kunze devotes a number of pages to an investigation of the "Thomas Rawlinson affair." This involves the dispute and settlement of a disagreement over control of Force Forge, owned by the Fells but claimed by Rawlinson after his service as forge steward. Rawlinson pursued his cause in the meetings of the Society of Friends and waged a long-term battle against the powerful and revered Fell family in order to lay claim of ownership to the forge. The case was eventually settled with the Fells signing the forge over to Rawlinson. Like most public disputes over things of financial significance, the records of the proceedings reveal a great deal more "truth" than does the final disposition of the matter. This kind of attention to social history is characteristic of the book as a whole. For the scholar familiar with Crosfield and Ross, the book by Bonnelyn Kunze will have a familiar feel to it. Kunze begins her work with appropriate attention to the family history of the Fells, as well as to their economic and domestic existence. She wisely includes by permission Isabel Ross' helpful "Chronology of Margaret Fell's Life."

Her own amplification of the Ross chronology includes important dates in the Rawlinson affair, as well as information on Margaret Fell's later publications omitted by Ross. In fact, the chronology just mentioned is itself an indication of how Kunze both reflects and differs from Ross, et al. Like its predecessors, this book devotes significant time to the biography of the Fells of Swarthmoor. With these earlier works she is appreciative of the historical insight that the Fell household accounts offer the contemporary scholar, and she gives them appropriate acknowledgment. This has the effect of further validating the most fruitful efforts of earlier Fell scholars, and reflects the overall tone of Kunze's contribution. And because this path has been well traveled by earlier publications, the landscape Kunze lays before us has a familiar feel. She meets us here in a way that remains respectful towards the contributions and then leads rapidly into more challenging critical terrain. At the same time, her views have been influenced and directed by the forty-plus years of scholarship that stand between her and the last important work on the Fells. This influence is most important in Kunze's discussion of Margaret Fell and the Women's Meetings in the early Society of Friends, and in her exploration of the roles gender, religion, and class played in the relationship between William and Gulielma Penn and Margaret and George Fox.

Her more careful consideration of this material (as well as the Rawlinson dispute) in the Fell biography adds dimension to the previously haloed, hagiographic portrayals of the Mother of Quakerism. Kunze recognizes the caveats concerning reconstruction of the past by scholars of the present, but she also has a feel for the ability of past voices to inform the present with subtlety and grace, particularly where they are enlivened by careful study of social context and sensitivity to the common experience of human existence shared across time. In addition to these other virtues, the work of Kunze advances Quaker scholarship when she includes an examination of Margaret Fell as theologian. A reading of Fell's publications alone makes it apparent that she was a force of some reckoning wherever she chose to take action. Yet her theological contribution to early Quakerism is usually overlooked. Delightfully, Kunze recognizes the importance of Fell's contribution:

> Fell's life spans the years when Quaker theological development was fluid. Her published and unpublished works, including a recently discovered theological tract, amount to approximately seven hundred pages. This documentary evidence gives us one of the few in-depth feminine perspectives available from the first-generation Quaker theological debates.[6]

For all of this there are minor drawbacks to the Kunze work, particularly in her discussion of Margaret Fell's theology. Kunze does not exercise an adequate command of Christian systematic theology in that she uses key terms improperly.

In scholarly writing it is often the case that an innate appreciation for detail is expressed in an examination so close as to be unreadable. *Margaret Fell and the Rise of Quakerism* avoids that and overall is better for it. However, as in the earlier discussion of Margaret's marriages and her theological development, an example here points out why sometimes working in more detail is better than less. In discussing Fell's Christology, Kunze misapplies the concept of adoptionism when she confuses our being adopted into the family of God (the church) with adoptionism in Christology, a different theological discussion. After quoting a passage in which Fell speaks of believers being adopted into the family of God (with the associated passage from Galatians), Kunze notes that "these two statements do not give enough theological content to ascertain whether she was adoptionist in her thinking."[7] Here Kunze makes do with a footnote on adoptionism that is a summary of an article found in a theology dictionary. This note and the general context of Kunze's discussion make it plain that she is talking about adoptionism in Christology.[8] However, in the Fell material under discussion the subject was ecclesiology and not Christology. Thus the attenuated discussion of theological concepts led to the incorrect assertion that Fell was adoptionist in her Christology, a claim that is ultimately unsupportable.

A third type of Fell study is done by religious historians, a group that includes modern Quaker historians. Here they bring the contemporary sophistication of religious studies and social history to bear on the study of Margaret Fell's religious writings. William C. Braithwaite's excellent history of early Quakers is a prime example of this latter type of scholarship, as is the work of Phyllis Mack (*Visionary Women: Ecstatic Prophecy in Seventeenth-Century England*). Works such as these provide an instructive methodology when they place Margaret Fell in the context of larger historical concerns. This makes their scholarship quite helpful for obvious reasons. For example, this category of work is most likely to remind us that in the earliest days of what became known as the Society of Friends, the moniker had not yet been adopted. In the initial phases of the movement they were more likely to call themselves "Children of the Light," though they would later embrace the initially derogatory slur "Quaker" as a self-referential term. It was not until the time of the Restoration and the ascendancy of Charles II that the name "Society of Friends" was commonly used alongside that of Quakers, by which time the term Children of the Light had all but disappeared.[9] Such distinctions are useful in all Quaker studies.

At the same time, research of this third type does not seek to increase Fell scholarship per se, but addresses her as an aside or a means to some other scholarly end. Although there are helpful mentions made of things such as early self-redaction in Friends' history and the importance of Margaret Fell among early Quakers, these are largely under-documented from the standpoint of scholarship about her in particular. So, while we are cognizant of the distinctions that the chronology of names the Friends used for themselves implies, and as such attend to discrepancies that could lead to historical inaccuracies or falsehoods, the work of religious historians is not focused on why these distinctions have more than a passing importance to Fell material. When the lens is turned in the opposite direction, works such as the one before you are more likely to take note of the distinction between terms that refer to the Society of Friends, but use the names in an overlapping manner when referring to the adherents of the Quaker movement in general. On a closing and tangential note, there is a grammatical problem with the use of the term "Friends" in the possessive. By and large the name Friends is used in a manner similar to other religious groups such as Presbyterian or Anglican or any other Christian denomination. Care and attentiveness should make the context more obvious so that when the name is intended to convey possession it will be spelled Friends'.

## An Overview

The next foray situates the religious life and literature of Margaret Fell within its larger social context, giving special attention to those areas unexplored by other authors. This draws on both published and unpublished material written by Fell, as well as relevant material in works by other authors, in order to more adequately flesh out our analysis of Margaret Fell and her contributions. As was alluded to earlier, in recent years her basic biography has been adequately presented in existing works. However, a working assumption here is that the subtleties of affiliation and affection can be as informative in their own way as dates, names, and places. For this reason, a brief recollection of her story is warranted in order to highlight areas of her life that hold significance for our reading of Fell and her theology. This challenges current notions about her and encourages others to look in new directions for an understanding of the Fell corpus. For example, chapter 1 considers her conversion in order to argue that when combined with her social status, Fell's strength of character and conviction made her a de facto leader in the early Friends movement. This is supported by an account of her initial encounter with George Fox, an event in which Fox is usually cast as the dominant figure in the meeting. However, reframed in light of her superior social position and her actions in the Ulverston conflict, the oft-rehearsed story of Fox's visit to Ulverston tells us a great deal more about Margaret than it does about George.

Contrary to the usual interpretation, Fell is in fact demonstrated to be the more powerful figure in the narrative. In our efforts to gauge the place that Margaret Fell occupied in early Quaker leadership, it is helpful to remember that this affluent and personally dynamic, upper-class woman was the one whom George Fox first encountered. This will be born out in the new argument that Margaret Fell's intervention and protection, along with that of her husband and children, is primarily responsible for Fox's survival when so many of his counterparts met early deaths. Likewise, new analysis of Margaret's later marriage to George makes the case that it was an affectionate but largely political alliance entered into as a part of Fox's effort to reorganize the Society of Friends in the wake of decimating persecution. In expanding what George Fox meant to Margaret Fell, we show how her years as a religious Seeker become more significant in gauging her perception of Fox as he arrived at Swarthmoor Hall.

As alluded to in an earlier section, this examination pushes in a new direction by focusing upon Margaret as the wife of Thomas Fell.

The goal is to bring together all the available scholarship on Thomas Fell and use this to add depth to our understanding of Margaret Fell. Such efforts operate on a previously unconsidered assumption that the "long and affectionate union" between a prominent barrister and gentleman such as Thomas, and a gentlewoman with the capable intellect and strong will witnessed in Margaret, would have shaped the intellectual frame of reference of each partner. Investigation of her social location is enhanced by a number of contemporary sources, including the important testimony of early Quaker Thomas Camm. In the "Testimony Concerning our Dear and Honoured Friend Margaret Fox," recorded in the preface of the 1710 collected works of Margaret Fell, Camm provides a welcome window into the last farewells to that great woman.[10] This is an account of Margaret Fell's funeral and offers us information as to her overall status at the time of her death.

In addition the social and religious ambiguity of Seekers is highlighted in the earliest tract against them, the 1646 *Gangraena, A Catalogue and Descovery of Many of the Errors, Heresies, Blasphemies and pernicious Practices of the Sectaries of this time, vented and acted in England these last four years*, for what it adds to the shape of Margaret's own experience.[11] Finally, in support of a better understanding of Fell's written contribution to the theological discourse of her time, chapter 1 closes with a summary of her main theological tracts, most of which are likely to be unfamiliar even to present-day Quakers. An underlying assertion of chapter 1 is that rereading the Margaret Fell corpus in light of who she was and how she lived has the potential to render previously unnoticed textual subtleties visible to the attentive eye. Earnest attempts to capture the fullest measure from material written by, and about, Fell during her own lifetime should give careful attention to her social, religious, and historical context from the outset. Thus, the work before you is greatly indebted to the labors of numerous scholars who have previously investigated the life and thought of Margaret Fell. However, it differs from most of them by taking Fell seriously as a religious thinker and writer, something she herself most certainly did.

Chapter 2 sets forth something of the organic genius of early Quaker religious thought as a prelude to the theology of Margaret Fell in chapter 3. Although not George Fox's first female convincement, she was among the early northern converts to Quakerism. For this reason, chapter 2 somewhat parallels chapter 1 by examining the religious and historical environment out of which Quakerism was born. The central focus is placed on the years 1534 to 1689, from the Act of Supremacy under Henry VIII to the ascendancy of William and Mary, in order to establish the strong presence of millenarian impulses and eschatological speculation and their effect upon the religious climate of Reformation England. By tracing the development of a uniquely English Protestant eschatology to the reign of Henry VIII, it becomes apparent that the English rejection of papal authority, the ongoing Protestant Reformation, and the open identification of the papacy with various apocalyptic figures facilitated the rapid development of a distinctly Protestant hermeneutic for eschatological symbols and created a new sense of English nationalism. Three works are set forth as being both indicative and formative of the eschatological climate of this period.

We look in turn at John Bale's 1541 *The Image of Both Churches*, John Foxe's 1563 *The Acts and Monuments . . . from the Primitive age to these later times of ours, with the bloudy times, horrible troubles, and great persecutions against the Martyrs of Christ*, and Joseph Mede's 1627 *Clavis Apocalyptica*. This will demonstrate that these works influenced the intellectual, religious, and political world in their time and helped dictate the course of religious radicalism in sixteenth- and seventeenth-century England. This information, which has been considered by scholars from within a number of different disciplines as apocalypticism, again found the spotlight at the end of the twentieth century. However, this chapter considers English eschatology and radical Protestantism in showing Quakerism to be an organic and innovative theological response to the religious climate of the age. Indeed, in view of the social and political circumstances that nurtured the religious thought of Fox and other early Children of Light, their theology was an inspired synthesis of ideas that spoke directly to—and for—the times in which they lived.

To accomplish this goal of focusing on eschatology, my argument moves to consider a sampling of radical groups that were part of the English Reformation and the Revolution that followed: the Sabbatarians, the Levellers, the New Model Army, and the Fifth Monarchists. This makes it possible to accurately gauge where Quakers fit in the overall scheme of English Radical Reformers. Against this backdrop it can be argued that the Friends movement and its theology was in large part a response to impulses and failed ideologies of earlier radical groups. Such a move advances scholarship forward by making the connection between the intense but unrealized chiliastic impulse of the time and the unfolding eschatological framework of Quakerism. What distinguished the eschatology of Fox from that of other millennial radicals was the strongly realized eschatology of Fox and other first-generation Friends. This emphasis upon an inner, spiritual, and realized eschatology was a unique contribution of the Quakers to English religion. As with the Sabbatarians, the

Levellers, the New Model Army, and the Fifth Monarchy Men, a strong eschatological mindset encouraged Quakers to challenge the religious, social, and political realities of the period.

This is the larger religious and historical context in which Margaret Fell wrote and disseminated her religious material, and this backdrop makes the advances of chapter 3 more tenable. From there, the project breaks new ground in approaching her theology in a systematic manner, giving special attention to her doctrine of the Triune God, Christology, hamartiology, pneumatology, ecclesiology, and how these effect her overall soteriology. This is done with an eye toward seeing her eschatology as it gave shape to her theological thinking, for although Mother Fell was not a trained theologian, she certainly had a powerful theological and hermeneutical voice among early Quakers. She admonishes her readers:

> Now, reader, in soberness and singleness of your heart, read this following treatise [A True Testimony] without an evil eye and a prejudiced mind. Let the truth of God have place in the heart. Let the light of Christ in your conscience seriously judge, weigh the things therein contained, (according to the scriptures) prove all things, and hold fast that which is good.[12]

She published letters and tracts rather than massive theological tomes, but her publications are still theological literature. As shall be seen, Fell was not a scholar in the traditional sense, but a popular theologian and religious activist who used her publications to present Friends doctrine and to correct public misconceptions concerning Quaker belief and practice.

In chapter 3 it is made clear that Fell saw herself functioning in a prophetic role, speaking the word of the Lord to the people of her day. Her battle was with the established church and its apostate practices instituted "after the flesh," and she challenged them in public discourse at every level. Working in a time when populist movements were flourishing and the individual human conscience was increasingly seen as the locus of personal freedom, Margaret Fell chose the avenues most likely to lead to widespread dissemination of Quaker ideas. One need only look at writers such as John Bunyan (whose own release from prison was facilitated by the intervention of early Quakers) to realize that thoughtful and intellectually engaging independent authors can influence the church more than academic theologians.

The theology of Margaret Fell is broadly Christian, with many of the same key terms and themes one would find in authors of her time, yet there were distinctive elements. Like the other Quakers of her day, she held that Christ had come fully in the Light, shining in the conscience of all people. This Light is the source for all divine revelation to the world across time. It will become evident that although her understanding of the second coming changed somewhat over time, she maintained an obvious and consistent realized eschatology. She held that the second coming of Christ has begun and he is come again in the flesh as his truth rises in the hearts and minds of those who dwell in the Light. He is now revealed in the eternal spirit of Christ, who is come among us as a teacher and guide, ending all outward laws and covenants and replacing them with a new law, written inwardly on the heart. It is here, inwardly in the cleansed self, that Christ lives and comes in the flesh as our bodies become the temple and dwelling place of God.

Margaret Fell insisted that these outward things included the Sacraments, showing deference based upon rank or other honor from the hand of man, the paying of tithes, and the swearing of oaths of any kind. Old forms no longer play any salvific role; they keep the conscience in the darkness and if humans search there, it is in vain. The witness to the coming of Jesus Christ in the flesh has been missed, because it is revealed inwardly by turning toward the Light and that made manifest of God within. The day of his coming has arrived and continues to arrive. Now is the time of prophetic fulfillment wherein human beings are taught directly by Jesus Christ himself and judged by the Light. This chapter also addresses the common assumption that Margaret Fell moved away from Trinitarian theology as she came to see it as unnecessary from a Quaker perspective. Instead she conceived of the Light as the Triune Godhead expressed as Father, Son, and Spirit.

Although her theological efforts are primarily as an apologist for the Quaker movement, her eschatology is most important in terms of Fell's work in the Friends mission to the Jews. The mission to evangelize the Jews was one in which Friends had an early and focused interest. This interest was a reflection of their theology of the Light in every person, and for Fell can be traced directly to her eschatology and her soteriology. This again pushes into new territory in scholarship on Margaret Fell. Until now, her perspective on salvation and the Jews has not been discussed in depth, and certainly not as an expression of her own theology. For this reason, a portion of chapter 4 is spent looking at the history of England and the Jews. This will set forth what Fell could reasonably have been expected to know about Jewish religious tradition and practice.

By the time of Margaret's first encounter with George Fox, the Jews were already long-suffering objects of Christian prejudice, superstition, and slander, often promulgated from the pulpits of the church. Stories of Jewish vampirism, cannibalism, and desecration of the communion host flourished in England alongside tales of ritual murder and kidnapping of Christians (particularly children). Though there is ample evidence from a variety of sources that English Christians found these accounts credible, the most obvious example is seen in the 1295 expulsion of Jews from England. This was decreed by royal writ from the hand of Edward I, and was a response to the drowning of a young boy in a cesspool a few miles from a large Jewish wedding. Public panic and outrage was so strong that any Jew found on English soil after the expulsion deadline was subject to the penalty of death. Jewish emigration to England became a possibility again in the seventeenth century, when the interests of influential members of the English and Jewish communities converged. In England, the Reformation generated an interest in Hebrew studies so that Scripture could be studied in its original language.

That philosophical community also looked to Hebrew as a possible new universal language, capable of replacing French and Latin as a supplemental language for English academics. Likewise, philo-Semitic movements increased interest in the Hebrew language and the Jews. All of this, and the eschatological hope and apocalyptic expectation which had grown to be commonplace, led to the invitation of well-known Amsterdam Jewish leader Rabbi Menasseh ben Israel to attend the 1655 Whitehall Conference.[13] (We have kept the variant spellings of his name in this chapter where they are taken from another work with an alternate rendering. The spelling currently preferred is Menasseh ben Israel.) The rabbi too had his own eschatological motivations for traveling to England, though the journey to Whitehall had a tragic ending for him and his family. For Margaret Fell, as for many others, this visit was a sign of the last days, and she was not alone in addressing her work to the Jews.

This had radical implications for Fell's eschatology, which provides its own lens for exploring Margaret Fell's 1666 *Women's Speaking Justified*, and her 1660 work *A Declaration and an Information from Us, the People Called Quakers*. These provide a focus for our look at the two most famous aspects of Fell's ministry: her defense of the spiritual equality of women and the Quaker peace testimony. Here again the importance of her eschatology for the development of these aspects of her ministry is discernable. An exploration of Fell's role as a woman religious writer turns us again to her social and historical context. As a sort of prolegomena, we begin with learned aristocrats such as Elizabeth I of England and Marguerite, Queen of Navarre. This will conclude with a brief look at the literary debate surrounding the so-called *querelle des femmes*, and also at the arguments made on behalf of women by Marie Dentière.

Chapter 5 also includes Mary Ward's efforts in founding the Institute of the Blessed Virgin Mary as a place to educate young women, and notes the importance of the well-known Lady Eleanor Davies and the Quaker Elizabeth Hooton. Margaret Fell rests between Davies and Hooton, including the similarities she shared with both. From there our attention is turned to *Women's Speaking Justified* and a discussion of Fell's case for the public ministry of women, demonstrating that her realized eschatology is the bedrock of her arguments in favor of women's preaching and teaching. Without this eschatological groundwork in place, attempts to read this text merely as an example of the history of feminism or the history of biblical interpretation are overly reductionist. The move to read Quaker material in light of their eschatological predispositions is not new, but the careful treatment of Fell's own eschatology as witnessed in her work for women in ministry is.

Chapter 5 also includes a treatment of Fell's *A Declaration and an Information from Us, the People Called Quakers*. With attention focused on the idea of Quaker pacifism and Margaret Fell's perspective on this, our next point of contact is the Lamb's War. As a concept, the Lamb's War evokes militant vocabulary and imagery. By their use of Lamb's War terminology, the Quakers aroused the fears of the English citizenry and contributed to outbreaks of persecution. This has led many historians to conclude that the articulation of the Friends' peace testimony was more an act of political expediency than of consensus and conviction. The idea that pacifism was not a widely held belief among early Quakers, but emerged instead as a response to the political pressures that accompanied the restoration of the English monarchy, is disputed. Drawing upon an unpublished early letter from Margaret Fell, it is simple to show that by 1653 she had articulated a Quaker pacifist position. By building upon other material that supports her early and active apologetic role on behalf of the Children of Light, it is possible to challenge the claim that there is no evidence for a consistent belief in pacifism among early Friends. The contention that Fox published the first public articulation of the Quaker peace testimony is disputed, and the credit rested at the door of Margaret Fell.

## Moving Forward

Throughout this theological study of the Mother of Quakerism, the essential eschatological horizon for her life and thought will be our leitmotiv. Although in each of these chapters the primary goal is to delineate

Margaret Fell more clearly from her contemporaries both inside and outside of the Quaker movement, this work is not an attempt to replace other Society of Friends icons with one of Margaret Fell. The point is to clarify her contributions and to enhance a reading of them by providing a more nuanced context, in an effort to add a greater depth of perspective to the origins of the Society of Friends generally. Margaret Fell was not seeking to be original in her religious writings, but instead desired the exact opposite. She sought to make it clear that the Light of which Friends spoke was the same Triune Godhead taught by Jesus Christ and the apostles. Her goal was not to be a standard bearer for new doctrines, but to be a faithful witness to the one true God. For Fell, the biblical promises of God the Father—who is Light—are fulfilled in the coming of Jesus Christ, the Lord and the Light. These are actuated by the Holy Ghost, the Spirit of the Light, which proceeds from Father and Son.

# 1

# Margaret Fell
*An Overview of Her Life and Work*

Theology, like every significant human endeavor, reflects the lives, values, and needs of a people at a particular place and time in history. In an almost poetic interdependence, a full explication of any theological literature cannot be done properly without an understanding of its historical milieu. To understand Margaret Fell's written contribution to the theological discourse of her time better, we have to find our way into it. One means is to follow her biographical footprints and by that to walk ourselves through her main theological tracts. This supports our purpose in this chapter, which is to place the religious literature of Margaret Fell in its historical context by attending to an overview of her life and work. Bear in mind as we move forward that for First Publishers of the Truth such as Margaret Fell true religion was as much about inward conversion as it was about outward proclamation. For them the Light that is Christ Within is ultimately a call of love answered by the individual within the conscience and not through participation in outward forms of religion such as communion or baptism. For those first "Children of Light," the established church appeared appropriately moribund, for religion had filled itself with outward signs and symbols, practices, and proclamations that were now meaningless. Christ himself was present once again on earth, old things had passed away, and new things were being accomplished through those who walked in the Light.

Such was the experience of Margaret Askew Fell Fox, who lived through much of the seventeenth century. During a time of intense religious and political ferment in England, she emerged to provide important leadership to a radical Protestant movement, the Society of Friends. In this capacity, she was a voice for freedom of conscience and religious expression. This said, the perception of Fell's contribution to Friends religious history has been colored by her marriage to George Fox, the man widely held to be the founder of Quakerism. Although Fox has been rightly granted historical preeminence in the formation of the Society of Friends, the popular notion of George Fox as the fountainhead of all things Quaker is plainly incorrect. The weighty contributions of others have been well documented, and there is ample evidence that Fell was an important leader in her own right. As Nicholas Morgan noted in 1993, she "became 'a tender nursing mother unto many', adapting to her role as a Quaker matriarch with the ease which one would expect from a leading member of local society."[1] For most historians, however, she has been rendered nearly invisible by the shadow of her more famous second husband, and has not received the attention she merits as a writer.[2]

## The Social Location of Margaret Fell

In keeping with the priorities and sensibilities of the first Quakers, little is recorded of Margaret Fell's early life. The scant details of her early years come generally from a short autobiographical relation written in 1690 and published after her death.[3] She was born Margaret Askew in 1614 at Marsh Grange near Dalton, in the county of Lancaster, England.[4] She was one of two daughters who were bequeathed property and money by their father John Askew, a well-established gentleman landowner and member "of an ancient family, of those esteemed and called gentlemen." Upon his death Margaret received her half of "a considerable estate that had been in his name and family for several generations."[5] Although we do not know the particulars of her father's death, we may infer from Margaret's brief remarks that his provision for her would have allowed her to live comfortably unmarried if she had so desired. It is certain that she was able to read and write well, something that was still uncommon at the time.[6] He also imbued her with sufficient stature that his daughter Margaret would be considered a suitable mate for the barrister and future Lord of the manor at Ulverston, Thomas Fell.

By her own account, the major event in her early life was her 1632 marriage to Thomas Fell (1598–1658). While still in her teens, Margaret entered into a long and affectionate union with the socially prominent heir of good estate, and apart from some notable trips she spent her life in the north running the Fell family home at Swarthmoor Hall. The union of Askew and Fell was advantageous to both parties. Thomas was the anointed descendent of a nouveau riche, wealthy, and influential Lancaster family from whom he had inherited his father's recently acquired gentry status and estate. Margaret was a morally upright and intelligent gentleman's daughter from an old and honored family. Together the Fells bought more property and profited "from both legal office and shrewd purchases of forfeit estates and fee-farm rents under the Commonwealth."[7] Separately they were privileged, but together they were a force with which to be reckoned. Through the agency of their union, they improved the fortunes of their household. By the standards of the day, their home was large and attractive, resting on a somewhat stark moor with the sea and the mountains in the distance. Their household eventually became quite large and at times Swarthmoor Hall was near to bursting with the Fells' eight children, servants, and the frequent guests who found their way to the Fell estate.

In any case, Margaret oversaw the comings and goings of staff, a family of eight children, and the unusually high number of visitors who made their way to her remote North Country home at Swarthmoor Hall. Thus, although there is no doubt that Margaret Fell deferred to her husband, as the lady of the house she also exercised a tremendous authority in her own right. Such observations help us better estimate the power and authority Margaret Fell wielded through her natural giftedness, her own social standing, and the rank and capacity conferred upon her by her husband's considerable status. In her early life she was already remarkable for so many reasons, and had she but held herself with industrious dignity to the rank and later remnant which was hers by birth and marriage she would have prospered and died well. She chose of her own volition to do something else and by this, religious history itself was greatly altered. So as we attempt to gauge the place that Margaret Fell occupied in early Quaker leadership, it is useful to remember the affluent and personally dynamic upper-class woman whom George Fox first encountered on his visit to Ulverston in 1652.

## Margaret and Thomas Fell

Margaret and Thomas gained in social currency because of their marriage, and her increased importance in the local community made her a woman of unusual influence in the politically and socially remote north of England where she lived. As we have already begun to grasp, she was not inclined by nature or design to be passive toward this state of affairs and there is evidence that both duty and affection held Margaret and her husband in a mutual and healthy bond. For this reason it is imprudent to try and completely separate Margaret's personal and intellectual development from the influence and accomplishments of her husband during the course of their life together. To do so is to unnecessarily divorce ourselves from available historical information and fly in the face of common human experience in favor of a more ethereal divination. Here the words of esteemed Quaker writer John Punshon are useful, "History is a mirror for human nature. That's why it is fascinating, and why it is not self-explanatory."[8] If we are to understand the direction of Margaret Fell and the Society of Friends we must get a grip on the social prerogative that she exercised on their behalf. This includes her intervention during their thousands of imprisonments, as well as her involvement in forming Friends polity.

Margaret was more than just a socially well-placed landholder and religious activist. She was the wife of a judge, and with him was involved in some of the earliest legal defense of Quakers. She would have contributed to the direction that early Friends took in their legal defense. One example is her 1654 *Letter to Judge Hugh Wyndham*.[9] Margaret Fell wrote to Judge Wyndham concerning the case of Cuthbert Hunter, a man imprisoned because he chose to be married in the manner of Friends rather than going before village priests. In her letter Fell adopts a two-pronged approach that reappears in other letters. She both defends the legality of Quaker marriages and explains at length the true nature of the Light. In this she addresses a legal question of great importance to the Children of Light. In customary style she blends her legal response with a longer apologetic for Friends belief and practice. By 1656 she issued another response in *To Friends, An Epistle on Marriage*. According to Elsa F. Glines, this letter "shows Margaret Fell, the clear-headed, well-organized woman who understands the necessity to satisfy legal and social requirements for a valid marriage."[10] She does not seem intimidated by the power of the law, which is helpful because of the seemingly endless legal troubles of the first Quakers. Her long-term involvement in their organization and strategic response make it well worth our time to probe her biography further. Although she seems to have shrunk from little, in this case her bold response to matters of the law makes most sense in the context of her long marriage to a barrister and judge.

It would be wrong on many levels to insinuate that their intimacy created a mirror consciousness. But it is certainly likely that Margaret learned a great deal from her many years living so closely to a major legal and political figure in the county of Lancaster. Thomas served his country as vice-chancellor of the duchy and county palatine of Lancaster for two terms, as a judge of the assize in the northwest (Chester and North Wales circuit), as member of the Long Parliament (1647–1649), and in the last four years of his life, as chancellor of the duchy of Lancaster.[11]

Yet for all of this, Thomas Fell is of primary interest to us where it deepens the understanding we have of Margaret. At the least we know that as chancellor, Thomas Fell would have had an official London residence at Duchy House in the Strand, presided over the duchy council and the duchy court at Westminster, and enjoyed a substantial salary drawn from litigation fees. Judge Thomas Fell "held one of the highest, most influential and most lucrative offices in the Kingdom. As chancellor of the duchy of Lancaster he stood in a distinguished lineage that included Sir Thomas More and Sir Robert Cecil. When considering his role in the history of early Quakerism the power and influence of such an important statesman should not be underestimated."[12] Indeed, no historian presented with this type of evidence about Margaret's life should choose to let it pass unexamined.[13] At the same time, she herself preferred to focus a good deal more on her second husband and her life after their meeting. This dissonance is one more challenge to scholars as we address the question of how best to honor who she was.

Ulverston is located in the north of England and Margaret Fell was a northerner by birth and by affection. The vicissitudes of her northern life, her education, her secure economic situation, her social rank as a member of the landed gentry, her marriage to the heir of a respected Lancaster family, and her membership in a persecuted religious sect all contribute to an understanding of who Fell was. In the seventeenth century the 200- to 250-mile journey to the capital city of London left northerners somewhat socially and politically insulated from their southern fellows. Then, as now, the north received minimal attention from the south except in times of political or social unrest. Northerners have historically been viewed as hardy, self-reliant though often poor, provincial folk.[14] Fell's deep connection to this geographical region is of significance because it was in the north that George Fox found his earliest successes and established his strongest following among early Friends.

Margaret Fell's influence among northern Friends from 1652 onward is well documented.[15] According to Quaker and scholar Christine Trevett, the Fell home at "Swarthmoor Hall was the cradle and powerhouse of Quakerism . . . the Hall became the postal sorting office for the movement, a place of rest and recuperation for Quakers traveling in their various ministries, and for more than thirty years it was the setting for meeting for worship."[16] Yet simply judged on the merits of social position and without considering her subsequent contributions, Margaret Fell is undoubtedly one of the most significant of George Fox's northern converts. Bonnelyn Young Kunze holds that "her class and wealth enabled her to become a powerful leader and pierce through traditional gender constraints of her era, and thus awe people in a way that Fox could not."[17] Most readers are likely to be familiar with the story of Fox's first visit to Margaret's home at Swarthmoor Hall and her subsequent convincement. Although both Fox and Fell wrote published accounts of this meeting, a far more interesting record is found in a long unpublished letter written by Margaret in 1679.[18]

The familiar events, such as Fox's confrontation with Rector Lampitt during a "lecture day" meeting at St. Mary's in Ulverston, are present.[19] Fell recalled that Fox entered the church building during the meeting and began to speak on the Scriptures. His message so angered the rector and several members of the congregation that Reverend Lampitt commanded the church warden to expel Fox from the premises. Fox and Lampitt had met the day before while each was calling at Swarthmoor Hall, and as historian H. Larry Ingle wryly notes, these two men "did not hit it off well."[20] Fell herself writes, "But when he came to touch them then they grew weary, and very angry, and so set the Churchwardens to haul G[eorge] out: But I stood up in my pew and looked at the Churchwarden: and he stood behind G[eorge] F[ox]: and let him alone, and G[eorge] F[ox] spoke on a great while."[21] In this account, Fell's reproving glare halts Fox's removal from the hall for some time. Here her implied directive carries more weight than the rector's spoken word. This reading makes a great deal of sense in the context of our analysis, because as Lord of Ulverston Manor it was Margaret's husband who secured Reverend Lampitt's appointment to St. Mary's. In fact, when Fox is finally removed from the church it is only through the intervention of Judge John Sawrey, a Member of Parliament who was also present in the meeting house.[22]

In the encounter we see a tug of war between personalities and ideas happening in a public space on the basis of power. That power is based upon things like religious conviction, personal ability, and social rank. When we interpret this narrative against the backdrop of Margaret Fell's social location, she is positioned high in the authority structure of her local community. Awareness of this dynamic gives us a different read on the drama that unfolds, and on the historical significance of this situation. Of all the participants in the story, Fox is lowest in power and rank, whereas Margaret Fell is subject only to a male of approximate rank with her husband.[23] In any case, the connection between Fell and Fox was immediate and long lasting, and the Fell home at Swarthmoor hall became a meeting place for Friends worship.[24] Of this important event, biographer Isabel Ross writes:

Thus began a half-century of work for the Quaker fellowship, a work in which there was a remarkable co-operation between the founder (till his death in 1691) and a woman who was frequently addressed as "our nursing mother." By her own personality, her social position, her education, courage, genius for friendship, and the gift not only of seeing essentials but of holding on to them even against the pressure of her friends, she gave stability to the movement, especially in the early days before any organization had been created by George Fox himself.[25]

Margaret Fell's social position, particularly as the wife of a judge, afforded the Lancaster Friends a degree of protection they did not often enjoy in other meetings.

For this reason, Swarthmoor Hall became central to the development of the Society of Friends and served as a base of operations as the Quakers firmly established themselves in the north of England.[26] That Margaret herself was aware of her unique status among Friends is seen in a letter from 1667. There she recalls that "we [Friends] kept our integrity and met together—At our house at Swarthmoor with my husband's consent: And he being the chief magistrate in the Country, they could not fall upon us in persecuting us as their hearts desired."[27] For this reason, Judge Fell's death in 1658 marks the end of a watershed period in Friends history, and a gradual but dramatic shift in Margaret's personal fortunes. Thomas Fell's death deprived Friends of his solid political and legal power, but Margaret was also released from a restraining influence on her actions, freed in conscience from those social obligations and proprieties to which she seems to have acquiesced out of deference to her husband. And though she could not know it at the time, she was now far more vulnerable to those who opposed her participation in the Society of Friends.

In a sense one could say that the death of Judge Fell began her second life as a Quaker. From this point, free of any concerns for her husband's social sensibilities, she also became a target for those who had been held at bay by his good offices.[28] In the first few years after Thomas Fell's passing Margaret was able to pursue her activities on behalf of Quakerism with a new openness, and she began a period of increased visibility and activity beyond Lancaster and environs.[29] One of her first efforts as a new widow shows us something of the form this transition and freedom would take. To set the scene: Oliver Cromwell, a man with whom she had many interchanges both by pen and in person, was gone. His son Richard proved less than capable of leading the nation, and it became clear that England would have her monarchy. In a letter of

1660, Margaret again sat down with pen in hand and hurriedly sent off a welcoming letter reminding Charles II of his duties, given by God for the protection of others. She hoped that this new king would ease the sufferings of Friends. Yet we know from other historical sources that the king himself had little of the power she imagined, and even where he agreed with her, Charles II was not strong enough politically to grant an outright edict of toleration.

### The Trials of Margaret Fell

As her activities exceeded social convention and breached expectations for the gentle widow of a respected judge, she became a fair target for others who despised religious nonconformity or simply coveted some part of the Fell estate. Within two years, George Fox would be arrested during worship at Swarthmoor Hall, and Margaret Fell would complete the peace testimony and deliver it to Charles II in London. In 1663, she undertook a thousand-mile journey throughout England, visiting various Friends Meetings, accompanied at several points by Quakers such as George Fox and William Caton. By 1664 Margaret had been arrested, tried, and convicted of crimes against the Crown for her refusal to take the Oath of Allegiance. Stripped of her citizenship she began the first of her incarcerations at Lancaster prison. Though the conditions were bleak and mean, some part of her was newly energized and she wrote six of her most important publications, including *Women's Speaking Justified*.[30] A year after her release from Lancaster in 1668, Margaret Fell and George Fox were married. During their marriage they seldom resided together, given the time which both spent in jails, on missionary journeys, or traveling in ministry. Margaret Fell, now Margaret Fox, continued to organize Friends for mutual support during periods of persecution. Her work organizing Women's Meetings and defending the autonomy of those meetings took on greater importance, and as Bonnelyn Young Kunze has written, "one of Margaret's greatest single accomplishments in her Quaker career was her pivotal work in the establishment of separate women's meetings which she commenced shortly after she was released from Lancaster prison."[31] She traveled widely, including eight more trips to London, the last of which took place when she was over seventy years old. In London, she met with King Charles II, just as she later would with James II, to plead the cause of religious freedom for Quakers.

To reiterate a key point of this chapter, social location reveals a great deal about the importance of Margaret Fell for the early Society of Friends. Her encounters with kings and other government leaders were ones for which she was well suited. We have likewise noted she was from a "great family" in her own right and had married well. As Nicholas Morgan has successfully demonstrated, "whilst Friends did enjoy an astonishing ease of access to the throne . . . for the most part personal petitioners to the sovereign were being carefully chosen by Friends from as early as 1660."[32] Fell was pressed into service early after her convincement in part because she was quickly judged by Fox to be an able theological expositor.[33] This would not be any original personal design of her own prior to her convincement. Margaret appears to have been content in the north and remained there even though her husband Thomas was frequently in London on his own political and judicial errands.[34] Also, she and others within the early Friends movement were aware that Margaret was much more likely to gain an audience with those of higher social rank. George Fox and others of his ilk had their own gifts to give to the cause, and so they did.

## Margaret Fell as Religious Writer

To say that Fell was a match for any writer of religious polemic or apology in her day may be faint praise given the tenor of the times, but a review of her published material shows that Margaret Askew Fell Fox was intelligent, extremely well versed in Christian Scripture, and passionate about her faith.[35] Reading her correspondence likewise reveals that she possessed a firm will, an independent mind, and the capacity of a natural leader who was not easily intimidated. In the context of the nascent Friends movement, Margaret Fell's nature and station make it difficult to envision a situation where she would not emerge as a leader of some sort. The assertion, then, is that rereading the Margaret Fell corpus in light of who she was and how she lived has the potential to render previously unnoticed textual subtleties visible to the attentive eye. Earnest attempts to capture the fullest measure from material written by, and about, Fell during her own lifetime should give careful attention to her social, religious, and historical context from the outset.

A brief but adequate example comes in Thomas Camm's short, four-page "Testimony Concerning our Dear and Honoured Friend Margaret Fox," included in the 1710 collected works of Margaret Fell.[36] This gentle and understated testimony comes from a fellow northerner who had known her since his Quaker convincement in 1652. Camm remarks on points we have already noted in this chapter, but his unadorned testimony is yet another insight into the value of context for scholars interpreting historical documents. Let us first consider his observation that Margaret willingly walked "in the narrow way of the cross, choosing much rather to join with, and suffer affliction, and all manner of reproach for Christ's sake, with the people of God, than to enjoy the pleasures, treasures and glory of this world, which she had a share of above many."[37] This comment has been interpreted in various ways, but a look at the readings given it by influential modern Fell biographers Bonnelyn Young Kunze and Isabel Ross should serve our purposes adequately. Kunze sees here that Margaret Fell's social standing did not protect her from the suffering common to the human condition.[38] At the opposite end of the spectrum, Ross reads this as testimony to Fell's warmth and hospitality.[39]

Certainly both biographies are well worth reading, and they make fine arguments. So whichever direction we choose, it is clear that Camm's words may also be taken as evidence of what Quakers knew and accepted about Margaret Fell—that she enjoyed greater social rank and prerogative than most, that she willingly and openly identified with the Friends cause and suffering, and that this was accepted with approval by Friends generally. In a similar vein, Thomas Camm recalls that this woman was gifted "with qualifications many ways for a considerable service in his church, in which she shined as a morning star." For a northern Quaker long accustomed to Friends' strict humility and the avoidance of vanity, this is very generous speech. Here, since the day he penned it in 1706, has been a witness to her significance in the work of early Friends. Writing after her death in 1702, Camm also tells us something of Margaret Fell's funeral, which he attended along with many other Quakers. Though he focuses upon the work and service of Friends, he seems to find it just and noteworthy that there were persons "of great quality and degree in the world" who attended her farewell.[40]

This somber attention to setting a farewell, reviewing the life of the deceased, and recording the words of the person on the death bed were common and significant practices for Friends. Though on its own this minor notice goes generally unmentioned by scholars, it still remains informative for students of Quaker history. Her death occurred almost ten years after that of her second husband, the Quaker icon George Fox. Likewise, almost everyone she had worked alongside in the early days of the movement was long dead, and her own public persecution and humiliation had taken place almost forty years prior. Yet in Camm's comment we see evidence of her lingering social standing, despite decline and imprisonment after the death of Judge Fell. Thomas Camm at the very least found her status a source of credit to the Society of Friends generally.

Having considered more carefully the aspect of Fell's social location, we move to reintegrate it with her religious life and ministry. Meeting

George Fox in the summer of 1652 and the subsequent convincement of Fell and most of her family at Swarthmoor are clearly major events in Margaret's religious journey. However, her quest for authentic Christian faith did not begin in 1652, but in the paths of her youth.[41] Throughout her early years she was an active enquirer, entertaining various religious teachers in her home where they often held private religious services and engaged in theological discourse.[42] Like many thoughtful Christians of her age, Margaret's formative theological experience was as a Seeker.[43] The Seekers' domain was the inward, spiritual experience of the individual believer, and the seventeenth-century crisis of faith that enveloped many and led them into seeking would prove particularly important for women. As Phyllis Mack has written, many of the powerful women religious leaders who emerged during the mid-seventeenth century (she includes Fell) had been Seekers of some sort. She notes, "Many of these literate women were not merely witnesses of the upheavals of the Civil War; they had been active seekers among the profusion of sects and independent churches that proliferated during the 1640s."[44]

The chaos and relaxed social boundaries of the English Civil War period allowed women like Margaret Fell to give wider rein to their intellect, and this seems to have been a watershed moment when women were able to visibly participate in the exchange and development of religious ideas. The Seeker phenomenon was key in this because it was a socially tolerated form of religious nonconformity. Generally speaking the Seekers were persons who were troubled by conflicts within the church and so chose not to participate in organized religion, opting instead for an inward attitude of waiting upon God. They were also deeply committed to the Christian faith, and this was born out in their pious lives. Because Seekers lived out their devout faith, and because their distress over the church was shared to some degree by almost everyone in England, society made a space for these religious dissidents. Even Oliver Cromwell, whose daughter was a longtime Seeker, admired the depth of their Christian commitment. Like most he seems to have accepted the seeking as a legitimate spiritual response to the confusion of the times.[45]

This said, Seekers were not a welcome phenomenon to the church generally. One of the earliest discussions of Seekers is found in the 1646 *Gangraena, A Catalogue and Descovery of Many of the Errors, Heresies, Blasphemies and pernicious Practices of the Sectaries of this time, vented and acted in England these last four years*.[46] Written by the Presbyterian minister Thomas Edwards, the book addressed 176 heterodox doctrinal positions circulating around England in the mid-seventeenth century. Though many of the wayward ideas Edwards saw afloat in the Christian tide would have found safe harbor among Seekers, it is doctrinal error number 97 that best captures the Seeker position:

> That there ought to be in these times no making or building of Churches, nor use of Church-ordinances, as ministering of the Word, Sacraments, but waiting for a Church, being in readiness upon all occasions to take knowledge of any passenger, of any opinion or tenet whatsoever; the Saints as pilgrims do wander as in a Temple of Smoak, not able to finde Religion, and therefore should not plant it by gathering or building a pretended supposed House, but should wait for the coming of the Spirit, as the Apostles did.[47]

The Seekers with whom Margaret Fell identified early on emerged as a movement in England in the 1620s, and arose as an expression of dissatisfaction with the divisions, theological disputes, and perceived corruption in the church. Although Seekers would not usually have identified themselves by this title, the name applies broadly to those individuals who, confused or discouraged by the attenuated spirituality and perceived apostasy of the established church, abandoned institutional Christianity. But not all seekers left the church and its practices entirely. Some such as Margaret Fell found a home of sorts in the Independent churches, and Thomas and Margaret participated in church worship together during her seeking years. Although both Fells "had a preference for the dissenting tradition," their social position allowed them to remain in attendance at the local parish church.[48] Like other Independent-leaning persons of privilege, they used their position to secure a local pulpit distanced from the practices and views of the Church of England. It was common enough at the time for the wealthy to use their "influence to install more left-wing clergy in their parish. Thus, rather than leaving the church as less-privileged Seekers did, local elites could seek within their own parish."[49]

In the case of the Fells, they chose to support the ministry of independent Reverend Lampitt in their Ulverston parish church. Given his work in Parliament, this arrangement probably reflected Judge Fell's political predispositions as well as his religious preferences, but it also seems to have accommodated Margaret's Seeker spirit prior to her encounter with George Fox. Though Margaret never addressed this aspect directly, it is likely that her attendance also reflected her sense of obligation to her husband and her position in the community. Whatever her motivation for continuing in church attendance, there is little reason to doubt Fell's own appraisal of her seeking years. Her extant writings are all post-convincement, but to the end of her days she remained critical of established religion and what she perceived to be its affection and preference for "empty forms" and hypocrisy.[50] According to Quaker historian Douglas Gwyn, "That keen sense of hypocrisy and institutional laxity is key to understanding the Spiritualist sensibility in general, and the seeking spirituality in particular."[51] This kind of human disappointment can be deep, lonely, and lasting.

To shelter them from the religious storms that tossed their faith, Seekers turned inward to the relative security of personal revelation and primitive Christianity. Unable to find the type of earnest Christianity they desired in the established church and burdened with disappointment at the failures of England's Protestant movement, they found what spiritual footing they could.[52] Awaiting a new work of the Spirit, most Seekers adopted a proto-church posture that eschewed the formal structures and practices of Christendom. Seekers set aside sacraments and liturgy as they looked for Christ to bring forth his new apostles, the holy and prophetic guardians of true Christianity's restoration. The expectation was that new leaders would emerge and, led by the Spirit, would rouse England to shake off her inter-Nicene squabbles and papist-influenced apostasy. Until then Seekers waited in expectation of revival, living in a spiritual distress marked by anticipation, hope, and despair. Margaret Fell herself certainly bore a patina of resigned disappointment over her inward glow of spiritual longing and expectation. This in itself is not surprising considering her close relationship with Judge Fell, someone whose career bound him in varying degrees to court life and politics in London during the upheaval of the seventeenth century. This would have supported her conviction that the church was compromised and corrupt.

Whatever sway Judge Fell's opinions held over his wife, she was herself earnestly spiritual from her earliest days. Her childhood spent with her father, whom she described as "a pious charitable man, much valued in his country for his moderation and patience," is the probable seed of this and perhaps even of the anxious piety sometimes apparent in Fell. Looking back on this time in her life, Margaret would later say of herself:

> [I was] one that sought after the best things, being desirous to serve God, so as I might be accepted of him; and was inquiring after the way of the Lord, and went often to hear the best ministers that came into our parts, whom we frequently entertained at our house many of those that were accounted the most serious and godly men, some of which were then called Lecturing-Ministers and had often prayers and religious exercises in our family. This I hoped I did well in, but often feared that I was short of the right way. And after this manner I was enquiring and seeking about twenty years."[53]

The conscientious piety of the Seekers is apparent in Fell. For her, like so many others, the suspension of outward obedience to the religious powers of the day was not a barrier to individual Christian practices or an attendant personal holiness. Although other groups such as the Ranters displayed antinomian proclivities decried by critics, Seekers were known for their earnest spirituality and deep commitment to Christ and his teachings. Gwyn observes:

> Their dualism between inward and outward, spiritual and formal, is based not on metaphysics but on an intense aversion to hypocrisy, the contradiction between nominal righteousness and the actual sinfulness, alienation, and pride. The Constantinian politics of the Reformation goaded this sensibility unbearably among individuals of uncommon introspection and scrupulosity.[54]

From her position of privilege, Margaret kept her ear to the ground awaiting signs of Christ's new work. The residents of Swarthmoor Hall had a reputation for welcoming itinerant preachers who traveled through the north, and here Thomas and Margaret would have encountered the full range of religious ideas in circulation at the time.[55] A number of those visiting the Fells were lecturing ministers, individuals who traveled the north of England and Scotland "to preach and explicate scripture usually in less than formal religious occasions and often outside the recognized church structure."[56] Margaret's place at the heart of this hospitality reflects, at least in part, her interest in spiritual life and the theology that framed it. This frequent exposure to the religious and devotional teachings of visiting preachers and teachers, combined with intelligence from Judge Fell's trips to London, would have kept Margaret current on the ideas and events that were in circulation in the wider world.[57] We know, for example, that she was aware of George Fox's presence in the north long before he came to Swarthmoor Hall.

## Margaret Fell and the Coming of George Fox

From her home, Fell kept abreast of news. She had heard of the developments surrounding Fox and his teachings in the north and had received word of the persecution and imprisonment of his recently convinced followers. According to Fell, "Several were brought to prison at York for their testimony to the truth, both men and women, so that we heard of such a people that were risen. *We did very much inquire after them.*"[58] It makes sense, then, that her own waiting and expectation contributed to the welcome extended to Fox and to her ready acceptance of the Light. It also provides some clue as to the level of Margaret Fell's own theological thinking prior to her convincement. From this we also get a better idea of circumstances that enabled Fox to rapidly gather such a committed group of believers in his travels across the north. As we set forth previously, the woman whom George Fox met on his first visit to Swarthmoor Hall was a person of consequence and superior social position, both by birth and by marriage.[59] Her husband Thomas was a high-ranking judge and a religious independent whose service with Parliament, support for the independent pastor Reverend Lampitt and the parish in Ulverston, and record of judicial protection of religious dissidents show him to have been a tolerant and open-minded man for his time.

In contrast to her husband, Margaret Fell was much more the privileged yet earnestly pious religious pilgrim who lived the tenuous spiritual existence of the Seekers. In Fell's case she found an end to her searching in 1652. It was then, with the arrival of George Fox at Swarthmoor Hall, that Margaret's transformation from Seeker to prophet—one who speaks the word of God into a specific situation, time, or place—began. George Fox had himself spent years in spiritual searching, confronting many of the issues that also confounded and concerned Seekers. Fox, an unusually serious and sensitive child who grew into an earnest and somewhat unconventional man, had spent his youth in anxious vexation. He was deeply grieved by the hypocrisy and "wantonness" of his fellow Christians.[60] After an apprenticeship in trade, Fox traveled throughout the country during the chaos of the English Civil War. This early itinerancy was the setting for his spiritual journey through despair and disillusionment into rapture, visions, and divine illumination. By the time he made his way to Swarthmoor Hall in the summer of 1652, Fox was an experienced preacher with an aptitude for rhetorical persuasiveness and an evangelist's zeal.

The distinctive elements of his theology were well in place, and George Fox had the support of a growing number of followers who worked alongside him.[61] Douglas Gwyn expresses a similar view:

> By 1650, Fox's personal transformation was more or less complete and most features of his ministry were in place. Although he was still an obscure figure, he had formed a significant network in the Midlands. He was noted for a keen discernment of spiritual states, faith healings, moral rigor, socioeconomic concern and apocalyptic warnings.[62]

His personal manner was forthright, and he eschewed a number of social conventions he believed to be prohibited by Scripture. Most notably, Fox scrupulously avoided showing "honor below" to anyone regardless of social rank. He addressed all persons with the familiar "thee" and "thou," and refused to bid a good morning or good evening to anyone.

Fox likewise refused bow or show obeisance, and refused to take his hat off for another, rejecting "hat honor" as unbiblical.[63]

It is interesting that Margaret Fell, who certainly counted as Fox's social superior, was not put off by his manners or the more eccentric aspects of his person such as his much remarked upon outfit of leather breeches and coat. On the contrary, she readily accepted him into her home and within a short time of their meeting had embraced the message he brought with him. Within days she and most of her household were convinced of the truth of Fox's teaching. The ease with which she accepted George Fox and his teaching is no doubt a credit to his persuasive message and convincing presence, for Margaret and her family had hosted and learned from the best preachers that traveled the north. But it is important to remember that the convincement of Fell was a milestone in her own spiritual journey. At the time of their initial encounter, Margaret Fell was a Seeker with a longing for God and an enquiring mind. As such, she would have been waiting for the appearance of a new apostle, the Lord's anointed who would lead believers out of apostasy. From her writings we also see that she was deeply influenced by the eschatological expectations of the age. Her intellect and her religious desire were both challenged and fired by Fox's visit, and she remained fiercely loyal to him for the remainder of her life.

For his part, George Fox was certain of his message and its truth. We get a sense of his presence and convictions in this somewhat lengthy passage from his journal. He writes:

> I was commanded to turn people to that inward light, spirit and grace, by which all might know their salvation, and their way to God; even that divine spirit, which would lead them all into Truth, and which I infallibly knew, would never deceive any. But with and by this divine power and spirit of God, and the light of Jesus, I was to bring people off from their own ways, to Christ the new and living way; and from their churches; . . . and off from the world's teachers, made by men, to learn of Christ . . . and off from all the world's worships, to know the spirit of Truth in the inward parts, and to be led thereby; . . . off from all the world's religions, which are vain; that they might know pure religion, . . . off from all the world's fellowships and prayings and singings, which stood in forms without power; . . . And I was to bring people off from Jewish ceremonies, and from heathenish fables, and from men's inventions and windy doctrines by which they blowed the people about, from sect to sect; . . . their schools and colleges for making ministers of Christ, who are indeed ministers of their own making, but not of Christ. And all their images and crosses, and sprinkling of infants, with all their holy-days (so-called) and all their vain traditions.[64]

From this one can see that the familiar prejudices and concerns of the Seekers were addressed, as were other nonconformist issues such as antipapist sentiment and eschatological expectation. He spoke to Margaret's spiritual condition and it changed her destiny. Having faced years of persecution, imprisonment, and physical and financial ruin, she would look back upon her meeting with Fox and at the end of her life would write, "in the year 1652, it pleased the Lord in his infinite mercy and goodness to send George Fox into our country, who declared unto us the Eternal Truth, as it is in Jesus . . . I and my children and a great part of our servants were so convinced and converted unto God."[65]

After her convincement she began her long and remarkable career as a Friends religious leader. In the first years of her convincement, the movement was blessed with a great number of capable and energetic preachers and organizers known in later times as the "Valiant Sixty."[66] Although George Fox was germinal in the growing gathering of Friends, he was but one of several persuasive and dynamic personalities that carried the message of the Inward Light through England and beyond.[67] In such an environment a woman of Fell's temperament quickly found an outlet for her resources and talents. Early on she organized social support structures for ministering or suffering Friends and became a vocal apologist for Quaker practices. Much of this activity was centered in Swarthmoor Hall, and the Fell home became an unofficial northern headquarters for Friends. According to Friend and scholar Christine Trevett, the introduction of Quakerism into the Fell household changed the structure of family life and made Swarthmoor Hall a unique domestic environment in its time. She has observed, "Swarthmoor was a place of integration, where the domestic and mundane integrated with the ministerial and ecstatic. Such integration was a commonplace requirement of Quakerism, especially for its women. But things happened on a larger scale at Swarthmoor, the 'mother-house.'"[68]

Fell was a true believer in George Fox and his message, and her leadership was energetic and earnest. Fox was indeed fortunate in securing Margaret's allegiance early in his work and over the course of his life he and his ministry benefited greatly from her unwavering support. How much of Fox's own survival and emergence as the founding father of Quakerism can be credited to the intervention and support of Margaret Fell and her husband Thomas is open to debate, but that they intervened for Fox on several occasions is well documented. Likewise, "she became a 'tender nursing mother unto many' adapting to her role as a Quaker matriarch with the ease that one would expect from a leading member of local society."[69] In an earlier time than ours, when the portentous but gentle power of the woman's breast to sustain life made the term "nursing mother" a compliment, Margaret was thus identified. Indeed her commitment to the fledgling Society of Friends expressed itself from the outset in care and support for imprisoned Quakers.

## Margaret Fell as Religious Writer, Advocate, and Apologist

Given her times, Margaret Askew Fell Fox was a remarkable woman author. She wrote books and pamphlets as well as a large number of letters, some of which were published. These demonstrate her vital faith, her prophetic role in English religion, and her pastoral role in the nascent Quaker movement. Her earliest religious writings are letters to other Friends, some of them already in prison. Fell's epistletory career began soon after her convincement in 1652 when she began a long career of voluminous correspondence with Friends. While these letters were certainly shared with others, they were not "public" documents in the modern sense. They were a mixture of the practical and the theological, written primarily for instruction, edification, and exhortation. At the same time, she began her more public work as a political apologist for Friends beliefs and practices, particularly to the king and others in power in England. Not surprisingly, there were few Friends who were better placed than Margaret Fell for this particular purpose, and the system of royal visitations and petitions made by Friends was pioneered by Margaret Fell and Friends leader Thomas Moore. On the basis of his research into Lancashire Quakers, Nicholas Morgan has written,

> The two prime movers of regular and planned visits to the King in the immediate post-Restoration years were Margaret Fell and Thomas Moore . . . Fell's personal record as a petitioner was prodigious. She began her career of solicitation in 1660 when she traveled from Swarthmoor to the capital, having been "Mov'd of the Lord to go to London, to speak to the King concerning the Truth, and the Sufferers for it." Her work in the capital was vigorous and systematic: she wrote and circulated papers to all the royal family.[70]

As she began her work in 1653, the main power in the land was Oliver Cromwell. He had dissolved the Long Parliament in April of that year. Fell wrote four letters to Oliver Cromwell, none of which were published in toto, though they were summarized in her *Works,* published after her death.[71] From the outset, Margaret Fell adopted a strong biblical, prophetic-apocalyptic tone with the Lord Protector. The first sentence of the lengthy letter sounds a theme that we find over and again in Fell. She writes, "I am moved of the Lord to write a warning to thee from the Lord God of heaven and earth that thou harken to the light of God in thy Conscience."[72] In this letter, written a year or so after her convincement, she did not ask for any particular protection, "for I utterly deny protection as from man."[73] Instead she writes that her concern is for his soul, that he would not be led astray by corrupt advisers and other "hypocrites," especially in the light of the soon-coming reign of Christ on earth.[74] However, in her other epistles to Cromwell she did appeal to his previous promises to bring "liberty of Conscience" and to "execute Justice," especially with respect to those in government, church, and court who were persecuting Friends.[75]

The Society of Friends came of age during one of England's most active periods of pamphlet publication, and they readily availed themselves of printing technology to broadcast their evangelistic, apologetic, and prophetic messages. They were aware from the outset of the power of print. The First Publishers of the Truth were willing to respond to the published claims and attacks of others with writings of their own. Like other Quaker leaders Margaret Fell was quick to the pen in the early years of the Friends. To those who were persecuting the Friends she could write with powerful prophetic prose which condemned in no uncertain terms both the persecutors and the actions they undertook in the name of God. In one early example Margaret wrote a letter in 1652 to Justice John Sawrey, the same man who had then recently expelled Fox from the parish church in Ulverston against her wishes.[76] In a no-holds-barred condemnation of his actions, she calls him a "seeming professor" of Christ, but really an agent of Satan, and a persecutor of the truth. She goes so far as to condemn his family as well. "The Devil is the father of lies, and thy family practices much in that trade." She utterly rejects the "lies and scandals which you have raised of me," and of "my friends and family."[77] The letter concludes with a stern call to repent and to turn to the Lord.

Of course, this letter is not only about Friends but about a personal attack on her and her family as well as George Fox. We attend to it primarily because it indicates Fell's approach to all those who would persecute Friends: a biblical-prophetic condemnation of their works in no uncertain terms, followed by a call to repentance and to listen to the inward teacher, the Light of Christ. Not long after sharpening her pen against Sawrey, Fell's first major period of published writing began in 1654 and continued for six years. In 1654, just two years after her convincement, she wrote *An Epistle to the World, Priests, and People concerning the Light* . . . .[78] This letter gives us a valuable insight into the growing prophetic consciousness of Fell and forms the basis of her first published work *False Prophets, Antichrists, Deceivers Which are in the World . . .* (1655).[79] This short pamphlet is a rhetorically powerful condemnation of those who were persecuting the Quakers, using terms drawn from biblical apocalyptic literature. However, it is more than this. It is a general condemnation of the empty outward forms, those "Means and Ordinances" or church practices, which Fell and the early Friends found unbiblical and unwarranted.[80] The Christians were "poor, blind People" that wandered in these last days. They had been led astray by the false prophets and followers of the antichrist predicted in the New Testament and now appearing in the "latter days." Such false teachers must be tested according to the Scriptures, and according to the Light of God in our conscience.[81]

The depth of Fell's concern for the spiritual condition of Christians was related in part to a powerful vision she experienced at this time. In an editorial aside at the end of her epistle *To all the Professors of the World . . .* (1656) Fell relates,

> as I lay upon my Bed, I saw a Vision of all the Professors in the World, and it appeared unto me, as a long, torn, rotten House, so shattered, and so like to fall, as I thought, I never saw a thing like it in all my Life, so miserable Old and Decayed, and so ready for Destruction; And a Pity and a Tenderness rose in my Heart to the People; and so in the Motions of God's Spirit I writ this Paper aforesaid.[82]

Like some other women of her time, Fell saw herself as a prophet to whom the Spirit of God had come, granting her visions and a powerful word to speak to the people of her time and place. The influence of this prophetic vocation upon her theological work is evidenced in its focus upon practical theology, including ecclesiology, evangelism, apologetics, and ethics.

Not only did Fell write to her fellow Quakers, to the leaders and governors of her time, to the established clergy, and to Christians in general, but she had a specific call to the Jews. Fox preached a gospel that was for all religions throughout the world, but Fell was the first to focus Quaker missions specifically on the Jews.[83] Her first major publication was *For Manasseth-ben-Israel* (1656), which was soon followed by *A Loving Salutation to the Seed of Abraham* (1657). Though it is doubtful that Rabbi ben Israel ever read Fell's work, both tracts were translated into Dutch and Hebrew for distribution by Quaker missionaries.[84] Fell's prophetic word to the Jews of her day was powerfully stimulated by her eschatological hope, as we shall demonstrate later in this work. Her concern for "all the professors of the World" and for the sorry state of the church (in what she obviously believed to be the last days) led to the publication in 1656 of *A Testimony of the Touch-Stone*, printed together with *A Tryal of the False Prophets* and *Some Ranter Principles Answered*.[85] Taken together as a corpus, most of Fell's main eschatological ideas, such as the present indwelling of the Light of Christ as "Christ come in the flesh," can be found somewhere in this three-fold publication.

In addition to presenting her eschatological convictions, these works provide us with a long summary of her practical ecclesiology and of the standard Quaker complaints against the "gathered" churches of the day. These are chronicled primarily as evidence that the established Church in England was Christian in name only and also to bolster Friends' contention that their persecution was in fact proof that they were true followers of Christ. This is in keeping with H. Larry Ingle's observation that, "Fox saw the sufferings of himself and his followers not as evidence of wrongdoing on their part but as a sign that they were faithfully following God's will."[86] In 1658, two major events further influenced the direction of Fell's religious work: one personal and one national. With the death of Oliver Cromwell and the leadership failures of his son Richard, the struggle for succession led to a period of political upheaval that would lead eventually to the restoration of the monarchy in 1660. The second major event was the death of Thomas Fell, leaving Margaret a widow. The death of the judge left her with more control over the family wealth as well as a new type of liberty wherein she was free from her obligations to her husband and his career. At the same time the considerable protection that Judge Fell's office provided for her and other Friends quickly fell away. The timing for this was unfortunate on many fronts, as it came on the eve of renewed persecution of religious dissidents in England.

In the first years of the Restoration, the period when the monarchy was officially reinstated under Charles II, the effects of long months of imprisonment in England's damp prisons resulted in the deaths of many important Quakers and decimated the nascent movement. Nicholas Morgan has noted that, "as far as the future of the Movement was concerned, the most important legacy of this period was the vacuum created by the deaths of the majority of the early northern Quaker ministers and leaders."[87] In the midst of these events, Margaret Fell wrote a pamphlet to the leaders of the army. Not surprisingly, her epistle *To the General Councel and Officers of the Army . . .* (1659) is an appeal for liberty of conscience and just treatment of the Quakers. Yet it is also an eloquent testimony to Fell's continued hope for the full reign of Christ to come upon the earth. In the opening paragraph, for example, after asking them to "do Justice," she wrote, "And oh!, that your eyes were open to see what the most high is doing in this his day of power."[88] At the end of the letter, just above her name, she describes herself in this manner: "From a true lover of true Peace and Righteousness which is coming to rule, for he hath taken upon him his great power and therefore the Nations are angry."

Although not included in her *Works*, this tract highlights Fell's eschatological hope in the midst of troubled political times and reveals a woman stepping forward into a great historical moment. In the following year, 1660, she published a number of her most important and lengthy theological tracts and in many ways came into her own as a prophet, teacher, and practical theologian. In part she was stimulated by the new political realities that surrounded the return of the king, Charles II (1661–1685). These led her to act as not only as leader, minister, teacher, and preacher of the gospel but once again as emissary to the king. With a new king, Friends were once again compelled to establish communication with the Royal Court. In addition, they had to identify themselves as loyal subjects and distance themselves from Interregnum activities. The type of political maneuvering deemed prudent during this time can be seen in Fell's early visit to Charles II.

When Margaret Fell visited Charles II in July 1660 to petition for Fox's release from prison, she was accompanied by Quaker Ann Curtis. Ann Curtis was the daughter of Robert Yeomans, a royalist sheriff who had been hanged almost twenty years earlier for his loyalty to the Crown. King Charles was apparently impressed, for Margaret Fell was granted three more visits with the monarch within the next week.[89] During this time she delivered *A Declaration and an Information from Us, The People Called Quakers* to the king on August 22, 1660.[90] This summary statement of Quaker principles written to the king and Parliament is signed by Fell herself, but also undersigned by Fox and twelve other Quaker leaders. This is the first fully public document to articulate the Quaker peace testimony, a subject to which we will return in a later chapter. For our purposes here, it is enough to note that its main purpose is to explain in general the truth as they understood it. In terms of politics, Fell argues that Quakers were good subjects of the king and that their principles in no way undermined the new monarchy. She also issues familiar calls for justice in the treatment of persecuted Friends.

The return of the king also meant the return of the bishops, and of the traditional structures of the Anglican Church. In this context, when there was a national debate about the nature of Church of England governance, Fell published an appeal to them in the 1660 *This is to the Clergy*. While there was little new in her condemnation of the traditional privileges and practices of the Anglican clergy, it did provide a summary of her ongoing critique of the established church, a perspective which she held in common with Fox and other Quaker prophets and teachers. Written directly to the clergy of the Church of England in the midst of a national debate about the episcopacy, it provides a summary of her complaints about their power, wealth, and legal privileges (or in negative terms, their greed, corruption, and partiality). She warns them against oppressing the followers of conscience, that is, of the Lord, lest they be destroyed by the soon-coming king. She writes, "Consider this, and see what the Lord is doing, and do not willfully shut your Eyes against the Hand of the Lord, lest you fall into utter Ruin and Destruction."[91] Another major summary document written in this time is her booklet *A True Testimony from the People of God*. This doctrinal tract was written "to all the teachers in the world, who go under the name of Christian."[92] Fell is writing to all Christian leaders in the name of Christ, inviting them to come to the truth. Her primary thrust here is the charge that they ignore the work of the Spirit and deny the Light of God shining in our hearts, "by which God teaches his people Himself." The testimony of Christian teachers "of the world" is the letter of the Scripture without its spirit and power.[93]

The last of the 1660 publications would be her most general and universal tract and was written to all Christians. In her booklet *An Evident Demonstration to God's Elect,* Fell addresses the doctrine of faith, something all Christians would have in common. From her perspective, those who merely own the name Christian are apostate, lacking faith but claiming to have it. True faith is a gift of God and has as its focus the Son of God, Jesus Christ. But faith must be tested and tried against the Scriptures, and also against the truth as we know it in the Inward Light of God. She claims this point as the major purpose of her booklet: "And so Friends, this is the very end of my writing, that you even would contend for the precious Faith in every particular."[94] The overall tone of this work is not condemnatory, but irenic and persuasive. The content of the publication is a general and by now familiar call to all believers to accept the truth, believe in Christ, and follow the teachings of Scripture and the Light of God in our conscience.

The flurry of activity that attended Margaret in the early years of her widowhood surrounded her as she came into full prominence in 1660. Fell was very active for the Quaker cause during the eighteen months she spent in London, and "her work in the capital was vigorous and systematic: she wrote and circulated papers to all the royal family."[95] In her autobiographical testimony, Fell records that she had visited Friends Meetings, given papers to those in power explaining the doctrines and principles of Friends, and spoken to all of the main members of the royal family. Things were going along well she tells us, "until the Fifth Monarchy Men raised an insurrection and a tumult in the city of London."[96] The views of this religious and militaristic group were millenarian and their nearly successful insurrection created a sense of panic among many, generating a backlash against religious nonconformists of any stripe.[97] The year 1661 brought wide-spread persecution and imprisonment of Quakers and other religious dissenters following the failed Fifth Monarchy uprising led by Richard Venner.[98] In the wake of this massive roundup, Margaret Fell worked incessantly through correspondence to calm the populace and direct activities that might free the more than 4,000 Friends who had been arrested.

From her earliest days as a Quaker, Margaret was involved in providing for the defense and support of persons arrested on the basis of religious belief and practice. A good percentage of her letters to magistrates and political leaders involved claims about the illegality of the writs and warrants used to arrest and imprison. A classic example is *A declaration of M:F: to all magistrates concerning the wrong takeinge upp & Imprisoninge of G.F.* There she writes a detailed explanation of improper procedure in the arrest and detention of George Fox. Her charge is against Henry Porter, who was the mayor of Lancaster. In addition to acting beyond the authority of their office, she alleges that Porter and his constables had violated Fox's rights as a prisoner. She writes,

> But he contrary to Law, (if he had taken him lawfully) denyed any bayle & clapt him up in close prison; After he was in prison, a coppy of his Mittimus was demanded, which ought not to bee denyed to any prisoner, nor noe lawfull Magistrate will[.] that soe hee may see what is laid to his charge, but it was denyed him.

But the sheer number of arrests made arguments of this nature fairly ineffectual, and the effect of the arrests on Quakers was devastating. The power of this determined attack on the personal liberties of English citizens was especially devastating for the leadership and those with key roles in the organizational structure of early Friends. Thus it was that "this infant structure, firmly settled in the north, was swept away in the storm of persecution which broke over Friends in the immediate post-Restoration years."[99]

In the years after the Fifth Monarchy uprising in London until the death of Charles II, Quakers and other nonconformists suffered under a number of acts aimed at reining in dissidents. Quakers were oppressed, fined, and imprisoned throughout the land, and their meetings—which had long been declared illegal—were frequently interrupted by officers of the law. Despite these setbacks Fell continued to work to free hundreds of imprisoned Quakers including George Fox. Her efforts were rewarded when the king ordered the release of Quakers in prisons throughout the land via two proclamations (May and August, 1661).[100] But Friends were slow to see any relief from these edicts as the proclamations were effectively rendered impotent by the local officials who chose to delay acting upon the new orders. For anyone troubled by the king's release of the Quakers, their disappointment was soon eased. In 1662, Parliament passed the so-called Quaker Act which required everyone to swear an oath of allegiance to the Crown if called upon to do so.

## Margaret Fell and the "Quaker Act"

Based upon their interpretation of the New Testament teachings of Christ, Quakers believed it was a sin to swear oaths. Friends refused to do so, citing their liberty of conscience by which they were bound to follow the teachings of Christ. The summer of 1663 was an especially difficult time that prompted Fell and her daughters to make a long journey of about a thousand miles, during which they visited and encouraged Friends throughout England. Soon Margaret would have her most important day in court. In 1664, George Fox and Margaret Fell alike were arrested and questioned before a judge and jury, then imprisoned in Lancaster Castle. In Margaret's time before the court, the judge at the assizes made an offer to her: she need not swear the oath of allegiance if only she would cease holding religious meetings in her house. She refused to do this on biblical grounds, and on the grounds of the liberty of conscience. It is clear in reading her responses that she grasped the gravamen of the court's complaint and intended to argue her position on the merits. She would be satisfied with nothing short of a full hearing before her peers. However, the Crown and its court desired only her religious conformity and it was their habit to use criminal charges to secure this. It was apparent from early in the trial that neither citizen nor court would be satisfied by this tribunal.

It should be said that in the account of the trial found in her *Works*, Fell was treated with courtesy befitting her station as a gentlewoman and a widow. She was offered many opportunities to avoid the penalties that loomed.[101] Though he was certainly no victim, it is obvious that the judge did not wish to impose any penalty upon Margaret Fell. She simply left him little room to maneuver. In August, the judge passed a sentence of praemunire upon Fell, effectively denying her rights as a free English citizen. Her estate and property were forfeit to the king and she was imprisoned under a life sentence. Though she used the events of the trial to publicize the abuses of the court, this was all the satisfaction it would afford her. In many ways her life was now changed beyond recognition. The persecution of the Friends was reaching its apex and no one would be safe from the storm.[102] Such an atmosphere, so toxic to the intricacies of personal liberty, would not be addressed by rule of law or the pull of popular opinion alone. Still, Fell would not be silent. During her four-year imprisonment in Lancaster jail from 1664 to 1668, she wrote numerous letters defending herself, Fox, and other friends to judges and magistrates, as well as pastoral letters to Friends who were likewise in chains.

The first of the main tracts she published while in jail was written in the initial few months of her imprisonment: *A Call to the Universal Seed of God* (1664).[103] This work is an appeal to attend to the inward, spiritual worship, which is real Christianity, and leave all outward forms as having passed away. Christ has now come, the Seed of God promised to Eve (Gen 3:14), and shines inwardly through the Spirit. This tract contains her longest reflections upon Christology and centers upon the eschatological fulfillment of Christ. In these last days Jesus has come in the Spirit. He has "risen in the hearts of His People . . . here is the place of public Worship, which Christ Jesus has set up . . . and hither must all nations flow."[104] The focus of the soon-coming day of Christ's lordship is centered on the church rather than on political reign. This tract was the first fruit from one of her most productive periods in terms of theological literature. She went on to publish five of her main theological tracts in the years 1666 to 1668, in addition to a long series of extracts from the Bible summarizing the Scriptures for the education of Friends.[105]

Fell held meetings for worship with other Friends in Lancaster Castle and engaged in theological debate with other nonconformists.[106] This context of debate may have provided the stimulus for her published defense of women's speaking in church meetings in 1666, and her long condemnation of the practices of the clergy in other denominations in *A Touch-stone: or a Tryal by the Scriptures* (1667). In the written record Fell seems to have adjusted her rhetorical stance and altered the apocalyptic tone of works addressed to those who were not Friends. In her letter to King Charles II (1666), there is no longer any mention of the coming Day of the Lord's Wrath. God is presented as a greater Lord than even the king, who sees and judges now what the king is doing to the Quakers and to Fell herself.[107] It is interesting to read this in view of the fact that 1666 also brought the Great London Fire. Though the attendant loss of life and property was a tragedy, the news confirmed in groups such as Quakers their sense that something of vast historical import remained at hand. The eschatological significance of the numbers 666 most assuredly added an extra element of spiritual intrigue.

This theme is a common one in her letters to those in power, namely that God is Lord over all, sees all we do, and will judge it. However, earlier (1660) in her second letter to Charles II she set forth this theme in more apocalyptic terms.[108] The Quakers are identified as God's own people who like Israel, "he [God] is delivering . . . from under Taskmasters, that they may serve him in freeness of spirit." Therefore the king should take care not to stop his ears to their cries, for "they have a testimony for the Lord, and he will bear them witness, when he comes to make inquisition for Blood."[109] Even after 1661 she would write to Quakers reflecting upon the book of Revelation: "now her Manchild that was caught up unto God [i.e. Jesus], is coming to Rule all Nations with his Rod of Iron." However, no such language appears in writings addressed to non-Quakers after 1661 and there is less of an emphasis upon the political implications of her belief in the soon coming day of the full millennial reign of Christ.[110] We know from her letters to Friends that she still held to these beliefs, but after the Fifth Monarchy uprising she did not dwell upon them in writings to non-Quakers.[111] In keeping with this slight shift in emphasis, when she mentions the soon coming Reign of Christ upon all the earth, she asserts that He is coming to judge the church, not the kingdom.

The first period of imprisonment in Lancaster Castle (1664–1668) was the most productive of her life in terms of theological literature. In part, this is because of her 1667 summary of the Bible, *The Standard of the Lord Revealed*, published for the instruction of Quakers. This book is of primary interest because it reveals something of the biblical hermeneutic of early Quakers and demonstrates the high level of competence Fell brought to Scripture. Their concerns can be seen in what is kept and abstracted by Fell, and what is left out. The books of Genesis, Exodus, Psalms, and Isaiah, for example, are the major focus of the Old Testament section. The Gospel and letters of John, the letters of Paul, and the book of Revelation are all important for them from the New Testament. At one hundred and thirty-two pages, this work is the longest of her publications and is not included in her *Works*. In the same year Fell published her most famous work *Women's Speaking Justified*. The importance of this tract for Margaret herself is evidenced by the appearance of a second edition, published with some replies to questions and criticisms in 1667. None of her other tracts received a revised edition.

The main concepts of *Women's Speaking Justified* follow from her earlier ecclesiological works. Christ has now come in the Spirit, in the

Inward Light. In the latter days, the prophets and apostles predicted that the Spirit would fall on men and women. These days are now, so both daughters and sons shall prophesy (cf. Joel 2:28-29, cited by Peter in Acts 2:17). The main body of this tract is taken up with biblical interpretation, including her reading of those passages in Paul's letters that seem to limit women's leadership in the church. The revised edition of this tract was published together with Fell's longest theological work *A Touch-stone: or a Tryal by the Scriptures* (1667). These works focus upon the practices and privileges of the clergy, and this practical, ecclesiological focus may explain why they were published together. The *Touch-stone* is an organized review of all the "false practices" of other churches which, according to Quakers, were contrary to the gospel of Christ. It is the negative side to the positive ecclesiology presented in her *Call to the Universal Seed* two years earlier. It is a summary of all the main objections the early Quaker leaders had to the church practices of other denominations, aimed especially but not solely at the clergy of the Church of England.

Fell closed this most active period of her theological writings from prison with another appeal specifically to the Jews, *A Call unto the Seed of Israel* (1668).[112] This tract was her last published, and was included along with some supplementary material on the Light, written to all people, Jews and Gentiles, who seek after the truth.[113] Though other tracts such as her *A Call to the Universal Seed of God* were written to both Gentiles and Jews, in this work she returned to a focus on the people of Israel alone. One can only assume that in the midst of all her concerns for her family, estate, and freedom, and the continued oppression of Quakers throughout the land, she must have retained a passionate concern for the Jews and a desire that they might come to Christ. Further evidence of this comes from her quest to have her tracts to the Jews translated into Hebrew and/or Latin.[114] The mission to the Jews was not making much progress, and it may be that she felt a fresh restatement of her position would be helpful in the advance of the truth among the children of Israel. At the same time she attached two open letters and twenty-five "queries" written to Gentiles and Jews concerning the nature of the Light of God, a subject so important in her address to the Jews alone. In this supplementary material she specifically considered the question (which must have been raised by the critics of Quaker theology) of whether the Inward Light is natural or supernatural.

## Margaret Fell as Quaker Leader: The Last Decades

In 1668 the petitions of Fell—and of many others on her behalf—pleading for understanding and liberty of conscience finally bore fruit. The king ordered her release, and in June she regained her freedom. During the period of this latest imprisonment, religious persecution had taken a high toll on the Society of Friends, particularly in the northern meetings, a loss that "pays tribute to the efficacy of English gaols in removing undesirables."[115] After her long absence from Swarthmoor Hall, she returned home to attend to her neglected personal and financial affairs, which included the celebration of her daughter Mary's marriage to a Quaker physician, Thomas Lower. Mother Fell again took up a leadership role in the Weekly Meeting in her home, and among the Quakers in Lancaster. She and her daughter Rachel also traveled to Friends Meetings and visited Quakers who remained imprisoned.

Her recent imprisonment and her prison correspondence and publications had secured Fell's position as a weighty voice among Friends at a time when losses had pushed the Society of Friends into disarray. As the Society struggled under siege, the remaining Quaker leadership was hard pressed on all sides. In response, the traditionally northern orientation of the Society shifted to London and the south. As Nicholas Morgan observes:

> The Quaker response to the nationwide sufferings of Friends, and to the deaths of so many of the early ministers and leaders, was encapsulated in George Fox's attempts, beginning in 1668, to rebuild the organization that had existed before the Restoration. There were to be two major changes of emphasis: the first was the shift to London, "a more convenient place"; the second was the predominance of George Fox.[116]

This new orientation toward London, with the emphasis upon establishing rules and procedures, and the new emphasis upon the authority of the Yearly Meeting gradually emerged over the next few years.[117] Mother Fell supported this by her travel and communication as she sought to encourage the movement throughout England, which included her final visit to London in the summer of 1669.[118]

During this period of reorganization, an event that Fox and Fell had been discussing in recent years came to pass: their marriage. In his own *Journal*, Fox noted that he had "seen from the Lord for a considerable time before that I should take Margaret Fell to be my wife."[119] Fell herself wrote of their wedding plans immediately after she was released from Lancaster Castle in 1668, in a way that assumes they had already agreed to it. According to Margaret, "Then he told me, the time was drawing on towards our marriage, but he might first go into Ireland."[120] True to his word, after he returned to England from Ireland, Fox met Fell in Bristol for the nuptials. On October 27, 1669, they were married before a large meeting, after the fashion of Quakers.

Although they shared a deep affection and respect for one another, the union of Fox and Fell was primarily entered into for the benefit of the Society of Friends.[121] Apart from their personal attachment and affection, the primary motivations for Fox and Fell seem to have been political, theological, and strategic. Politically, the marriage itself addressed issues raised both inside and outside the Society of Friends concerning the relationship between George Fox and Margaret Fell. They had long worked closely together in the Society of Friends, and their close association was such that critics of Quakerism looked upon it as a scandal.[122] The theological symbolism may be seen in an October 2, 1669, letter written by George Fox to all the meetings in England. From his perspective the marriage was itself a testimony that all might come out of the wilderness to the marriage of the Lamb, and to marriage as it was in the innocence before the Fall.[123] The strategic value came in giving official standing to the reality that Fox and Fell had long ago become mutual partners in ministry and leadership.

The case for this interpretation of the marriage as a strategic maneuver is supported by details already discussed. We know that Fox had such confidence in Fell's abilities that soon after her convincement he began asking her to respond to critics of Quakerism when he was away from the north.[124] And as we have seen above, George had felt for a "considerable time" that he and Margaret should wed. However, it was not until Fox had begun his effort to rebuild and restructure the Society of Friends in 1668 that such an arrangement was made.[125] Soon after their marriage Margaret returned north to Swarthmoor Hall while George remained in the south. This arrangement benefited their efforts to reorganize and consolidate power within the maturing Society of Friends. Already a fire-tested powerhouse of the north, Margaret was now also the wife of emerging Friends icon George Fox. In this way, George's authority and presence among northern Friends would have been reaffirmed even as he devoted most of his attention to activities in the south.

The advantages of this second marriage were considerably less for Margaret than for George. While she benefited in some circles from her relationship with George Fox, she suffered greater for it in others. It greatly strained her relationship with her own son George Fell, and temporarily cost her possession of Swarthmoor Hall. At the same time, the added weight of her role as Fox's representative in the northern Society seems to have anchored her once again, for she rarely traveled to London after that time. This left her increasingly isolated from southern Friends and from the new generation of leaders emerging there. Such isolation, and the perception among younger Friends that her work was an extension of Fox himself, also contributed to George Fox's hegemony in later Quaker histories. It certainly placed her at a disadvantage when she found herself in conflicts such as the long-lived Quaker schism led by northern Friends John Wilkinson and John Story.[126]

As we alluded to previously, this union of George and Margaret may have appeased some critics, but it greatly displeased her only son, George Fell. George was the son and heir of Judge Fell and educated as a gentleman of the day. Like his father, he studied law at Gray's Inn in London. As the male heir he was certainly within his rights to expect some portion of his father's estate. In addition, George Fell did not adopt Friends beliefs and openly opposed his mother's marriage to a commoner who was ten years younger than she.[127] Though young George has been painted in a poor light, it is difficult not to feel some sympathy for him and his actions. His mother, sisters, and boyhood companions all immersed themselves in the Quaker life which in turn brought unending humiliation and estrangement for him personally. And though there is ample evidence that George Fell was often cruel to his mother, he seems somewhat justified in his determination to keep Swarthmoor Hall from falling to Margaret and the Quakers. Thus when Margaret Fell became Margaret Fox, her son argued that she was no longer the widow of Judge Thomas Fell. Young George believed (with some justification) that he had been unfairly deprived of his inheritance of Swarthmoor Hall, and her alliance with Fox remained a bitter pill to her son.[128] He struggled to keep the despised George Fox from depriving him directly or indirectly of his inheritance and also, in some final way, of his mother. George Fell therefore moved to legally win possession of Swarthmoor Hall and his father's estate.[129]

According Judge Fell's will, Margaret had possession only while she was a widow, and since she was now married their son sought to gain control of the estate.[130] As Bonnelyn Young Kunze has noted, "Family correspondence conveys the bitterness of the battle for Swarthmoor that ensued."[131] Due to George Fell's machinations, Margaret was forced back into jail in April 1670, under the old sentence of praemunire. She was quite ill during this imprisonment and endured the horrors of English prison for over a year. The action was settled in an unexpected manner when son George died in October 1670. It is difficult to know what this would have meant to his mother. In the historical record there is ample evidence that she was a loving mother who expected a great deal from her children. Her only son had rejected the testimony of the Light and lived a life antithetical to Friends values. That truly would have wrenched her passionate heart. The Friends' narrative portrays George as a heavy drinker who was overly influenced by his wife and the company of others with his social station. He made himself an enemy of all things Quaker. As a religious crusader and visible standard of the Society of Friends, Margaret must have had mixed feelings about her son and would probably have viewed his death as a consequence of his work against them.

No matter what her disposition, we know that with the death of George Fell his mother Margaret petitioned to have Swarthmoor Hall and the estate settled on her unmarried daughters, Susan and Rachel. The king granted this in April 1671, and in the same document he released Fell from prison. Thus Swarthmoor Hall—an important Quaker institution, meeting house, and center for Friends activities—remained in the hands of Quakers. However, the matter remained a source of antagonism into the next generation.[132] Regardless, from the point of their marriage, George Fox and Margaret Fell continued to labor over the reorganization of the Society of Friends. The system of Monthly, Quarterly, and Yearly Meetings was strengthened and organized with London rather than Swarthmoor Hall at the center. Fox made a long visit to America from 1671 to 1673, in part to help organize Friends in the colonies. This was still a time of persecution in England, and many fines were leveled against Friends for disobedience to the Second Conventicle Act, which "sought to enforce conformity by seizing the goods rather than the person of the offender."[133] This practice of fines rather than imprisonment was extremely effective in creating hardship for the Quakers. Fell was herself fined a total of one hundred pounds, a large sum for the time.[134] From the outset Friends had organized their resources in support of members who were fined or jailed. With the push for reorganization in the late 1660s, Fox and Fell also labored for stronger and more autonomous Women's Meetings.

Early Quakers were well known for their teaching concerning the equality of women and men in the Light. This led to a loose organization of Women's Meetings initiated by Quaker women in London around 1657 and separated from the Men's Meetings. As part of the general purpose of organizing the various branches of Friends, Fox circulated a letter about Women's Meetings, their governance, and their purpose prior to his journey to the colonies in 1671. Although we will address this topic in a later chapter, some information is helpful here. The exact origins of the

Women's Meetings are not fully known, but London appears to have had the first such, in two meetings—the so-called Box Meeting, and the Two Weeks' Women's Meeting.[135] However, Margaret Fell played a "pivotal role in organizing the separate women's meetings."[136] Starting in 1671, Fell held a monthly Women's Meeting in Swarthmoor Hall. She and her daughters were prominent leaders. Women's Meetings spread from London to Kendal, Bristol, and Lancaster, then later to other regions of Friends activities, though not without some resistance from the Men's Meetings.[137] Their main activities were charitable, working with the poor and imprisoned, especially to those in the circle of Friends. Margaret and her daughters, particularly Sarah Fell, Rachel Fell, and Isabel Fell Yeamans, were all quite active in the leadership of the Women's Meetings, especially in Swarthmoor, Lancaster, Bristol, and London. Ross summarizes their work in this way: "For well over thirty years Margaret Fox and her daughters had been among the chief creators of Women's Meetings, which were not only of vital importance for the education and development of Quaker women, but of very great value to the Society of Friends in general."[138]

In 1673 Fox returned from the American colonies and sailed into a fresh assault on nonconformist religion. Parliament had passed the Test Act that resulted in persecution which lasted until 1685. George was arrested and imprisoned in Worcester, then moved to London, where he was held for more than a year. During this time Margaret made her sixth journey to London to petition the king for religious freedom.[139] She was also able to arrange her husband's release. At the time of his release he was in such poor health that he "spent twenty-one months in all, having returned there with Margaret and her daughter Susannah Fell . . . in the summer of 1975. By April, the notable Quaker leader William Penn was staying with him and he was being well looked after."[140] On his recovery Fox made for London to address some of the issues that continued to cause distress and dissent among Friends. By George Fox's trip to London in 1677, Margaret was sixty-three years old. In this year she published her last theological tract *The Daughter of Sion Awakened*. The outline of this tract is not unlike her précis of biblical themes published ten years earlier.

*The Daughter of Sion Awakened* is a summary of the history of salvation from Adam to Christ, with special focus on the true church. She asserts that a new day has arrived, one in which the true Light of God is shining in the hearts of all people.[141] She examines several biblical metaphors for the people of God—tabernacle, temple, Holy City, Jerusalem, bride, body—all of which she used to emphasize the contemporary work of God through the Light, and the dwelling of God within his people. They are included in her benediction: "And blessed and happy are all the Faithful, that are constant, true and obedient to the Lord's Eternal Light, Spirit and Truth."[142] Her work was headquartered in Swarthmoor Hall, and Margaret continued her work with Friends while her husband George embarked on yet another evangelistic journey. In the fall of 1678, Fox returned from London and Holland to see his family, coming once again to rest and work with Friends in the north. From her correspondence we know that Fell missed her husband very much and had anxiously awaited his successful return.[143] This was to be his last visit to Swarthmoor, and in the spring of 1680 he left once again for London and the south of England. There he remained, battling frequent health problems for the remainder of his life. He corresponded with his wife and often stayed in the homes of Fell's married daughters near London.[144]

The last of Margaret's single daughters were married in the 1680s to Quaker men. Sarah Fell married William Meade in 1681, and the couple moved to his home in London. Rachel Fell was married in 1683 to Daniel Abraham. Daniel gave up his family home in Manchester, the city where his family had made their fortune. He chose instead to live with Rachel and Margaret at Swarthmoor.[145] This same period saw the last years of the reign of Charles II (1680–1685). There were again widespread fines, oppression, and imprisonment of nonconformists, including many Quakers. Margaret, her daughter Rachel Abraham, and son-in-law Daniel Abraham were called up before old enemies of Fell and Fox, the brothers William and Roger Kirkby. The Kirkbys were judges in Lancaster, and they saw the Abrahams jailed and Margaret fined. The judges also saw fit to take many of her cattle from Swarthmoor.[146] In 1684 a seventy-year-old Fell made yet another journey to London, helped by her children, to petition on behalf of her family and of persecuted Friends in general. She was able to see her husband and other family members, and sought to present her case for religious tolerance to the Duke of York (James, soon to be king) and to Charles II. Her last meeting with Charles II was unsuccessful. He had lost patience with the dissenters for political reasons, and he was dismissive of Fell to the point of refusing to receive the paper she had written for his attention.

Margaret waited until the death of the old monarch to present her case before the new king, James II.[147] After gaining audience with the new king, her efforts were greeted with little enthusiasm. Thus, "Fell's attempt to resurrect the informality of the 1660s with the new king was equally fruitless: James was still in the first 'Anglican' phase of his reign, and his response to her plea for relief from persecutors was simply

'Go Home, go home.'"[148] By this response we can get some sense of how much her political and social clout had diminished over her years as a Quaker. James II would eventually stem the persecution of Quakers by the Crown and the established church, but by that time William Penn had replaced Margaret Fell as the gentle-born Quaker of choice in the Royal Court. James II issued a general pardon in 1686, followed by the 1687 Declaration of Indulgence for all nonconformists. This brought a general pardon for nonconformists, including Roman Catholics, and later in the month a royal warrant released Friends from prison and returned to them some of the heavy fines they had been paying.[149] This liberty was made more secure by the Glorious Revolution of 1688, when William and Mary of Orange ascended the throne of England. William III and Parliament then passed the Toleration Act (1689), ending the legal avenues for the persecution of Friends.[150] The Friends' long struggle for religious liberty had born fruit in the lifetime of Fox, Fell, and the remaining first generation of Friends.[151]

George Fox died in 1691, leaving Margaret a widow for the second time.[152] Mother Fell wrote a testament to her late husband published in his *Journal* as well as her own autobiographical recollections later published in her *Works*.[153] Though Margaret would reside at Swarthmoor for most of the eleven years she lived after the death of her second husband, she did make one last sojourn to London from 1697 to 1698, at the age of eighty-three. Her purpose generally was to settle the will of her husband and to visit the London Meetings and her family in the greater London area. At this point in June of 1698, the great Margaret Fell found herself unwelcome by many in Friends leadership in London, and some in the Yearly Meeting were reported to have made unkind remarks about her with regard to her age.[154] Despite this, Fell "once more took upon herself the heroic mantle of the early 1660s delivering by the hand of her daughter a letter to William III written in tones entirely redolent of 1660 and 1661."[155] There she reviewed in brief the former times of suffering, praising God and the king for their present liberty of conscience.[156]

Her next great pulpit would be her deathbed, which was a time filled with spiritual power derived from the proximity to death. This was especially true of early Friends' practice where testimonial and last words were considered particularly weighty things. From her bedside, family, visitors, and attendants took note of what she said and passed on what they saw as significant. This, in turn, was passed on to an attendant from within the Society of Friends which in the case of Margaret Fell was primarily her family. Deathbed visitors included her children and other Quakers who might have good cause to pay their respects at this final going. She was almost eighty-eight years of age and on the verge of leaving this world. She was surrounded by her children and others who hung on and collected her last words. Margaret Askew Fell Fox passed from life in 1702 at her home in Swarthmoor Hall. Her body was interred a few miles away in the burial ground belonging to the Swarthmoor meeting house. As was the custom within the Society of Friends at the time, all work for her funeral and any ceremony included were conducted by them after the manner of Friends. Ten years later her daughters and sons-in-law edited and published her *Works*.

# 2

## A Measure of the Times

In the last chapter we explored the life of Margaret Fell, particularly her conversion, arguing that her combination of social status, strength of character, and conviction made her a de facto leader in the early Friends movement. However, it is important to acknowledge that another factor contributing to Fell's prominence was the time during which she aligned herself with Fox and his message. In those early years, as George Fox and others convinced of his message traveled and preached, the support of the Fells and Swarthmoor Hall filled a critical role in the development of the Society of Friends.[1] On an organizational level Swarthmoor became the hub of northern activities, and the north was the base for Quaker efforts throughout England and beyond. The Hall was also the "heart and hearth" for the nascent Friends movement. Looking back on those early days at Swarthmoor Hall, William Caton reflects on the Fell family and the work of the Lord in their midst:

> Oh, the love which in that day abounded among us, especially in that family, and oh, the freshness of the power of the Lord God which then was amongst us . . . And hence came that worthy family to be so renowned in the nation, the fame of which spread much among Friends, and the power and presence of the Lord being so much there with us, it was as a means to induce many even from far to come thither, so that at one time there would have been Friends out of five or six counties.[2]

No doubt the course of Quaker history was changed by Margaret Fell and her work, and one cannot help but believe that she would have been a formidable presence in any age. At the same time, her actual significance for Fox and the new movement was predicated on the needs and opportunities of the hour. If a woman such as Margaret Fell had joined the Society of Friends in later years, when the likes of statesman William Penn and theologian Robert Barclay had already entered the stage of Quaker history, her role as a religious leader and thinker could not help but be diminished. This is not to slight Mother Fell, because it can be said of many great leaders that their destiny found them, not vice versa. The point here is that her rise and influence were made uniquely possible by the confluence of events around her, and if this is true for Fell it is even more so for the movement on which she exerted such influence. To aid our understanding of this, we will situate the emergence of Quakerism within the larger context of the English Reformation from which it sprang. For practical purposes, our discussion will focus on the years 1534 to 1689, from the Act of Supremacy under Henry VIII to the ascendancy of William and Mary.

Quakers were millenarians, and so we will turn our early attention to the effects of millenarian impulses and eschatological speculation upon the religious climate of Reformation England. From there we will look at religious radicalism and dissent during the period and the development of a specifically English Protestant eschatology. Against this backdrop we will situate the emergence of the Friends movement and the unique theological innovations that propelled its growth. We will attend specifically to religious, social, and political trends that fueled a pervasive interest in the end times, and the influence that these trends exerted on the course of religious radicalism in sixteenth- and seventeenth-century England. This period, marked by tremendous social, political, and religious upheaval, also straddles the intellectual migration from the medieval to the modern world. It was a time of transition—a social paradigm shift engendered in large part by the effects of a rapid population increase upon deteriorating feudal structures, emerging Enlightenment ideals, and the influence of the Protestant Reformation.

### English Eschatology from Henry VIII to the Bloodless Revolution

Despite the fusillade of new ideas that barraged the institutions and traditions of Reformation England, the people of this period continued to conceive of their symbolic universe in predominantly religious terms.[3] The conceptual union of cross and Crown retained its dominance of a sociopolitical landscape in which "religion was both the legitimizing ideology of the rulers and . . . the revolutionary idiom of the ruled."[4] The kingdoms of heaven and earth had thinly veiled borders, and Christian scripture possessed an almost undifferentiated religious and social authority barely conceivable to the modern mind. Despite the diminishing power and authority of feudal church structures, the conceptual world of the Christian religion continued to dominate the social and political landscape of England in the sixteenth and seventeenth centuries. According to historian Howard Shaw, religion for the English was "an all-embracing force that shaped their ideas and gave meaning to their lives."[5]

In this context, political issues were frequently cast in religious terms, and political battles coalesced around matters that would otherwise appear entirely theological.[6] Biblical eschatology, with its vague political undertones and evocative apocalyptic imagery, provided a rich source for political rhetoric that accommodated the turmoil of the time and yet nurtured a sense of destiny among the English people. Bernard McGinn, who edited the second volume of *The Encyclopedia of Apocalypticism*, touches upon this when he writes, "The most fundamental appeal of apocalypticism is the conviction it holds forth that time is related to eternity, that the history of man has a discernible structure and meaning in relation to its End, and that this End is the product not of chance, but of divine plan."[7] Of course, eschatological speculation and chiliastic expectation were not new pastimes introduced into the West in the sixteenth century. Indeed, Walter Klaassen has argued that "it is possible to trace an unbroken tradition of apocalyptic thought through the centuries," noting that, "from the late thirteenth century onwards specific popes or the papacy as an institution were increasingly identified as the Antichrist."[8] But the combination of Henry VIII's political goals with a Protestant vilification of the Catholic Church and a rising tide of nationalism created a peculiarly English apocalypticism. This "led not to the pursuit of a millennium but to the aspiration after nationality, not to the expectation of a messiah out of the blue but to the idea of an hereditary monarch called by the grace of God to rule the realm and defend the faith, not to the desire to cast down the mighty but to the resolution to cast out the interloper."[9]

We can trace the development of a uniquely English Protestant eschatology to the reign of Henry VIII (1491–1547) and his politically motivated break with the Roman Communion. Better known for his marital difficulties than his theological genius, Henry was nevertheless awarded the title "Defender of the Faith" by Pope Clement VII for the king's treatise against the Reformation ideas of the Protestant Martin Luther. However, with the Reformation Parliament (1529–1536) Henry VIII, aided first by Thomas Cromwell and later by Thomas Cranmer, broke with the Roman Communion and established the Church of England. When Parliament passed the Act of Supremacy in 1534, Henry

VIII was confirmed as the Supreme Head of the Church of England, and by 1536 the Catholic Church had been stripped of its English lands and prerogatives. With this, the monarchy began the transition from the medieval concept of ruler as chief lawmaker and overseer of civil behavior. The king now more closely approximated the modern idea of ruler as the ideological symbol of the state.

The English rejection of papal authority, the ongoing Protestant Reformation, and the open identification of the papacy with various apocalyptic figures facilitated the rapid development of a distinctly Protestant hermeneutic for eschatological symbols. Although as early as 1520 the "great protagonist of the Reformation, Martin Luther, had himself identified the Papacy with the Antichrist according to the prophecy contained in the Book of Daniel."[10] The pivotal English work in this area was *The Image of Both Churches*, part one of which was published in 1541, with a full text published in 1550. The author John Bale (1495–1563), who had served as a Catholic monk before his conversion to Protestantism, "hoped to convince the entire English people that their participation as a nation in the struggle between the godly and the unrighteous was essential to both their individual and corporate salvation."[11] The work contained a paraphrase of the book of Revelation and a detailed, verse-by-verse exposition of the text.

In the context of the Protestant Reformation, the English rejection of the papacy was interpreted by Bale as evidence of a special divine direction for England. Operating within this framework, Bale examined the biblical prophecies in the book of Revelation and connected them with specific historical or contemporary occurrences. Not surprisingly, he "saw the protestant reformation prophesied in Revelation."[12] Bale's approach to Christian Scripture as history and prophecy influenced the new apocalyptic tradition in England by knitting together medieval Latin and Protestant vernacular interpretations of the Apocalypse.[13] By establishing a chronology of events which tied Christian Scripture directly to human history, Bale formulated a new interpretive paradigm which endowed English Protestant eschatology with its particular historical cast. To apply the observations of McGinn: placed within the context of God's unfolding plan, English religious and political struggles were part of the ongoing and ultimately triumphant struggle of good over evil. The chronologies of Bale and others gave the English a new perspective on their past and a larger sense of their own history, a history with an eschatological framework. In this way, "a new element entered the apocalyptic tradition—the passion for chronological calculation of the future."[14]

Bishop Bale's chronological approach to eschatology encouraged the development and publication of similar timelines for end times, and "by the late sixteenth century, scholars replaced vague feelings about the imminence of the end with more precise calculations about its arrival."[15] This scholarly interest in end-times chronology helped establish its respectability and focused millennial expectations on contemporary events. Such was the intellectual environment in this time of peculiar foment that Enlightenment luminaries such as Sir Issac Newton wrote Bible commentaries which included extended discourses filled with end-times speculation.[16] Indeed, the esteemed Newton was himself a millennialist who wrote over a million words on matters religious.[17] More importantly, the identification of the pope as antichrist continued to anchor the formulation of these timetables, and "by the time of Elizabeth I, the doctrine that the Pope was Antichrist had acquired a theoretical respectability which seemed to rescue it from the subversive dangers of medieval heresy and tie it safely to monarchy."[18]

The Crown by now clearly recognized the inherent advantage of identifying the pope and papacy with the antichrist and Babylon and fostered the perception that the papacy was the enemy of the true church.[19] For this reason, the English political and religious leadership encouraged the publication of *The Acts and Monuments . . . from the Primitive age to these later times of ours, with the bloudy times, horrible troubles, and great persecutions against the Martyrs of Christ. . . .*[20] Written by John Foxe (1516–1587), the *Acts and Monuments* was known commonly as the Book of Martyrs. The work "was designed by the author to set before his countrymen in overwhelming detail a conception of universal history and of England's place in history, a conception which continued to prevail in the English mind long after the book had gone out of fashion, though not out of use and memory."[21] *Acts and Monuments* enjoyed widespread popularity and exerted tremendous influence on the formation of the religious opinions and national outlook of English Protestants during the period, and copies were eventually in every cathedral church, and chained to many parish lecterns.[22]

John Foxe accepted the eschatological presuppositions of his good friend John Bale and the work instilled in the multitude of its readers "the idea that the Church of Rome was the relentless foe of their country."[23] The popularity of Foxe's Book of Martyrs also facilitated the widespread dissemination of Bishop Bale's apocalyptic paradigm. And "because men like Bale and Foxe so firmly fixed a chronological apocalyptic interpretation of the history of the Christian church, their framework gained wide acceptance and lay embodied at the presupposition level in works which concentrated on other issues."[24] Works inspired by Foxe followed, and "a tide of opinion concerning the second coming of Christ and the end of the world had begun to flow early in Elizabeth's reign and would not ebb until its high watermark had been reached in the middle decades of the seventeenth century."[25]

In addition to the contributions of Bale and Foxe, the Cambridge biblical scholar Joseph Mede (1586–1638) is significant for the influence his views were to have on the eschatology of English religious radicals.[26] His work *Clavis Apocalyptica* appeared in Latin in 1627, with an English translation in 1642. This translation and publication were sponsored by the Long Parliament.[27] Although Mede's interest in eschatology was fueled by reading Foxe, his approach differed significantly from earlier work.[28] A respected scholar, "Mede, exercising his philological skills and announcing his discoveries in an understated way, founded a school of English millennial thought which continues to the present day."[29] Mede was a premillenialist who applied the seven seals of the book of Revelation to specific historical periods and argued for two judgments on either side of a literal thousand-year period, during which Satan would be bound on earth.[30] As we will see in the next section, Foxe and Mede become signposts for divergent paths in English apocalypticism.

Yet for all of this interest in end-times chronology, the perception of a rapidly approaching apocalypse would not have gained such a hold on the collective consciousness of England had it not provided the populace with a useful vocabulary and explanatory scheme.[31] The apocalyptic symbolic universe of calamity, replete with famine, plague, war, and immorality addressed the reality of life in sixteenth- and seventeenth-century England.[32] Likewise, apocalyptic thought reflected the polarized view of the universe that shaped the thinking of English Protestants during this period. "They believed that transcendent forces of good and evil strove to control the universe and linked each individual to one side or the other."[33] Because good would ultimately vanquish evil, banishing it for all eternity to outer darkness, it mattered that one be on the winning side. Given this mindset, "it was obvious to Puritans and their fellow Englishmen that the confrontation between Protestantism and anti-Christian Rome was already rapidly separating the world into diametrically opposed camps."[34]

In a culture that viewed all of life through a religious lens, such an explanatory scheme proved quite compelling. For example, the influence of apocalypticism on eschatology presented itself in an almost paranoid cultural preoccupation with popery and the antichrist. This ongoing identification of the papacy and "Romanish" practices with the antichrist could not help but shape the development of English ecclesiastical polity and practice.[35] Of course, not all speculation was vitriolic or nationalistic or radical, and it is worth remembering that prior to "the millenarianism . . . of the mid-seventeenth century, contemporary with them, and long after them, there existed such a moderate doctrine of the last things which focused primarily on the belief in Christ's second coming."[36] At the same time, the schismatic tendencies of Protestantism were exacerbated by this widespread use of apocalyptic terminology with its dualism of light and darkness, good and evil.

From its original introduction as propaganda in support of the English monarchy, the use of apocalyptic imagery to demonize the political opposition became common practice. This is mirrored in a similar movement from identification of the antichrist with a political power to identification of the antichrist with anyone who does not share one's political or religious ideology. So it was that in a period of intense confessional debate, apocalyptic thought accustomed people to conceive of conflict with the natural law as sinful. The term *antichrist* "ceased to be an exclusively ecclesiastical power and could be a symbol for any kind of political power—monarchy, the Lord Mayor of London, Parliament, the rule of the gentry, the protectorate of Oliver Cromwell."[37]

## Eschatology and Religious Radicalism

To this point we have treated the apocalypticism of the English Reformation period as a general category. As we expand our journey, a greater degree of distinction becomes necessary. Down one path stands the tradition we shall call the Magisterial Reformers. Magisterial Reformers were influenced by the millennial views of Augustine as represented by writers such as John Foxe. They believed they were living in the last days, and that the second coming of Christ would soon occur, ushering in eternity and the fulfillment of the church. Down a second path we find the Radical Reformers.[38] The views of the Radical Reformers may be seen in writers such as Joseph Mede, who held the position that Scripture mandated a literal second advent followed by a thousand-year reign of Christ, and then the judgment and eternity.[39] They believed that, "as God's chosen instrument to herald the new millennial age, their task was not a reformation but a restitution of what they believed to be Apostolic Christianity."[40] Although radical religious dissidents had been active in England since the mid-fourteenth century—largely through the work of John Wycliffe (*c*. 1329–1384) and the Lollards—our interests will be served just as well if we focus on Radical Reformers in the sixteenth and seventeenth centuries.[41] For our purposes, and in the interests of economy, we will consider four groups: Sabbatarians, the New Model Army, Levellers, and Fifth Monarchists. Other groups—such Anabaptists, Baptists, and Ranters—which could be included in our current discussion appear in other sections of this work.

By the reign of Elizabeth I (1533–1603), the Sabbatarian movement had migrated to England from the Continent.[42] Sabbatarianism, a dissident Christian practice that reemerged during the Reformation, embraced the Jewish Sabbath as the true day of rest advocated by Scripture and early Christian tradition.[43] Openly and actively opposed by leading reformers such as Martin Luther, the movement nonetheless gained adherents in all branches of Protestantism and in English Puritanism in particular.[44] "Saturday Sabbath" is the central tenet of this dissident practice, and Saturday Worship its hallmark. The use of the Jewish day for rest and worship was accepted in the Christian Church until A.D. 364, when it was forbidden by the Council of Laodicea.[45] It had also existed in some form in the Celtic Church from the outset.[46] Although not identified as holding apocalyptic views, a number of Sabbatarians were associated with the millenarian Fifth Monarchy movement.[47] And as we will see in a following chapter, the pro-Judaic—though not always pro-Jew—impulse of many Sabbatarians led to a revival of interest in the Hebrew language among scholars. A related development, philo-Semitism, was to have its own repercussions for English eschatology.[48]

Beyond Saturday observances, practices varied to include observance of Jewish dietary restrictions and other customs they believed to have been a part of the early church. Sabbatarianism reached the height of its power in the sixteenth and seventeenth centuries, and its influence on all forms of Protestantism may be seen in the number of Sabbatarian practices that survive today in groups such as the Seventh-Day Adventists, the Seventh-Day Baptists, and the World Wide Church of God.[49] In England, the Sabbatarian movement has historically been identified most readily with the Anglican priests John Traske (1585–1636) and Theophilus Brabourne (1590–1662).[50] Traske was the more radical in his views, and the more able preacher. Brabourne was the more capable and motivated scholar, and his works were influential with Sabbatarians long after his death. John Traske and his wife Dorothy Traske (c. 1585–1645) are associated with the Traskites, a sect which adopted a more strict adherence to Mosaic law than that favored by other practitioners at the time. His first two publications in 1615, *Christs Kingdom Discovered* and *A Pearle for a Prince, or a Princely Pearl*, expounded his views on Sabbath practices and on baptism. For the latter he was arrested and briefly imprisoned. In 1617 John and Dorothy Traske were married in London, and they established a Traskite Sabbatarian congregation. As other such congregations appeared in England, John Traske was again arrested.

His appearance before the Star Chamber, and the penalties there imposed, led Traske to recant his views publicly in the 1620 publication *A Treatise of Libertie from Iudaisme, or An acknowledgement of true Christian libertie, indited and published by Iohn Traske: of late stumbling, now happily running againe in the race of Christianitie*. John continued in ministry, primarily as an itinerant minister, and appears to have eventually given up promulgation of his Sabbatarian practices entirely. However, his wife Dorothy continued to work in spreading her husband's message, with the result that John Traske was arrested again in 1636 by the High Court of Commission, whose task it was to stem the spread of Sabbatarianism. He again renounced any affiliation with Sabbatarians, and after a brief imprisonment was released in London, where he died shortly thereafter. For her part, Dorothy Traske seems to have carried on with Sabbatarian teaching after her husband renounced his views in 1620, and she became far more important for the movement from this time on. She never recanted her religious views.

With an M.A., Theophilus Brabourne became the early scholar of record for English Sabbatarianism.[51] Brabourne was no follower of Traske. Rather, "what linked Traske and Brabourne was their insistence that the seventh day should be observed as the Sabbath, but to associate them more closely . . . is not warranted by the evidence."[52] A committed Anglican, Brabourne's efforts were directed toward integrating Jewish Sabbath observances into the Church of England. His first work *A Discourse upon the Sabbath Day* appeared in 1628. In it, he presents scriptural support for his Saturday Sabbath convictions, and these arguments and ideas often reappear in his later work. Brabourne was neither as radical nor as visible as Traske. However, his writings also brought him to the High Court of Commission as early as 1634. One result of this was Brabourne's carefully worded recantation of Sabbatarianism. However, he would long insist that this was not an indictment of the movement or its ideas.

The English Reformation was in many ways more a product of law than spirit. In a time of suspicion of all things papal, the popular religious and political concern over the presence of "Catholic style" practices in such things as church hierarchy, the use of vestments, the presentation of the Sacraments, and the placement of the altar further alienated Protestant sectarians from the Church of England.[53] For many, their eschatological interpretation of history or their fear of association with the antichrist and his works drove them to separate entirely from worship in the established church. As the rising popular millennialism turned attention toward the second coming, England was rife with religious sectarians who claimed prophetic knowledge concerning the time of Christ's appearance on earth. As Ball notes, "The interest shown in these symbolic predictions in the mid-seventeenth century was neither a new phenomenon, nor a sudden development of thought. In much the same way as belief in the imminent second advent, this absorption with prophecy can be traced back to the earliest years of the Reformation."[54]

Publication of various chronologies of historical events supposedly leading to the millennium contributed to the sense of expectancy and the subsequent need for vigilance.[55] This instilled sectarians with a sense of urgency and militancy that, not surprisingly, was perceived by those in authority as a threat. Early attempts to suppress independent and separatist religious gatherings, such as the Conventicle Act of 1593, used fines and imprisonment to deter illegal religious gatherings and enforce the conformity of religious practice which was a cornerstone of English government. However, given the apocalypticism that framed separatist religious beliefs and practices, such persecution was interpreted as evidence that the Church of England was indeed infected with remnants of the antichrist.[56] This perception fueled the resolve of many sectarians to continue political defiance in the name of righteousness. This trend toward political defiance in the name of religion was fueled not only by fear of popery, but by the subtly democratic sensibilities of Calvinism and radical Protestantism.[57] Royal authority in the period under consideration still rested upon feudal foundations. Respect for the authority of the monarchy was undermined by the habit of disobedience that developed through suppression of Protestant sectarianism. It was also challenged by the Reformation emphasis upon personal salvation, unmediated by any earthly institution.

This emphasis fostered the emergence of a peculiar sensibility that rejected socially mediated authority structures in favor of immediate divine guidance. Such an approach to religious revelation bred a view that the only valid human authority was one that acted in accordance with the religious ideology of a particular individual. The potential impact of such a posture on social and political stability became apparent during the English Civil War period. Here, the power of apocalyptic and millenarian anticipation was marshaled on behalf of Parliament in the form of the New Model Army. The New Model Army was a reconfiguration of three parliamentary armies that, for a number of reasons, initially had not seen much success against royalist forces. This new army, pulled together in an attempt to refocus resources and to circumvent political infighting in Parliament, was not intentionally organized around religious ideology.[58] However, the New Model Army's stunning military success was in many ways directly attributable to religious motivation. "Animated by a militant faith and having an apocalyptic, millenarian vision of England's destiny," the religious motivation of this political instrument made a distinct difference in its conduct and accomplishments.[59]

The New Model Army, particularly in the early years, was better disciplined and enjoyed higher morale than the royalist opposition. Likewise, the sense of fighting in the service of God against the forces of the antichrist imbued the soldiers with a confidence and a ruthlessness "directly traceable to the New Model's peculiar religious stamp."[60] As S. J. Barnett has observed, "Set against the background of unprecedented revolt and civil war across mid-seventeenth-century Europe, the English Civil War of the 1640's contributed to the production of a heightened quasi-apocalyptic atmosphere in the minds of many English Protestants."[61] Standing as they were at the edge of the second coming, the social constraints of the past proved unable to inhibit the actions of the New Model Army as it challenged the authority of the king. Protestant doctrine which encouraged notions of equality among the elect also generated a "solidarity based on a shared conviction of righteousness." This in turn "produced many feats of extraordinary courage which in turn hastened the collapse of enemy morale."[62] The belief that the New Model was an instrument of divine action was buoyed by its military success.

The power of such a conviction emboldened men of mean estate to battle their king and to contemplate a millennial kingdom led by the righteous under King Jesus. Such confidence led many members of the parliamentary forces to intervene in local civilian affairs, enforcing the puritan reformation of social customs, suppressing immoral behavior, and battling the agents of the antichrist. In a similar vein, members of the New Model Army often protected local Independent and separatist congregations from violence on the part of their more orthodox neighbors.[63] It is, however, an unfortunate fact that the same eschatological beliefs that facilitated the formation of the Commonwealth would haunt it until its demise. The primacy of unmediated divine guidance over earthly authority liberated many a conscience in the New Model Army's battle with the forces of the monarchy. Yet the same arguments that allowed men to reject the earthly authority of a king ultimately generated schism and rebellion in the ranks of the New Model Army. When the New Model Army proved victorious, the trial and execution of Charles I and Oliver Cromwell's ascendancy to leadership appeared to many to be the beginning of a new age. "With the end of the Monarchy came a suspension of censorship, which resulted in an explosion of tracts . . . often highly apocalyptic. It was widely believed that the Lord was doing a truly new thing in England, the very kingdom of God might soon be established there."[64] Even the letters of Cromwell himself reflect a certain chiliastic concern.[65] However, disputes over the shape and direction of the Commonwealth quickly arose between factions within the parliamentary forces.[66]

The religio-political movement that became known as the Levellers was one important faction, representing the more radical social views present in the parliamentarian party at the close of the English Civil War. Although primarily viewed as a political movement, historian Brian Manning makes it clear that "the Levellers sprang from the radical religious groups of the period."[67] Comprised in good measure of New Model Army members, these Independent separatists championed a more egalitarian social system. Leveller reforms called for the abolition of the monarchy and dissolution of the House of Lords, religious liberty, election for public office, and universal suffrage for "free-born" men. They advocated for the poor and argued that people could come to a correct understanding of the Bible and Christianity without the assistance of educated clergy.[68] Likewise, "the Levellers saw a parallel between the capacity of all men to discover for themselves true principles of religion and the demand that the laws of the land should be accessible to all citizens."[69] When the new Commonwealth failed to meet their expectations, Levellers continued the militant struggle to realize an England that reflected their vision and their conscience.

Though there were many who took leadership roles in the movement, John Lilburne (c. 1614–1657) is most consistently placed at the helm of the Levellers and is generally considered to be their most important leader.[70] According to Fenner Brockway, Lilburne "was the truly dynamic figure, cruder and fiercer . . . but of spectacular courage."[71] He was an early supporter of Oliver Cromwell (1599–1658) and a former army officer who eventually opposed the Protectorate. At the Grand Council Meeting that began on October 25, 1647, the Levellers openly backed the New Model Army's demands for back pay and presented for approval a constitutional document, the "Agreement of the People," that promoted and supported their agenda.[72] Known as the "Putney Debates" (1647–1648), this meeting placed Lieutenant-General Oliver Cromwell and Commissary-General Henry Ireton (1611–1651) as representatives of the "Grandees" in a face-to-face confrontation with the "Agitators," many of whom had been Cromwell's allies in the civil war. The divisions between Cromwell and the more radical opposition had not yet destroyed the goodwill between them, and Rufus Jones remarks that "how strongly the religious spirit dominated the debate can be seen by the fact that Lieutenant-Colonel Goffe and Lieutenant-General Cromwell, with the unity of all present, called for a solemn day of waiting for the guidance and direction of God in their deliberations."[73]

Schism further confronted Cromwell in 1648 with the Leveller rebellion. In March 1649 the writings of Leveller leaders were condemned as seditious and the writers confined to the Tower. In April a large detachment of Levellers, several of whom had fought under Cromwell only a few years earlier, captured the standard from the colour-sergeant in London.[74] In the following days many defected from the parliamentary forces, and whole brigades were in open revolt and aligned with the Leveller cause. Despite this support, the Leveller rebellion in the army quickly succumbed to the superior organization and numbers of the remaining parliamentary forces, and the movement became a minor footnote to history.[75] John Lilburne moved to Amsterdam for a few years, though he continued to write and publish. He also involved himself in plans "for the overthrow of Cromwell and the establishment of a limited monarchy in England."[76] He returned to England and was exiled by Cromwell to prison on the Isle of Jersey and was eventually confined to Dover Castle in 1655. There, Lilburne became a convinced Quaker and was released not long before his death in 1657.

The religious and political environment that gave rise to the Levellers readily produced other challenges to the authority of Oliver Cromwell and his government.[77] The next significant schism occurred in the form of the Fifth Monarchy Men, a millenarian group that took their name from Daniel's vision of a fifth and "everlasting kingdom to follow the four great world monarchies."[78] Like Cromwell, the Fifth Monarchists were Independent in religious practice, and many had served in the parliamentary forces. However, the millenarian tenor of the times brought them into sharp conflict with the aims of the government, and the "militant and exclusive self-confidence of the Fifth Monarchy Men" put them on a collision course with the government.[79] The Fifth Monarchy movement emerged as a religious and political entity after the dissolution of the Barebones Parliament in 1653 had once again dashed the hopes of millenarians.[80] Fifth Monarchists were "bitterly disappointed over the untimely end of the Parliament of God-fearing men that had dispersed before completing its work of preparing England for the rule of the saints."[81] This millenarian expectation of the rule of the saints under

King Jesus was the unifying sentiment among the Fifth Monarchists, who believed that Cromwell had subverted divine will with the dissolution of the Barebones. Believing Cromwell to be the primary obstacle to the establishment of King Jesus' reign, they were initially prepared to remove him by force if necessary.

Since the Fifth Monarchy Men included many former members of the New Model Army, this was not a threat to be taken lightly. At the same time, despite claims that they were prepared for armed insurrection and waited only for a sign from heaven, the majority of Fifth Monarchists appear ultimately to have had no taste for the anarchy that would follow such an enterprise. When a noteworthy uprising did finally occur in London, it was by a small, fanatical band that had ultimately been turned away by the leaders of the Fifth Monarchy Men.[82] However, the history of the Fifth Monarchy Men is exemplary of the fate of other radical reform movements with chiliastic expectations, which as we have seen included the Quakers. The Fifth Monarchists continued to appear in the occasional plot against a government leader. Rumors of Fifth Monarchist uprisings circulated from time to time, and their schismatic diatribes continued, though they appeared with less frequency. However, the ultimate fate of Fifth Monarchists and their beliefs was to fade not with a bang but a whimper.[83]

The Fifth Monarchy Men responded to the failure of their eschatology by maintaining a confrontational posture toward the government. In this, they reflect the struggle to maintain their eschatological vision in the face of disappointment with the pace of reform and its failure to incarnate their millennial hopes. For others the unfulfilled apocalyptic expectation was internalized, and many eventually found common ground with the realized eschatology of the Quaker movement.[84] In looking at the religious positions of radical groups such as the Levellers or the Fifth Monarchists, it is tempting to see Quakerism as a direct outgrowth of earlier teachings. As H. Larry Ingle notes, "to many critics, it seemed that in Quakerism the Levellers had gathered to pray."[85] However, it is more appropriate to understand the Friends movement as a response to impulses and failed ideologies of earlier radical groups.

According to Bernard Reay, "Leveller and True Leveller or Digger ideas do recur in Quaker literature. Winstanley and the Leveller leader John Lilburne became Quakers . . . Yet there is no evidence of any substantial continuity between Levellers and Diggers and Quakers."[86] It is more correct to see that the Society of Friends developed in response to the failure of this eschatology in general, and to the disappointed millenarian expectations of religious and social reformers in particular.

Likewise, the radical populist and egalitarian ideals that toppled Charles I also imprinted themselves upon the social consciousness of the emerging Friends movement, allowing the teachings of Fox and his companions to speak to the times and restore reason to the tumult of the age. This said, Quaker teachings did not develop in isolation, and to argue this in the case of Margaret Fell would be to ignore the drumbeat already heard. Like all the early Quaker leaders, she was greatly influenced by George Fox and the early band of preachers he gathered around himself.

## Apocalyptic in Early Quaker Thought

When he was released from prison in 1651, George Fox moved north to begin his life's work, drawing around him some of the main separatist leaders in Yorkshire, such as James Nayler and William Dewsbury. The young Fox already had experienced a number of visions and "openings" from the Lord; the main shape of his theology and religious fervor were set. All of the early leaders of the Quaker movement were highly prophetic-apocalyptic, and their fervor fit the tenor of the times, as we have seen in this chapter. Indeed, all of the earliest Quaker publications are in the category of prophetic and apocalyptic tracts for the time, proclaiming the judgment of God and the need to turn from sin and live henceforth in the Light of Christ.[87] This strong message of repentance and apocalypse was often acted out in symbolic and visible public actions and open-air preaching. For example, in the town of Selby after her convincement as a Friend on hearing the preaching of Dewsbury, Elizabeth Tomlinson went through the town proclaiming in a loud voice, "Repent! Repent! For the day of the Lord is at hand. Woe to the crown of pride. Woe to the covetous professors."[88] This example is not unusual. On the contrary, it is typical of the early Quakers, including Fox.

Early in his ministry in the north, Fox walked barefoot through the cathedral city of Lichfield shouting "Woe unto the bloody city of Lichfield."[89] Again in 1652, Fox recounts this incident of open air preaching in Kendal:

> I was moved to open my mouth and lift up my voice aloud in the mighty power of the Lord, and to tell them the mighty day of the Lord was coming upon all deceitful merchandise and ways, and to call them all to repentance and a turning to the Lord God, and his spirit within them, for it to teach them, and tremble before the mighty God of Heaven and earth, for his mighty day was coming; and so passed through the streets.[90]

Notice the reference to the Day of the Lord that was coming, and the need to repent and take heed of the Light (Spirit) within. Fox tells us in the same passage from his *Journal* that "the power of the Lord was so mighty and so strong that people flew like chaff before me, and ran into their houses and shops, for fear and terror took hold upon them." Indeed, this frank and openly apocalyptic preaching drew powerful criticism and persecution upon the new sect. One of the most infamous events of this type is of course the prophetic-symbolic entrance by James Nayler to the English city of Bristol. There ringed by women extolling him, he rode an ass into the city mirroring Jesus' triumphal entry into Jerusalem. He failed to understand his audience and as we will later see, the mistake had a lasting negative effect upon Quaker reputations.

What distinguished the eschatology of Fox from that of other millennial radicals we have been surveying in this chapter? The difference is in the strongly realized eschatology of Fox and the early promoters of the Lamb's War. As Doug Gwyn has demonstrated in his excellent study *Apocalypse of the Word*, Fox had a strongly realized and spiritual eschatology.[91] Although speaking and writing in strongly apocalyptic terminology, Quakers saw the kingdom of Christ as having already come in the Spirit, but soon to spread throughout all the earth. For example, in a 1653 letter to Colonel West, Fell writes, "The warr is begun. Michall and his Angells, and the Dragon & his Angells . . . But the lamb shall overcome."[92] This in no way undermined the fact that the full coming of the Day of the Lord was also at hand. Rather, the coming of Christ fully in the Spirit was the initial act of the fullness of the kingdom about to come upon the earth. Thus Fox used both the present and future tense when speaking of the reign of Christ. Christ "is come and coming to reign," and "the mighty day of the Lord is come, and coming to all the world, and his salvation shall be known to all the ends of the earth."[93]

The Lamb has now come in the Spirit, in the Inward Light, and will make war against the followers of darkness (Babylon or Satan, etc.). For example, Fox could write in 1654 that, "A day of slaughter is coming to you who have made war against the Lamb and against the saints . . . The sword you cannot escape and it shall be upon you ere long!"[94] At this point we can better understand that incorporating the bloody imagery from biblical apocalyptic into their proclamations was not without its own negative consequences. It contributed to an increased fear of sectarian violence in general, and a fear of Quakers in particular. As Reay notes, "George Fox reported that it was being preached that 'Quakers would kill' and 'the Quakers would rise.' Ministers were warning their congregations that England was about to become another Munster."⁹⁵ Of course, given the material in the previous paragraphs it is clear that fear of sectarian violence was reasonable to a certain degree. At the same time, the letters and journals of Quakers and public attempts to address these fears by Friends themselves support the general conception that they were a peaceable group on the whole.

The symbolic imagery that was so alive for the Friends became a vehicle for them to convey the desperate affairs of the day and the spiritual war they saw at every hand. But symbolism is likely to be misunderstood unless a hermeneutic is set forward that interprets it correctly. Toward this end, James Nayler uses his 1658 tract *The Lamb's War* to clarify the eschatology of the early Quaker preachers:

> What Their Weapons Are: as they war not against men's persons, so their weapons are not carnal nor hurtful to any of the creation; for the Lamb comes not to destroy men's lives nor the work of God, and therefore at his appearance in his subjects he puts spiritual weapons into their hearts and hands; their armor is the light, their sword the Spirit of the Father and the Son, their shield is their faith and patience, their paths are prepared with the gospel of peace and good-will towards all the creation of God.⁹⁶

This is not to say that Friends were entrenched pacifists from the beginning.

Although Friends followed the example of George Fox and endured beatings and other physical attacks without returning violence for violence, they were not consistently pacifist in the earliest years. Bernard Reay has argued at length that increased Quaker visibility in 1659, when Friends moved towards "a militant revolutionary position," was a strong catalyst in the restoration of Charles II in 1660.⁹⁷ It was the Restoration, then, that led the Society of Friends to fully and publicly articulate an absolute commitment to pacifism. Reay argues,

> Before that time it is impossible to talk, as it is later, of the Quakers as a predominantly pacifist group. Self-preservation after the restoration of the monarchy in 1660, disillusionment with the effectiveness of political action, encouraged them to project their pacifism backwards.⁹⁸

However, we will see in a later chapter that Quaker leaders such as George Fox and Margaret Fell had articulated the concept of nonviolence at least seven years earlier.

The Quaker position was clarified in the 1660 *A Declaration and an Information*, written and delivered by Margaret Fell to Charles II. Although the 1660 publication is of more interest to us, it is also important to take note of George Fox's 1661 *A Declaration from the Harmless People*:

> As for the kingdoms of this world, we cannot covet them, much less can we fight for them, but we do earnestly desire and wait, that by the Word of God's power and its effectual operation in the hearts of men, the kingdoms of this world may become the kingdoms of the Lord, and of his Christ, and he may rule and reign in men by his spirit and truth, and thereby all people, out of all different judgments and professions may be brought into love and unity with God.[99]

The Quakers did expect the reign and rule of Christ and indeed believed that Christ had already come. Yet they often proclaimed that their kingdom was not of this world, and their revolution was one of peace and love, not mortal conflict. Ultimately the Quakers were pacifists because they believed the Lamb's War was a spiritual conflict.

This emphasis upon an inner, spiritual, and realized eschatology was a unique contribution of the Quakers to English religion. George Fox and the other early Publishers of the Truth were alike in their constant refrain that the kingdom was come "within." The reign of Christ has already begun, in the Light that now shines in every human heart. William Dewsbury tells of his looking to many sects, in order to find "where Sion was." In 1652 he heard Fox preach that the kingdom is not in outward observances or merely human forms, but the kingdom of God is within (cf. Luke 24:23). England thus must "harken diligently to the counsel of the Lord, which is the light in your consciences."[100] God is ready to teach his people directly, through the Light. While much of the teaching and practice of the Quakers can find root in earlier practices, in their realized eschatology and spiritualized kingdom, the Quakers brought a new voice into the chiliastic conversation of their age. Here was a genuinely new perspective, which endured long after other millennial sects had dissipated.

For Fox and the early Quakers, Christ had already come again into the world, and his reign was being established in the souls and bodies of those who accepted the Inward Light of Christ and followed the teachings of the Light in their daily lives. This emphasis upon the interior, experiential nature of religious life also reflected the reliance upon unmediated divine direction. The Quakers relied upon direct spiritual inspiration, the "leading of the Lord," rather than the established structures of the church, which they considered corrupt. As with the New Model Army, the Levellers, and the Fifth Monarchy Men, a strong eschatological mindset encouraged Quakers to challenge the religious, social, and political realities of the period.[101] With their internalized and spiritualized eschatology, and direct reliance upon the teachings of the Inward Light, radical Quaker religious fervor took on a personal form.

The "rebellion" in which the Quakers participated was marked by the consistent refusal to participate in various mandated religious and social practices that conflicted with the powerful leveling effect of Quaker eschatology. As Catherine M. Wilcox has observed:

> The sense that they were living on the brink of the final crisis of history created a great sense of urgency among the first Quakers. It left them without the option of compromise with the fallen world and its apostate Churches. The Judge of all the world was at hand, and the Quakers' task was to warn people of the wrath in store for those who ignored the Call of Christ (the Light) to repent.[102]

Living as they did in the last days, and all being equally the servants of the Light, Quaker teachings led to a radical, spiritual equality that overturned accepted social institutions. This steadfast resistance to such necessities of seventeenth-century life as the payment of the tithe, the use of last names in personal address (Quakers used first names and the more familiar "thou" rather than the formal "ye"), the doffing of hats to social superiors, and the refusal to swear an oath of allegiance: all these radically egalitarian practices led to the persecution of Friends.

However, this persecution was also interpreted by Quakers in eschatological terms. Like all the biblical apocalyptic literature, the early Quakers saw a stark division between the children of light and the children of darkness. There can be no compromise between the Lamb and Satan, between the followers of the Light and the works of the devil. Persecution therefore must be expected; but the Lamb and his people will have the ultimate victory. As Nayler puts it in *The Lamb's War*, "is God's love in you otherwise than it has ever been in Christ and all his saints, whom the world ever hated, whom God loved, and in whom he testified against the world unto death, and unto bonds, and persecution?"[103] Likewise, Fox, in a letter written to all Christians, compares those who persecute Friends to the Jews who killed Christ, to those who stoned Stephen, and to the Romans who killed Paul. He goes on to speak of the rise of truth in his own day:

> And the same power now is made manifest, and doth overturn the world, and did overturn the world, to the exalting of the Lord, and to the pulling down of the kingdom of Satan . . . The priests they incense all the ignorant people for fear their trade should go down; and the professors they show forth what is in them, full of rage.[104]

In the same year in a letter to the pope and all the kings of Europe, Fox warns them to "be not bitter, nor hasty in persecuting the lambs of

Christ, neither turn yourselves against the visitations of God . . . lest the Lord's hand, arm and power take swiftly hold upon you; which is not stretched over the world."[105] In the eschatological vision of the Quakers, persecution was to be expected; but woe to those who battled against the Lamb of God!

Despite their being persecuted for what were perceived to be antisocial practices, the pacifist Quakers were a far cry from the New Model Army, whose ruthlessness, valor, and sacrifice flowed from the apocalyptic, chiliastic expectation that the righteous kingdom of God would soon be established on earth. Equidistant between the two, the Levellers and the Fifth Monarchy Men are witnesses that the revolution fuelled by millenarian expectation is easier to begin than to end. As we have seen, apocalyptic imagery loosed for political purposes in a time of social disequilibrium quickly gained a power all its own, and the eschatological vision of a New Jerusalem proved to be the undoing for many. By turning the power of the millennium inward, in a spiritual direction, the Quakers were able to keep their eschatology after the "disappointment" of the return of the king in 1660.

With the restoration of the monarchy and the return of the Church of England to its previous foundations, the apocalyptic character of English religion was confronted with a crisis. However, because Fox and the other Quakers had an inner, spiritual expectation of the kingdom, their eschatology was able to absorb the "shock" of return to normalcy. At the same time, *Declaration* of 1660 marks a turn in the apocalyptic character of Quakerism. They were forced to distinguish themselves from actions such as the Fifth Monarchy uprising. While they could and did still write of the "Day of the Lord," the emphasis was upon the Inward Light, and the struggle against sin. Little of the strong, military, apocalyptic prose of the 1650s lasted very long into the new decade. There is a distinct drop-off of "trumpet blasts" and other prophetic tracts after 1662.[106] As H. Larry Ingle writes, "After 1660 Friends—seldom billing themselves as 'Children of the Light' anymore—evolved into a sect markedly different from the creative, exuberant, and confrontational company of the turbulent and exciting 1650s."[107] Yet the first generation of Quakers still retained a powerful expectation that the truth and the Light would spread through their efforts to the uttermost ends of the earth. This explains in part the abundance of Friends' missionary efforts worldwide.[108] The kingdom was still coming: not by the sword, but by the Spirit.

# 3

## The Kingdom of Light
*Margaret Fell's Theology and Eschatology*

As an early apologist, Margaret Fell championed Friends' beliefs and practices in a variety of contexts. As a First Publisher of the Truth, she is an important source of insight into the theological development of the Society of Friends and her extant correspondence and religious writings provide a window through which to view the rise of Quakerism. Her books, pamphlets, and correspondence are addressed not only to Friends, but to priests, rabbis, kings, and nations. Never merely a follower of George Fox, Fell was a proclaimer of the Light, ever working to clarify, defend, and promote Quaker beliefs. From the outset of her convincement by Fox, Margaret Fell gives us a unique perspective on the Quaker movement. Though expressed in terms unique to the Friends movement, Fell's theology is biblically based and surprisingly orthodox given the strong opposition which Friends' theology elicited among the church leaders and divines of the day. Despite the occasional confusing or poorly organized effort, she was often an articulate theological spokesperson for the Quaker movement. In the same way, her well-documented leadership of the Friends' organizational hub in the north of England and her persecution and imprisonment for Quaker religious practices gives her writing a clear pedigree.

Scholars and students of Quakerism also understand that the value of her religious writing rests in her readiness to challenge critics and her willingness to defend Friends' beliefs and practices in print. Having said this, it should be noted that in pursuing a systematic account of Fell's theology we enter into territory she herself chose not to explore. This "nursing mother" of Quakerism was a polemical and prophetic pamphleteer, a religious leader and practical theologian concerned primarily with her immediate audience and present pressing needs of the Lamb's War. Margaret Fell was not a scholar in the traditional sense, and in fact carried with her a distrust of the educated, professional clergy. According to Fell, schooled pastors received instruction in Scripture but "have not the inspiration of the Almighty, and motion of the Spirit of the Lord God, the same that gave forth the Scriptures, when they come to interpret them, and give meaning to them, being unlearned therein, they just wrest them to their own destruction and therefore they do not profit the people at all."[1]

What then, besides some quest for deep irony, would justify our efforts to corral her religious thought into the close quarters of the standard systematic loci? We shall discover that gaining a better sense of the overall shape of her theology in reference to the standard loci will enhance our appreciation of early Quaker thought, and her contribution to it. As we discussed earlier in chapter 1, Margaret outlived the majority of first-generation Friends. Because of this long period of productivity and publication, Fell survived long enough to become an anachronism in the very movement on which she had stamped her mark. Later Society of Friends leaders at times found her earlier work awkward for political or social reasons, and her later work problematic because her pen had become an unauthorized vehicle for dissemination of the Society's opinions. Thus, close attention to her writings reveals the clear impact of changing social and political realities on Quaker theology over a long and historically significant period of time, and while this came at great personal cost to Fell, it is a benefit to Quaker studies.[2]

Like others of her time, she was motivated by her belief that a new age was upon the earth. Margaret was thus filled with a feeling of urgency and a holy boldness evidenced in her letters and publications. Her place at the center of the emerging Quaker movement was marked by a sense of mission which, combined with her pragmatic nature and her no-nonsense North Country sensibilities, made her a woman neither inclined to waste time nor mince words. Fell's writings thus reveal a great deal about the dynamic origins of the Friends movement and its developing theology: its early eschatological fervor, missionary zeal, spiritual militancy, and boldness in the face of persecution. Fell's writings likewise convey the values and sensibilities of those First Publishers of the Truth, most of whom went early to the grave as a result of their convictions.

Because of this, it is important to make clear that we are not making claims as to originality in Margaret Fell's theology. Though she was an able and creative biblical exegete, Fell was very much in debt to George Fox as well as to others who were silenced by death before their influence gained a face. This said, there is sufficient evidence to assert that

Margaret Fell was theologically active in the earliest days of her conversion. For example, in recounting the early days of the Quaker movement she writes, "And the preists & professors in our parts began to write against us: And G:F: [George Fox] being gone out of the Countrey Frst [first] brought things to mee, & I answered them. And I was but young in the truth yet I had a perfect & a pure testimony of god in my heart. For god & his truth."[3] What we seek in this chapter is not to ferret out an elusive "originality," but rather to take Fell seriously as a practical theologian and to demonstrate the inner coherence of her theological ideas.

In order to convey a sense of Margaret Fell's own voice, we will rely in the main upon her own writings, looking to create a more nuanced picture of her theology. At the center of her theological vocabulary are two workhorse terms that shoulder the greatest burden in her writings: "conscience" and "Light." Because it is easier to capture, we look first to the term conscience. From there we will seek to get a rein on Fell's conception of the Light, a term whose frequent and varied appearances makes it all the more difficult to grasp.

### Quaker Religious Thought and the Concept of the Conscience

The conscience, broadly understood to be a kind of moral faculty which judges our thoughts, words, and deeds, is central to understanding early Quaker theology. The idea of a conscience lies deep in western culture, and by the time Margaret Fell began writing the notion was commonplace in English religious literature.[4] Although the validity of the concept is still generally affirmed, our current use of the term is desiccated and trivial when compared to the mystical, chain-breaking, revolutionary power the word had acquired in Fell's day.[5] For this reason, our study of her theology will be enhanced by a brief overview of conscience and its development as a concept. Placed in context, the significance of the term and how it relates to Margaret Fell and early Quakerism should become apparent as we move through this chapter. We begin with the notion of conscience in the Bible and follow it through to the time of the Reformation and the emergence of Quakerism.

From a biblical standpoint, the term appears most often in the Pauline Epistles. According to New Testament scholar Judy Gundry-Volf, the use of the word conscience there "refers uniformly to the inner tribunal which determines whether behavior (in the broad sense, including thinking, willing, speaking and acting) agrees with the moral norms and requirements affirmed by the mind."[6] The notion can be traced back generally to the Bible and to Greco-Roman philosophers. It gradually emerged as an important theme in Christian moral theology, gaining philosophical subtlety and theological nuance from the patristic period through the Middle Ages and into the Reformation and Enlightenment. For instance, during the medieval period an elaborate moral theology, casuistry, and priestly authority developed around the idea of a conscience. During the Reformation the concept was refocused and given new direction by the work of Protestant theologians such as Martin Luther and John Calvin.

The appeal to the conscience, or the freedom of the conscience, was a staple rhetorical gesture in Protestant literature dating back to Luther himself.[7] Luther's defense at the Diet of Worms (1521) was based not only on an appeal to the word of God, but also on an appeal to his own conscience, which was "captive to the Word of God."[8] In what is possibly his most important theological work *The Bondage of the Will*, Luther also argues that the conscience is captive to the laws of God.[9] In a significant departure from the more liturgical, corporate, and priestly emphasis of medieval theologians, Luther radically focuses on the conscience of the individual believer, which is captive to the word of God in the Bible. Luther and Calvin alike taught that only faith—as opposed to outward penitence and good works—can yield a clean and clear conscience. The inner certainty of the grace and forgiveness of God, based upon the word and the Spirit, became a central element of Reformation thought. Freedom of conscience became a rallying cry in the Protestant movement and its political revolutions throughout Europe.

This idea that all of us have been given a conscience by God, and before which each of us is morally responsible, is key to any explanation of Fell's theology. Its prominence in her thinking may be briefly demonstrated by a look at her prophetic word to the political powers of her age. Here we see some of her most cautious and careful writing, regardless of whether the letters were intended for subsequent publication or not. Her letters to Oliver Cromwell began in 1653, which was soon after her convincement, in the first days after Cromwell was made Protector.[10] From the beginning she was urging him to heed God and protect the rights of Friends, "appealing to and exhorting him to obey the Light of Christ in his Conscience."[11] Years later when Charles II was newly returned to England and the throne, Fell appealed once again for liberty of conscience in several letters to him. Her charge to King Charles II included protection of Friends, as she urged him "to let the Lord Jesus Christ have his Right and Prerogative, whose Throne and Sceptre is in the Hearts and Consciences of his People."[12]

In 1698, not many years before her death, Mother Fell wrote to the newly enthroned King William III. After she provided a brief history of the Quakers, she assured the king that "we were never found in transgression of any just or Righteous Law, but only upon Account of our Consciences towards God."[13] Although this kind of appeal to the liberty of conscience in religious and civil matters would have been common and well understood by English Christians of the seventeenth century, Friends' theology and practice pushed the boundaries of the concept both in religion and society. What Friends added to the general Protestant notion of a moral conscience was their teaching regarding the Light within. With the significance of the term conscience as a backdrop, we turn our attention more directly to Fell's theology and her conception of the Light.

### Casting Light on Margaret Fell's Theology

We will conduct our examination of Fell's theological perspective through the lens of "the Light." The Light as we discuss it here was a unique emphasis of early Quaker theology, and one that generated a great deal of confusion among those outside the movement.[14] In the case of Margaret Fell, the Light is a nuanced concept that serves as a unifying theme in her theology. As we will see, the Light is a co-referential term for the activity of the Holy Spirit and the present work of Christ. Our understanding of the identity and function of the Light will itself become more nuanced as we examine Fell's theology as an exercise in systematics. Toward this end we will explore Mother Fell's religious writings for an insight into her doctrines of the Triune God, humankind and salvation, eschatology, the church and the sacraments, as well as sin and Satan.

The enquiry begins with a look at the doctrine of God, beginning with Fell's view on the Trinity. Evidence that she accepted the Trinitarian nature of God is found in her 1660 publication *A True Testimony from the People of God*. There, in a clear articulation of the traditional Christian perspective, she writes, "Christ saith, If any Man love me, and keep my Words, my Father will love him, and we shall come unto him and make our abode with him. Here the Comforter, which is the Holy Ghost, which proceeds from the Father and the Son, is manifested, which doth teach all things."[15] However, such a clearly Trinitarian statement is rare in Fell's religious writing taken as a whole. More common are the situations where the distinctions of the economic Trinity can reasonably be inferred, though they are not made explicit within the text itself.[16] For example, in the opening of one of her general letters to Friends she writes, "Oh! Blessed and happy are all they that are come into this sweet Being of Universal Love, which would have all to be Saved and to come to the Knowledge of the Truth."[17] This quote is more representative of Margaret Fell's theological approach to distinctions within the Trinity.

Her theological exposition of the Trinity is weighted toward Christ the Son, with God the Father discussed primarily in relation to the Son.[18] The Holy Spirit—explicitly identified as the third person of the Trinity—makes even fewer appearances in Fell's religious work. As with her references to God the Father, God the Holy Spirit is discussed most often in the context of God the Son. This approach can be seen in her 1656 publication, *To all the Professors of the World*, where she writes:

> He [Christ] hath offered one Sacrifice, and for ever is sat down at the Right Hand of God, from henceforth expecting, until his enemies be made his Foot-stool. For by his own Offering hath he perfected for ever them that are sanctified; and of this the Holy Ghost is a Witness to us, in the fulfilling of the Everlasting Promise of the Lord God.[19]

This Christocentric approach is a part of Fell's theological methodology generally, and may go some way towards explaining her lack of interest in discussion of the Trinity.

Another possibility is offered by Bonnelyn Young Kunze in her chapter on Fell's theology. She believes that Margaret "had an astute understanding of the theological debate," and intentionally kept her treatment of the Trinity to a minimum. In this "she pursued a studied avoidance of . . . Trinitarian arguments because she no longer accepted them as central beliefs as a Quaker."[20] This is a possible explanation, though it would be more persuasive were it made about the work of a second-generation Friend. However, it seems clear from her extant communications with "priests and professors" that she saw the Light as a revelation of God through the Christ of Scripture. Although the doctrine of the Trinity is certainly not central to Fell's theology, her constant use of the language of the Trinity (Father, Son/Christ, and Spirit) would hardly be understandable if she had abandoned the Christian doctrine of the Trinity altogether.

An equally plausible explanation is that Margaret Fell retained her belief in the Triune Godhead after her convincement, but the concept of the Light became her new interpretive and explanatory paradigm. As we have mentioned, Fell does not see herself as operating outside of the Christian tradition, but believes herself instead to be explaining a revealed truth consistent with the Bible, "for the Scriptures were given forth from the light, and the spirit of God was in them who spoke forth the Scriptures . . . as they were moved of the holy ghost, and Christ Jesus who is the light."²¹ Referring to the teachings on the Light she insists, "This is not a new Doctrine, though it may seem so to many; because this Mystery hath been hid, and the Spirit of God, which opens this Mystery, erred from, and turned from, by those that have been Teachers of People."²² It is also worth noting that that the amount of attention her work devotes to each person of the Godhead is roughly proportionate to that assigned in important statements of Christian orthodoxy such as the Niceo-Constantinopolitan Creed.

In part, the problem with her articulation of Trinitarian doctrine arises from the blurring effects her constant references to the Light have on distinctions between the three persons of the Godhead as economic Trinity. For example, in her published epistle *A Letter to Francis Howgill, and others when they were Prisoners at Appleby*, she writes:

> God is Light and in him is no Darkness at all, the work that he works is in the Light, which is pure, and leads to purity; which Light testifies against all sin . . . And the Light which comes from Jesus Christ, which is the Messenger of the Living God, sent from God, may bring your Souls out of Egypt, and out of the Fall, from under the curse, which Disobedience hath brought upon all Men. Dear Hearts, this is the Day of your Visitation, and Salvation, if you be faithful and obedient, for the everlasting God, which is the Life, Light and Substance of Life, is risen, and arising, and raising up the Dead to hear the voice of the Son of God.²³

We can see that for Fell, "Light" is a multivalent term which here expresses aspects of God's nature and will and the redemptive revelation in Jesus Christ. Likewise, the description of the everlasting God as "Life, Light and Substance of Life" places the term into what could be read as a Trinitarian formula.

This look at Fell's doctrine of the Trinity also grants a better sense of her problematic use of the term Light, which she uses to describe God the Father, yet also to comprise the functions of the Holy Spirit and the present work of Christ. This is not modalism, but a reflection of the unity of the Godhead. To better explore this, we turn closer attention to the distinct persons within the Godhead (realizing that our initial descriptions will be amplified in the context of other loci). It is clear from reading the overall corpus of Mother Fell's writing that she embraces the general western understanding of God as a being of infinite power and the source of infinite goodness.²⁴ She sees God as immortal spirit, fully just and perfect in every aspect.²⁵ Under the powerful influence of the Gospel of John—which significantly shapes her theology—she identifies God, the "father of Lights," as the Creator who made all things through the Word.[26] She is generally careful to distinguish between Christ and the Father when speaking of creation—probably with the first chapter of the Gospel of John in the back of her mind.[27]

God the Father is immutable, inscrutable, invisible, and the ground of all being.[28] According to Margaret Fell, the "God that made the World and all things therein, dwells not in Temples made with Hands; neither is he worshipped with Mens Hands, as though he needed any Thing: For he giveth to all Life and Breath, and all Things, and hath made of one Blood all Nations of Men that dwell upon the Face of the Earth."[29] She affirms that no human concepts are adequate to the Divine Being, and unaided human language and thought cannot grasp the eternal God.[30] The connection between the human and the divine, between finite and infinite, is made only through the Light of Christ. In her 1654 *An Epistle of M. Fell to Friends*, she writes, the "Light opens the Mystery of God, and leads to the invisible God, which no mortal Eye can reach unto, or behold."[31] In the same letter she identifies this Light as the immutable spirit of Christ, "the Light which John bears witness to, which is come a Light into the World, and lighteth every Man that cometh into the World."[32]

In Fell's theology, the Light within is the present principle of salvation, "the Light of Jesus Christ, which manifests him in the Flesh."[33] For this reason, Fell urges others to "turn to the Lord God, and believe in the Light, which is rising and shining in your Consciences; he it is who is the Resurrection and the Life."[34] But what does Margaret Fell actually claim about Christ? Those who have read the early publications denouncing the Quaker movement might be surprised by the orthodox nature of many of her theological statements about Jesus Christ. She holds that he is the incarnate Word who took on human form, performed miracles, proclaimed God's truth, was crucified and buried, and rose again from death.[35] Fell likewise accepts the propitiatory nature of that death, and the blood of Christ as the foundation of the new covenant.[36]

That said, Margaret as practical theologian does not dwell on the particulars of the incarnation, only upon its benefits. Theological reflections upon the virgin birth, Joseph and Mary, or the brothers of Jesus are absent save the occasional "God sent forth his Son, made of a Woman."[37] While it appears that she had little interest in Jesus Christ as man, she also never doubted his historical reality as presented in Scripture. For her, these past truths are of little importance because the primary purpose of the incarnation is "for the Suffering of Death" which "hath wrought the Redemption of Man."[38] In her work *A Call to the Universal Seed of God, throughout the Whole World*, Fell writes:

Christ Jesus, who is elected and chosen of God, and precious, who was glorified with the Father before the World began, him hath he made Heir of all things, and the Propitiation for the Sins of the Whole World; by him, and in him, and through him, is the Restoration, and Redemption and Building up again, out of the fallen State of lost Adam, and of all Mankind in the Fall.[39]

In Margaret Fell's Christology, Jesus Christ is also "the fulfilling of the Law, and the End of the Law."[40] In Christ, the outward law of the old covenant is fulfilled and abolished. Jesus Christ's shed blood is the basis of a new covenant which is the inward law, and "by no other Way or Means under Heaven shall ye know the living God, but by this pure Light, and Law written in the Heart."[41]

It is in this, the explanation of the law written inwardly, that also we touch upon the place of the Holy Spirit in Fell's theology. In her 1656 publication *To all the Professors of the World*, she holds, "And of this the Holy Ghost is a Witness to us, in the fulfiling of the Everlasting Promise to us, in the fulfiling of the Everlasting Promise of the Lord God, who hath said, I will put my Laws in their Hearts, and in their Minds will I write them."[42] This Spirit is a comforter, guide, and teacher who reveals and empowers.[43] Here is also the same Spirit that moved upon the apostles and disciples of Jesus Christ after his death and resurrection, and now bears witness to the Light. This is the Light "from which all the Holy Men of God ever spake, as they were moved by the Holy Ghost, and from which Light all the Scriptures were given forth."[44] More importantly for Fell's theology, the revelation of the Spirit did not stop with the prophets of old, or with the closing of the canon. The revelatory work of the Holy Spirit continues in the present, guiding the Children of the Light.

As we noted earlier, Fell explicitly stated that the Spirit proceeds from the Father and the Son. At the same time she viewed the Holy Spirit, promised by Jesus and made manifest after his death, as the "Eternal Spirit" of Christ. In an important 1660 publication she writes:

> And again, the Apostles after they had received the Holy Ghost, and Power from above, when Christ was offered up and ascended, the Apostles having received his Eternal Spirit, and they going on in the Work of God, converted Thousands to the Faith, and did great and wonderful Works and Miracles by the Spirit of Christ which they had received.[45]

So for Fell, the Spirit that proceeds from God the Father and Christ the Son is the Eternal Spirit of Christ Jesus. In keeping with this she writes:

> And this is he [Jesus Christ] which God the Father hath sealed, that is come a Light which every one that believes in is sealed with his Spirit: Therefore it is good for all People not to quench the Spirit of the Lord Jesus, nor to grieve it . . . And who lives in Unity and the Spirit of the Lord Jesus, they come to have Fellowship with the Father and the Son.[46]

Notice that if the Holy Spirit is identified with the "Spirit of the Lord Jesus," then the last sentence is clearly Trinitarian. Here too, we see the usage of Light as a reference for Jesus Christ. Have we at last found the definitive referent of the term? Let us consider another example to test and see.

In her 1658 *A General Epistle to Friends*, Margaret Fell argues that both Jews and Gentiles are now part of a spiritual covenant, which replaces the outward covenant of the law:

> So that now Jew and Gentile that comes to the Light of Christ, by which they may come to the Father, even thro' him, who is the Light; for when the fullness of time was come, God sent forth his Son, made of a Woman, made under the Law, to redeem them that were under the Law, that we might receive the Adoption of Sons. God hath sent forth the Spirit of his Son into your hearts, crying Abba, Father.[47]

Here Fell is making a direct reference to Scripture (Galatians). This quotation, which is written to Friends and so is not a mere concession to the critics of Quakerism, has a clear Trinitarian shape. God the Father, God the Son, and God the Spirit are distinct in their functions. As in earlier citations, Christ is not assimilated into the Light, but is the source of the Light. However, a question of interpretation arises in the third phrase of the quotation, "thro' him, who is the Light." The Light cannot be the Father here, since the Light is the way to the Father. Neither is the Light identical with Christ, since the Light is of Christ. Given the overall shape of her theology, it is plausible to suggest that the Light here is the Spirit.

This explains her quotation from Galatians, where the Spirit of the Son is sent into our hearts. This Spirit of Sonship (adoption) is identical with the Light. Thus, while the present functions of Christ and the Spirit are often assigned to the Light, it appears that the Light does not become identical with Christ in every respect. Rather, in Fell's theology the Light becomes identical with the work of the Spirit. For example, in one of her earliest writings, a 1653 letter to Cromwell, she can speak of "the eternall light which is of god, & now is the spirit of the Living god made manifest."[48] Fell does make a clear distinction between Jesus Christ, God the Father, and the Light (or Spirit). There is one God, the Father of Lights who is also the Father of Jesus Christ. She holds that only Christ was crucified and raised from the dead.[49] It is the blood of Christ (rather than the Light) which is the basis of the new covenant and which cleanses us from sin.[50] However, the *present* work and reality of the Spirit become the same as that of the Light, and the *present* work of Christ is likewise identical with that of the Light.

Given that Fell articulates the Trinity as three persons, is there any theological assumption we have not examined that is responsible for this blurring of distinctions between their works? We can answer this in part by a brief look into her eschatology. Though we will explore her end-times concepts more fully later in the chapter, it is useful at this point to understand that for Mother Fell, the second coming of Christ had begun. However, it is not of the type generally expected or predicted by the traditions of the church.[51] The Lord Jesus Christ has returned inwardly as a Light in the conscience, the center of the moral, culpable self. Jesus Christ has come in spirit to dwell in those who hearken to the Light. As he is made manifest in the lives of believers, he is in fact come again in the flesh. In Fell's pneumatology, the Holy Spirit is a separate person of the Godhead, but the Spirit is Christ's. Let us consider again how Fell explained the coming of the Spirit when it fell upon the early Christians. She writes that the apostles "received the Holy Ghost, and Power from above, when Christ was offered up and ascended, the Apostles having received his Eternal Spirit."[52] Here the crucified Christ rose from death and ascended to heaven, at which point his followers received Jesus Christ's eternal Spirit: *Christ's* holy Spirit and power from above.

If this explanation is correct, then Fell's doctrine of the Trinity might be articulated thus: God the Father is Light, God the Son is the revealed Light which was made incarnate in Christ Jesus, and God the Spirit is the eternal spirit of Christ who brings the ongoing revelation of the Light. Accepting this construction makes Fell's Trinitarian theology more apparent in phrases such as "His Will is revealed in the Light, the Power is one with the Light, and works in the Light."[53] In this way she can also affirm that the Spirit proceeds from the Father and the Son. This Spirit working in the Light—the Holy Spirit—is the source for all divine revelation to the world: revealing God in the old law and covenant to prophets in the past, foretelling the salvation of the world through the incarnation, living among us and teaching us as the Lord Jesus Christ, and showing us the new law and covenant instituted in Christ's death and resurrection as recorded in Scripture. This Spirit is now revealed in the eternal Spirit of Christ come among us as a teacher and guide. In this way, the *present* work of the Spirit and the *present* work of Christ are the same.

This conception of the Spirit as an ongoing source of Christ's revelation shapes Margaret Fell's doctrine of Scripture. Her religious writings demonstrate that she respected Scripture, and her religious writings overflow with references to it. She believed that the Bible is a divine revelation of the Light, inspired by the Holy Spirit and spoken through the prophets and apostles.[54] It is the Light of God, "from which all the Holy Men of God ever spake, as they were moved by the Holy Ghost, and from which Light all the Scriptures were given forth."[55] At the same time, Fell held that Scripture as revelation was secondary in authority to that of the Light made manifest in the conscience. Because she believed the Spirit was the conduit for the ongoing revelation of the Lord Jesus Christ, Scripture was a limited revelation that would not be contradicted by the Spirit, but it did not close the work of revelation.[56]

Fell writes, "For the Holy Seed is risen, the Substance of all; and the Life of the Scriptures, which spoke them forth is manifested; the Word, which was in the beginning, which was with God, which Word was God; He who was dead is alive, whose Name is called The Word of God."[57] Her reason for this emphasis on the living Word was her understanding that the Holy Spirit as the witness to the Light within brings us the ongoing teaching of the Lord Jesus Christ. Defending this early Friends position in her tract *A True Testimony* (1660), she writes:

> So, the same Spirit that revealed the Son in the apostles revealed Him in us, for we neither received it of man, neither were we taught it by man, but the revelation of Jesus Christ . . . The Scriptures bear testimony with us, and we with them, and so are in the same Spirit which gave them forth.[58]

At the same time it should be noted that although Scripture was not the primary source of revelation, it was a significant and revelatory authority for early Quakers. Fell herself was convinced of the Light largely through Fox's appeals to, and explanation of, the biblical text.

The Bible retained importance for Friends and remained a source of reference and guidance. In support of this, Margaret writes, "And so now Friends, seeing that many when trials come upon them have been shaken, as you may see in the Scriptures more fully, therefore in the fear of the Lord God keep close and near to the word of Faith which is nigh in the heart."[59] Scripture is a sure word of God, but its truth is only open to those who have grasped the revelation of the Light at work in the present day. Of course, as an apologist and theologian, this placed her in an awkward position when confronting detractors of the Quaker movement. Scripture is a repository of divine truth, but those who read it and do not accept the idea that the second coming is now begun through the agency of the Light of Christ Jesus have not embraced the special revelation that makes the Scripture alive.

Her approach to this is to direct others to reexamine Scripture both to defend teachings of the Friends, and to encourage them to open again to the witness within. As her purpose and target audience changed, so did her documentation of biblical citations. In her epistletory works directed to Friends, Scripture verses are generally undocumented. Like other Quaker writers of this period, she shifts back and forth between biblical quotations and her exposition and amplification of them with little to indicate where one ends and the other begins. However, in her religious writings directed to the professional clergy or Christians outside the Society of Friends, she is frequently more careful in her use of biblical citations and included the text references.[60] Likewise, when she addresses the Jewish people in publication, Mother Fell uses only Old Testament references and stories, accompanied by notations of chapter and verse.[61] Given the care that she exercises in her publications to Christians and Jews, it seems likely that her more relaxed and flowing use of Scripture in documents to Friends is in response to the sensibilities of her intended audience.

In addition to defending Quaker teachings, Fell wrote as an evangelist for the Light. Some of her religious writings were targeted to a diverse audience of "professors" including the traditionally churched and the Jewish people. Though they all sought salvation, they were mired in darkness and so sought redemption through the dead rituals and practices of the Scriptures, whereof they had knowledge from without rather than within. In these circumstances, Fell's understanding of the universal availability of salvation and that of God within each conscience provides a means to reach out in proclamation and reproof to those outside the Light. She uses the Scripture, which those held captive to the outward law still accepted as authoritative, as a means of turning their attention to the inward Light of Christ.[62] In this context they are challenged to turn to the Light, and examine the Scriptures for themselves to see if the Quaker teachings are true.

From her epistles to those within the Quaker movement, it is clear that the Bible was looked to as an authoritative revelation whose truth is witnessed to by the Holy Spirit. Margaret Fell was herself extremely knowledgeable about the biblical text in English translation, and this was often her weapon of choice in later publications. Her approach at each point is from the perspective of Christian Scripture, which is given pride of place in each argument. Though this is consistent with other religious publications written during this time, it is important to note that Fell's use of the Bible is not so much about proof-texts as it is about her belief that Scripture, animated by the Spirit of Christ, brings genuine revelation to the reader. Thus she would have them "search the Scriptures, examine them honestly, and see whether ye are not deceived by them, who draw you from the Light, which is, and ever was, the Saints Teacher, and ever shall be."[63] Once Scripture has been faithfully presented, the reader—in whom the indwelling Light of Christ is universally present as a beckoning guide—must either accept or reject the truth of it. Of course, for Fell as for other sectarians across the ages, failure to interpret Scripture in a manner consistent with her reading was an indication of damnation and a rejection of true Christianity.

### Pneumatology: The Light of the Holy Spirit in the Conscience

Much of the work of the Light and the Spirit takes place in the conscience. God as Creator is the source of our moral consciousness, and Fell sees the conscience as the connection point between the divine Light and the human soul. She holds that all people are created alike in that they all have a moral conscience, and something of the Light is manifest in them all.[64] It is here where we first encounter "That of God" within us, and she beckons "all People, to the Light in your Consciences, which Christ Jesus hath enlightened you withal, turn your Minds."[65] Thus, the conscience—the point of contact between the human and the divine—is the starting point for Christ's salvific work. This pure Light is the sole broker for human salvation. She writes, "By no other Way or Means under Heaven shall ye know the living God, but by this pure Light, and Law written in the Heart."[66] The ultimate goal of this mediation is the reconciliation of humankind with a holy God, through "the Way, the Light, that convinceth you of Sin."[67] Margaret Fell sees salvation as universally available to all, because all have the seed of God in the conscience.

The Light of Christ is available to all through this general revelation, and in this sense the gospel of Jesus Christ has been universally proclaimed. However, while all persons are children of God, not all choose to become Children of Light. Early in her convincement, Mother Fell writes:

> For no other Name under Heaven, but by this Name Christ Jesus, who is the Light which John bears witness to, which is come a Light into the World, and lighteth every Man that cometh into the World; this is the Light that shines in a dark place, which you may do well to take heed unto, until the day dawn, and the day star arise in your

> hearts; and this you will witness if you be faithful to the Light; but if you turn from the Light, and hate the Light, then the Light makes you manifest that your deeds are evil, and that is your condemnation.[68]

The seed of human salvation has been placed within every person, but it is our response to this germinal presence that determines our eternal destiny.

In Fell's soteriology she is firm in her claim that we must choose to embrace the Light if we are to know the Living God and his salvation in Jesus Christ. In her publication *To all the Professors of the World*, we find Fell offering this challenge:

> To the Light in all your Consciences, which comes from Jesus, who is the Father's Covenant of Light and Life, the Lamb, who is the Light of all Nations that are saved, which now shines in all your Consciences; to this in you all do I appeal, that with it you may search and try your Standing, and Ground, and Foundation, which is in God the Father of our Lord Jesus Christ.[69]

Again we see in Fell's theology that general revelation is available to all because the Light is present in some measure within every human conscience. However, the Light is an efficacious presence only for those who positively respond to it and embrace it. At some point in every person's life, the person makes a choice between the Light and the Spirit or the darkness and the flesh.

The close connection that Fell draws between inner states and outward actions is grounded in her understanding of the indwelling Light as the agent for Christ's promised return. Christ is come again in the flesh as his light rises in the hearts and minds of those who dwell in the Light. In her theology, Margaret Fell does not view the physical body itself as inherently good or evil. However, the body is a potential dwelling place for Light or for darkness, and will come to reflect the nature of what is within it. Ideally, the body is intended as the dwelling place of the Light and the incarnate Christ. She writes, "Ye are the Temple of the living God, as God hath said, I will dwell in them, and walk in them, I will be their God, and they shall be my People . . . the Temple of God is holy, whose Temple are ye; and what, know ye not that your Bodies are the Temple of the Holy Ghost which is in you."[70]

The old law and covenant have ended, as has the need for the external temples and rituals that Margaret Fell referred to as "outward forms."[71] In our turning to, and waiting upon, the Light of Christ, our spiritual liberty is returned as we leave off the trappings of outward religion. For Fell, we are thus "freed from having your consciences subject to the Beggarly Rudiments and Carnal Ordinances, set up by Men, and established by Men's Laws, contrary to the Law of God, and contrary unto Christ."[72] However, those who reject the grace of God through Christ and Spirit do not understand the law written in the heart, and for them "there is a necessity, that those that are not guided by That of God in their Consciences, there must be a law for such to Rule and Govern them."[73] It is for those who are not of pure conscience that the governments must write laws, for they have not received the revealed truth of the Inward Light and law. This distinction offers an indication of how Mother Fell viewed the idea of liberty of conscience, something to which she often appeals in her work on behalf of Friends.[74]

This liberty is available to all in the freedom that Christ brings. As we have already noted, in Fell's theology God makes salvation available to all through Jesus Christ, but it is only given to those who choose it. In this choice we become open to God's special revelation and the divine mysteries, which to all "who deny the Light, shall be shut for evermore . . . ye shall never know them, but they shall be as a Book sealed unto you; the depth of the Mysteries of them ye shall never understand."[75] To perceive and understand God's special revelation, Fell directs us to "turn to the Light, and there ye will come to see; and learning there, in the Light, ye will come to see and know the Mysteries of God."[76] The corollary is obvious: if the Light does not dwell in us, then we become a dwelling for Satan. These are two distinct paths for Fell, one leading to redemption, the other to condemnation. As we turn our attention to the more subtle aspects of her soteriology, we will look first to Fell's explanation of the path to human redemption.

## Salvation in These Last Days

With human cooperation, the Light integrates transformationally with every human cognitive function. Mother Fell instructs us to "let this Light search you, and try you, and mind whether you have receiv'd the New Covenant, which is everlasting, which never shall be broken, which is the Law written in the Heart; which Law is pure, which law is Spiritual, Just, and Good."[77] As we turn our minds toward the Light, we are closely examined in our inward being, where the hidden habits of the heart are revealed. This process of divinely guided self-examination scrutinizes every aspect of one's life, and its goal is the cleansing of the soul. We see this in a number of Fell's religious writings, including her 1656 publication *To all the Professors of the World*. Here she admonishes, "To this pure Measure of God in your inward Parts, turn your Minds, that ye may come to witness Cleansing and Purging within, that ye may come to see the Uncleanness which proceeds out of the Heart, which defiles the Man."[78] In this turning, the true scope of one's own sinfulness is revealed as the corruptions of sin and moral weakness are revealed and laid bare. This inward cleansing is made possible through the atoning death of Christ Jesus, and the experience of cleansing reconciles us to the pure and holy nature of God and resurrects us from the dead.[79]

Moreover, we must take into account how Fell's eschatology altered her interpretation of biblical terminology. In this case, we are served by clarification of what she meant by "resurrection of the dead" and related terms. In the Light within, we have the hope of salvation that beckons us out of darkness and away from condemnation:

> And he that is the Supreme Judge in the Conscience is arisen, who purgeth the Conscience from Dead Works, to serve the living God; and the Voice is heard, which saith, Arise, you Dead, and come to Judgment; and the time is come and now is, that the Dead do hear the Voice of the Son of God, and they that hear do live; and he that believes on him, though he be dead, yet shall he live.[80]

By the testimony and proclamation of those who witness to the Light, "the Lord God of Life and Power hath visited you, and sent his Servants to awaken you, and to raise you from the Dead, that Christ might give you Life, which is now come, and coming."[81] This resurrection is not a bodily resurrection, but Fell's understanding of how the dead in Christ shall rise in the Eschaton.

The death to which Fell refers is spiritual, and we dwell in it so long as we remain captive to the darkness and the chains of outward forms. Mother Fell would have us look to "that which turns and draws your mind towards God, the Light that cometh from the Father of Light, turn to and there witness a Living Hope, which was that Hope that the Apostle Paul was called in question for, that hope of the Resurrection of the Dead; who was a Minister of God, who watched for the Soul, which your Ministers of Death know not; but their Labour tends to keep you in the Death."[82] Here we can see some of the subtlety of her hamartiology and a bit more of the importance she afforded to human volition in soteriology. The choice between redemption and condemnation is ours to make. All individuals make a choice that determines whether they belong to the Light or the darkness.

If we receive the revelation and reproof of the Light, we are resurrected out of the world, with its darkness and death, and reconciled with God. This reconciliation is the beginning of salvation. Cleansed, with the Light of Christ enthroned within us, our new life begins. This journey with the Light must be made in humility, as we seek to follow the Spirit. Fell instructs us to "receive with Meekness the Ingrafted Word that the Milk thereof ye may witness, and as new-born Babes, desire that you may grow thereby."[83] Our growth in the Light comes through "obedience to the Light which Shines in your consciences who hath left an Example unto all those that follow him; they must follow his Steps through Obedience, and through Sufferings, as he hath done who hath gone before, who is the Captain of our Salvation."[84]

The human self remains the center of divine transformational activity. In one of her many "epistles to Friends," Fell exhorts early Quakers to follow the moral guidance of the conscience, which is a witness for the living God:

> Therefore, my Dear Hearts, keep clear, keep your Consciences clean, keep out of Transgression in any wise or kind, against the liberty or freedom of your Consciences; keep to the just and the pure in you and your Consciences, at liberty therein, which witnesseth for the living God; and all outward prisons will then be little to you . . . So, my Dear Friends, Seal this upon your Hearts, that you keep clear your Consciences in the sight of God in every thing, now that he hath called you for Witnesses for him.[85]

The Light of Christ returns our spiritual liberty. For Fell, this is to be "freed from having your consciences subject to the Beggarly Rudiments and Carnal Ordinances, set up by Men, and established by Men's Laws, contrary to the Law of God, and contrary unto Christ."[86]

We see the incarnational flavor of Mother Fell's salvific vision in her understanding that the Light with the divine word is poised in the human soul, waiting to be engrafted and sealed within us. Likewise, her emphasis upon the necessity of the imitation of Christ through obedience to his example reflects the dual nature of our transformational relationship with the Light. In Fell's theology, as we dwell in the Light we are established in righteousness by the blood of Jesus Christ.[87] At the same time, our cleansing is ongoing and conditional. In her 1658 *A General Epistle to Friends*, she writes that we are made clean "by the Blood of the Son of God; which Blood, if you walk in the Light and dwell in the Light, will cleanse you for all Sin."[88] Believers are justified by Jesus Christ's atoning death and sanctified through the ongoing work of the Spirit. Thus we are instructed to abide "in the pure Eternal Light of God . . . and this is that which must sanctifie you and justifie you, and present you pure and holy in his sight."[89]

In Fell's theology, both justification and sanctification are made possible through Christ's redemptive sacrifice on the cross. Accordingly she writes,

> But this Man, after he had offered one Sacrifice for Sin, sate down at the right Hand of God . . . by one offering, Christ Jesus the everlasting High Priest, hath perfected for ever them that are sanctified. This is he that doth the Will of God . . . by which Will we are sanctified, whereof the Holy Ghost is a Witness to us.[90]

This sanctification is a process in which we participate as we learn to follow the Light in humility and patience. Through obedience to the Light of Christ—our inward teacher and guide—we progress toward spiritual maturity. This obedience is marked by certain intellectual virtues such as humility and love, which facilitate the work of the Light within us.[91] Here, in the presence of the Light, we begin to evidence Christ in our spirits and our actions.

Given this understanding of the Light's salvific mechanisms, the fact that Fell places an emphasis on works as a witness to the inward condition is not surprising. Our works in righteousness are an expression of our disciplined obedience to the Light and, as such, are a function of our moral agency. The idea that works are an essential testimony to the condition of the soul appears throughout her religious writings. In her incarnational spirituality, the true followers of the Light will act in accordance with the Spirit that dwells within them. Her position on this echoes the Apostle James when she writes:

> And so here ye may read your Faith by your Works. For the Apostle James saith What doth it profit though a Man say he hath Faith, and hath not Works; that Faith cannot save. See what Comparison James makes, Jam. 2.16. Even so Faith, if it hath not Works, is dead, being alone. Yea, a Man may say, thou hath Faith and I have Works; shew me thy Faith without for thy Works, and I will shew thee my Faith by my Works.[92]

In an unpublished 1654 letter to Jeffrey Elleston, she writes, "Thou professeth a god and a Christ in words (and soe thou doest a Conscience) but in workes denyes all: who denyes the light of Jesus xt [Christ] by which the Conscience is purged from dead workes, to serve the livinge God. But thou that denyes the Light shall never know what a Cleane conscience is."[93] The close connection that Fell draws between inner states and outward actions is grounded in her understanding that the indwelling Light is the agent for Christ's promised return.

Christ is come again in the flesh as his light rises in the hearts and minds of those who dwell in the Light. At the same time, Mother Fell does hold for the necessity of faith, for "without Faith it is impossible to please God; and that whatsoever is not of Faith, is sin."[94] By following Christ the Light, under the guidance of his Spirit, we are altered both in our inward and outward person; our inward spiritual transformation is always inextricably bound to our outward actions. For those who persevere in the Light, this transformation leads them "out of the World, out of the World's Ways, Fashions, and Customs; and this makes a Separation from the World, and this leads to God."[95] Mother Fell assures them that "if you are constant in Obedience to it, it will preserve in the Simplicity, and lead out of the Pollutions of the World, and the Filthiness of the Flesh; in that which is pure, where you worship God in Spirit and in Truth."[96]

By walking in obedience to our spiritual guide we learn true discipleship, as the Light of Christ becomes incarnate in us. This inward turning is made possible through grace, which is the free gift of God through the indwelling Light of Christ.[97] Given our previous discussion of the role of human free will in salvation, Margaret Fell's theology would seem to embrace what has elsewhere been called "prevenient grace." She writes, "No People can retain God in their knowledge, and Worship him as God, but first they must come to that of God in them."[98] As we have discussed earlier, Fell believed that we who are human need to be reconciled to God, but cannot initiate contact with the divine because of our Adamic nature. God, in his mercy, has implanted some degree of divine presence within our consciences that enables us to embrace the Light. This grace makes it possible to respond to the Light within, but does not compel us to do so.

Grace is the indwelling Light of Christ—which can mean the present work of Christ or the Spirit—and it is universal, offered for the reconciliation of the human and divine: a direct function of the Light within. Once we turn to the Light, we "are partakers of the free Grace of God, which brings Salvation; so let it be your Teacher and Leader."[99] This unmerited favor of God lies in God's provision of a "measure of God in everyone," and in our capacity to turn to it. Fell writes, "Now the free Grace of the everlasting God is offered to you this Day; and therefore return to the pure Light and Law written in the Heart."[100] The universal offer of salvation, and the role of human volition in conversion and divine revelation, also affects Fell's doctrine of election. Her theology differs significantly from the dominant Calvinist view of election, which held that only a select number of persons chosen by God were predestined for salvation, and these were God's elect.[101] Moreover, in Fell's theology, election is conditional.[102]

The elect are not predestined to salvation in the Calvinist sense. In her theology, Margaret Fell's use of the term refers to "the Elect, who dwell in the Light which comes from Christ Jesus."[103] Those who are among the elect have this status because of "Christ Jesus, who is elected and chosen of God."[104] Christ is elect, and he has become incarnate in those who embrace the Light.[105] Thus we are to "give all diligence, not to make only your Calling, but your Election sure."[106] She moves even farther from the dominant reading of election in her belief that those who have walked in the Light and begun the process of sanctification can "backslide." It is possible for any of us to fall away from the Light, even after a long obedience to it, if we turn from our knowledge of the Light and return to the ways of the world and the flesh.

According to Fell, potential candidates for reprobation include "the Backslider, and the Revolter, and the Disobedient Ones, and the Careless, and the Slothful, and those whose Minds are at Liberty, and will not abide in the Cross of Christ."[107] This perspective reflects the prominent role which Fell affords human volition in salvation. For this reason, Fell's epistles are filled with words of caution and encouragement to others to attend to the Light,

> so you may grow up as lively Plants in the Garden of God, which now he is dressing, and watering, and pruning, that to him Fruit may be brought forth, who is the Lord of the Vineyard, and the Husbandman, who purgeth every plant that beareth Fruit, then it may bring forth more Fruit; and every Branch that beareth not Fruit, he taketh away.[108]

At the same time, Fell's soteriology emphasizes that it was not God's intention in the incarnation to bring condemnation to anyone. Rather Christ was sent into the world to save us.[109]

God the Light desires our resurrection into life and salvation, out of death and into perfection. He likewise desires our reconciliation and redemption, for "all things are in God, who hath reconciled us unto himself, by Jesus Christ; and hath given us to the Ministry of Reconciliation; to wit, That God was in Christ reconciling the world to himself, not imputing their Trespasses unto them."[110] This reconciliation in Christ is not limited to humanity, for the "whole Creation hath long groaned under the Burden of Oppression and Corruption; the Redemption out of which, is through Christ Jesus."[111] Likewise, "the Redemption of the Body is through waiting in the Spirit of Adoption, whereby every Member may call God Father."[112]

In Margaret Fell's theology, the telos of the Light is not merely redemption, but sanctification unto perfection. She writes, "here is the

Coming of Christ the Second time without Sin unto Salvation: This is the great Work that God is working in this his day in the Hearts of his People, as it was in the days of the Apostles."[113] The path to perfection begins with justification and is ongoing in the sanctification that takes place in the Light. But salvation is not an end in itself, but something that comes to us as we dwell in Light and are increasingly conformed to the Spirit of Christ. Perfection is possible for the Christian in this life "for Christ saith, Be ye perfect as your heavenly Father is perfect."[114] Thus, in Fell's theology, perfection in Christ Jesus is our genuine goal, for "by his own Offering hath he perfected for ever them that are sanctified; and of this the Holy Ghost is a Witness to us, in the fulfiling of the Everlasting Promise to us, in the fulfilling of the Everlasting Promise of the Lord God, who hath said, I will put my Laws in their Hearts, and in their Minds will I write them."[115] The ultimate goal of the Light within is human reconciliation with God, through which it is possible to achieve a state of sinless perfection.

In her religious works, Fell holds forth for the possibility of human spiritual perfection in this present life. This perfection has only become available with the revelation of the Light come within, for "never was there any Perfection till now, that the Power of Truth is made manifest."[116] She embraces this doctrine early in her convincement and writes in 1656, "He that is borne of god sinneth not for the seed of god remaine in him, and he cannot sin because hee is borne of god."[117] An indication of how she understood the process of perfection may be found in a letter to her close friend William Caton (who was himself also convinced by George Fox). She writes to Caton, "In thy own Portion and Inheritance which is given unto thee, dwell continually, that a daily renewing, and an increase of his Government thou may'st feel, and a growing from Glory, to Glory, from one stature to another, unto a perfect Man in Christ."[118] Here, as in most other places, Fell interprets the biblical phrase "and his government shall be increased" to refer to the inward governing of the Light.

Margaret Fell does not argue for the verity of this concept of godly perfection simply by appeals to the revelation of the Light within. Perfection is also to be found throughout the whole of Scripture. In *An Epistle to the World, Priests, and People, concerning the Light, and for all People to Try their Teachers by the Scriptures*, Fell writes:

> And the Apostle Peter prayed, that they might be perfect, when they had suffered a while. And the Apostle said (who was a minister of Christ) that the Scripture was given forth by inspiration of God, that the Men of God might be perfect . . . Noah was a Preacher of

Righteousness, and he was a perfect Man. Abraham was a Friend of God, and God said unto him, walk before me and be thou perfect. And Lot was a Just Man and the Lord delivered him. And Job was a Perfect and Just Man and the Lord Preserv'd him. And David saith, Mark the perfect man, and behold the upright, for the end of that man is peace, Psal. 37. And Soloman saith that the upright shall dwell in the Land, and the perfect shall remain in it.[119]

This cascade of references comes at the end of the work and is primarily addressed to those whom she challenged to try their teachers by the Scriptures. By this point in the epistle, Fell has called those who teach against perfection "Ministers of Anti-Christ, and Upholders of Sin, and the Devils Kingdom."[120]

Although the idea of perfection was not new territory in theology— it has generally been associated with Pelagianism and antinomianism— the possibility of perfection ran contrary to the dominant teachings of Reformation Protestantism. To this Fell responds:

> And your Teachers tell you, *That you must never be perfect, but that you must sin so long as you are upon the Earth* . . . Try them by the Scriptures, and you shall find them contrary to the Doctrine of Christ, and of the Apostles, and not to have received the Gifts, which he gave to the Prophets, Apostles, and Evangelists, for the perfecting of the Saints.[121]

These teachers to whom she refers are primarily the clergy, who are out of the Light and from whom the gospel is hidden. And "if our Gospel be hid, it is hid to them that are lost, in whom the God of this World hath blinded the Minds of them that believe not."[122]

## The Children of Light vs. the Children of Darkness: Apocalyptic Dualism

One characteristic of Jewish and Christian apocalyptic literature is a strong dualism of light versus dark, and God versus Satan. The combat between these two powers in the last days does not allow for any compromise. With the coming of the Light of Christ to fight against the darkness, all people and nations are necessarily either followers of God or Satan. There are no other options. Though Margaret Fell believed in the universal availability of salvation for all human beings, she did not believe in universal salvation. Given her perspectives on the conscience, human free agency, and election, it follows that those who reject redemption are subjects of condemnation. "That of God" within us dwells alongside our natural inheritance, which includes a predisposition to choose the darkness over the Light. In Fell's theological estimation, human endeavor outside of the Light is marked by spiritual blindness.[123] This blindness metaphor is intended to convey an essential truth about the human race: we are born into a sinful world. Because we exist in "the fallen State of lost Adam, and of all Mankind in the Fall" we resist the Light.[124] Our nature is under the curse of the Fall, and we are inclined toward the world and spiritual darkness. Thus, says Fell, "your inside is Sin, Uncleanness, Filthiness, Pride, Envy, Wrath, Malice, Strife and Persecution; this is of the Devil's Kingdom of Sin, and this is the inheritance, and possession which ye possess."[125] Human beings are captive to this sin through a disobedient and rebellious nature.

In Margaret Fell's theology, sin is both an action and a condition (i.e., the result of an action). The task of the Light, which is come and is coming, is to bring our souls "out of the Fall, from under the Curse, which Disobedience hath brought upon all Men."[126] In our spiritual blindness, our affections are tragically misplaced as we willingly become obedient to the powers of darkness.[127] Of our own choice, out of our Adamic inclination to disobedience and strife, we deny the Light in each of us.[128] Salvation, then, involves the ongoing struggle between Light and darkness, where the human soul is the field of battle. Those who repeatedly choose the darkness and reject the Light increasingly conform to the world and to sin. This affection for the world gives rise to a variety of sinful tendencies within the human soul and an affinity with the dark forces at work in it. We come to love the darkness and hate the Light, and the outworking of this is our own damnation.[129] Those who are outside the Light dwell in sin through sinful actions and citizenship in a sinful kingdom.

We are born estranged from our Creator, into a world dominated by the flesh and the devil. These two spiritual forces opposing each other in the battlefield of humanity are oppositional and mutually incompatible. According to Fell, it should not surprise us that "there should be Opposition and Wars betwixt those two Kingdoms; the Kingdom of the Antichrist and Darkness, and Oppression, and Tyranny; and the Kingdom of Christ, which is in the Light, Power, Righteousness and Peace, Freedom and Liberty."[130] As we have already established, human beings must reflect one or the other of these two natures, dwelling in either the darkness or the Light. Sin is thus defined in part by analogy: sin is to darkness as righteousness is to Light. The world is of the darkness, and the domain of Satan, "for the Prince of Darkness is the God of this world."[131] In our spiritual idolatry we come to love the world and outward things rather than God. Because Fell holds that our outward comportment reflects our true spiritual allegiance, the outworking of a soul in darkness will be evil.

Condemnation under sin befalls all who discern the call of the Light and turn away from it. According to Fell, "That which hates the Light, turns from the Light, and that shall be condemned by the Light forever."[132] This condemnation is eternal, and the outworking of human volition. To avoid this end, she offers this warning: "And woe unto you, if ye do not hearken unto the Warning of the Lord God, who calls unto you for Repentance, and to return to the Light of Christ Jesus in your Consciences."[133] As we mentioned earlier, such a falling away was possible even for those who have turned to the Light. We constantly battle the darkness, both within and without, and we must keep our conscience pure in the Light by being low and humble before divine scrutiny. For this reason, Margaret warns early Quaker fellowships to avoid "the speaking in the Imaginations of Truth, both in your Speaking and Judging, that causes Divisions and Strife among you; and all this is cursed from God, and shut out of the Kingdom for ever."[134] Fortunately, the Light remains a voice in the conscience even in those who slip out of fellowship with Christ. Thus it is possible and most desirable, that all who fall away should return to the Light. This was the eschatological engine that drove early Friends in mission throughout the earth.

### The Second Coming, the Church, and True Worship

As she was born and raised in a time of intense eschatological speculation, and in keeping with the chorus of religious voices at the time, it is highly likely that Margaret Fell early on accepted the reality of a second coming. In chapter 2 of this work, we provided a sampling of movements and attitudes that instilled high eschatological expectations in many—some to the point of apocalypticism—which were prevalent in England in the years prior to the death of Oliver Cromwell. There we saw that, as the English people realized that the hoped-for social and government reforms would not be implemented, and that the hoped-or return of Christ—even the establishment of the New Jerusalem in England itself—did not materialize, they were left disappointed, angry, and confused. Some responded with military and political insurrection, or with the inward turn of continued spiritual seeking. Margaret Fell was of this second inclination, and the message of George Fox provided an account of Scripture that addressed wounds left by a failed eschatology:

Christ had indeed come again in the flesh to establish a new kingdom and reign upon the earth, but our expectations—built around traditions corrupted by darkness—led us to look in the wrong direction.

What Fox introduced to Fell was the exegetical importance of the concept that God is Light. This became the lens for a reexamination of the biblical text from start to finish and introduced a new interpretive paradigm wherein light becomes an attribute of God rather than an explanatory metaphor. With this new revelation, the "Way, which hath long been hid and hedged up, hath the Lord now opened and made manifest in this his Day; and the Law and the Testimony, which was sealed among the Disciples, is now opened; and the Word, which is the Light, is now revealed."[135] Thus, in Margaret Fell's theology, God—who is the Light—has chosen according to his own plan and purpose to begin the final chapter in Adam's story. For this reason God "made known unto us the mistery of his will . . . that in the Dispensations of the fullness of tymes, he might gather together all things in Christ . . . now is this brought to pass, & fulfilled."[136] The Light—Father, Son, and Spirit—has come among us in a unique new revelation that makes clear the mysteries of Scripture and the divine will.

With this new work of the Light and the Spirit, the present world with its sinful predilections and pride and vanity were beginning to pass away, "for this Darkness, and this Heathenish Ministry and dark Power hath long reigned. Now God hath raised up his glorious Light, and brought the Life and Immortality to light in your understandings."[137] In Jesus Christ a new and lasting covenant has been established that replaces those of the Old and New Testaments. Here the Lord "searches the heart, and tries the reins, and teaches his People, and writes his Law in their hearts, and puts his Spirit in their inward parts; and this is the new and everlasting Covenant which he makes with his People."[138] In this inward law, we are freed from the old ways of religion that have become captive to the power of the Prince of Darkness. The sacraments and rituals of the Christian faith are empty and without salvific efficacy, though the commands of Christ in Scripture remain valid when interpreted through the Light.

In keeping with Quaker beliefs, Fell teaches that in order to be obedient to Jesus Christ and his commands we must "Swear not at all," neither are we to seek or give honor, but to look to "the Honour that comes from God only."[139] We are not to show favor or respect based upon a person's degree of rank, social status, or possessions, "for if you respect Persons, you commit sin, and are convinced by the Laws as Transgressors," and we must especially avoid the swearing of oaths. Instead, "Let your Yea be Yea and your Nay Nay, for whatsoever is more than this cometh of Evil."[140] Likewise, the need for outward rituals and observances of the past is gone, and they have no salvific efficacy whatsoever. By her reckoning of Scripture, the Spirit of the Lord Jesus Christ has come again in the consciences of all human beings, and it is there that the temple—the place where the Light resides and is worshiped—is now established. It is "here you may see where the Lord will be worshipped, not in outward Temples, or outward Synagogues made with hands; But the time is come that the Lord will be worshipped in Spirit, in the inward man."[141]

This long awaited appearance of the Lord Jesus Christ come again was witnessed to by the fulfilling of biblical teachings and prophecies.[142] From Fell's perspective, the "Lord is pouring out his Spirit upon all Flesh, that his Sons and Daughters may Prophesy. And that we witnessing the pourings out of this Spirit upon us, and thereby Christ Manifesting himself in us, our Testimony is of him."[143] As human beings turn toward and accept the Light within, Jesus Christ—through the Spirit of Jesus Christ that bears witness to his coming—is established inwardly. Fell alludes to this in an unpublished 1659 letter to Friends:

> The Second Addam, the lord from Heaven, whose power is now Resen, and whose Light is now Shininge in the Consciences of men, but especially in his Saints, in whom he is to be Glorified, and Admired, as his name and Nature Ariseth and growes in them, and as his Image is Renewed. Soe there light Shines forth amongst men . . . [and] The image of the Invisable god growes.[144]

In this we are justified and sanctified, in which process Christ is made "incarnate" in the Flesh.

To understand her view of Christ come again more precisely, some effort must be made to clarify another underlying theological assumption in Margaret Fell's religious work. In her eschatology, Jesus Christ's return *in the flesh* has already begun. Through the paradigm of the Light, Fell perceives that the promised return of Jesus Christ is not fulfilled by the reappearance of a distinct, individual represented by a single physical body. Instead, Christ's return in the flesh is a spiritual one that occurs as individual persons experience the growth of the Spirit of Jesus Christ within them. In this way, each person "who is faithful and obedient to the Light, witnesseth Christ made manifest and come in the flesh."[145] Thus in some sense, Jesus Christ dwells in our bodies when we are joined into the body of Christ.

From her perspective, Margaret Fell believed that any other interpretation of the second coming missed the truth of the Light within if they denied the corporeal aspect Jesus Christ's reappearance:

> Some lookinge for a Christ cominge in the Cloudes of the Sky and in their minds Imagines a personall raigne and thus you are confused and Divided in your vaine thoughts & imaginations which makes you manifest that you know him not come at all nor cannot confesse him come in the flesh, and soe you are prooved by the scripture to be the Antichrists which John speakes of which shall be in the last tymes . . . therby we know that is the last tyme.[146]

For those who cannot accept this truth, Fell urges them to "turne to the light of Jesus Christ which will examine and search & try you, and bring you to know Christ within you, and soe bringe you out of the reprobate faith. This will let you see the mistery which is Christ within; and this will bring you to know him come in the flesh."[147] This principle of the Light made flesh is an essential point of doctrine for Fell, and serves as a litmus test of one's spiritual condition: "Every Spirit that confesseth that Jesus Christ is come in the Flesh is of God: and every spirit that confesseth not that Jesus Christ is come in the flesh is not of god."[148]

Here we see that in her theology, Mother Fell rejects the prevalent interpretations of the second coming in favor of a more realized eschatology. At the same time, she accepts other aspects of popular English end-times speculation and incorporates them into her religious writings. Where we can see a clear connection between Fell's eschatology and the commonly accepted views of the times are in those areas that express some aspect of the Quaker response to the failed eschatological expectations of those they sought to bring to the Light. For example, we discussed earlier a unique aspect of English eschatology prevalent in the early seventeenth century: England was the first truly Protestant country and therefore the place where Christ's coming again on earth would first be manifest.[149] In keeping with this, many also anticipated that the establishment of the New Jerusalem was to take place in England.[150]

Margaret Fell accepted this thinking to some degree. We can see this in her open publication to Rabbi Menasseh ben Israel where she asserted that it was "this English Nation . . . which is a Land of gathering, where the Lord God is fulfilling his Promise."[151] England was not itself the new kingdom of God, but was the place where the new revelation of the Light was first sent. As such, the people of England were first to hear the truth of the second coming proclaimed in their midst, and from there it was being carried forth to all the nations of the world. Thus England was the location where the standard of the Lord was first lifted and it was he "who hath set up an Ensign [England] for the gathering up of the Nations together."[152] This special role assigned England through the Children of the Light also gave impetus to their evangelistic endeavors because they "received his Testimony, and could set to our Seal, that this was true. And then we saw the great Concern that lay upon this, which is the Salvation of poor People's Souls."[153]

With regard to the New Jerusalem, Margaret Fell does not often refer to it in her religious writings. When she does it is a spiritual concept, "For Jerusalem, which is from above, is free, which is the Mother of us all; and who are here are one."[154] In a parallel to this, Fell uses the eschatologically weighted name Babylon as a symbol of the kingdom of darkness in several places, and even refers to herself as "one Redeemed from Babylon."[155] Since we know that she was neither Catholic nor ever inclined to be so, Babylon cannot here refer to the papacy or the Catholic Church (but would include the pope and papists).[156] In this way, both Jerusalem and Babylon are symbolic terms for the spiritual realms of Light and darkness.[157] Fell also makes particular use of the Old Testament stories of Daniel in the lion's den and Shadrach, Meshach, and Abednego in the fiery furnace. These stories appear in the context of religious writings that discuss the ongoing Quaker persecution, to which situation she likens them.[158] This imagery fits into Mother Fell's eschatology, in that she interpreted the persecution of Friends as a sign of the end times and their role in it.

As an argument for the truth of the Quaker conception of the second coming, and as a source of encouragement to suffering Friends, Margaret Fell frames their persecution in a biblical context. Those who suffer for Christ will rise with him, while those who persecute Friends "are of the first Nature, which is Cains, who slew his brother, and by this Generation all that will live godly in Christ Jesus, must suffer Persecution."[159] This persecution is in accordance with the prophetic word of Scripture and clearly delineates those who have Christ within from those who do not for, "Jesus Christ saith, Woe unto you, when all men shall speak well of you, for so did their fathers of the False Prophets."[160] Fell likewise contrasts the fortunes of those who hold that they are Christians but do not believe in the Light with the situation of Quakers, who do. She challenges, "high Formalists and great Professors consider now, who is persecuted for the Truth, and who it is that persecutes them."[161] And to Quakers she writes, "The same God you suffer for, and by same you are preserved, which Daniel, Shadrach, Meshach and Abednego was."[162]

Underlying Fell's eschatological phraseology and rhetoric is her need to convey an essential truth about the second coming, which is the reality that this Lord of Light is also the righteous judge of the earth. The time of God's judgment is at hand, and "the acceptable year of the Lord is proclaimed, and the day of vengeance of our God is come, and the

Prince of the World is come to be Judged; and the Day of the Son of Man is come, in which he is lifted up."[163] This divine judgment was not to be an inconsequential affair, "for Dreadful and Terrible is the Lord God to the Disobedient, and those that will not that he should reign over them, must be bound in Chains, and cast into utter Darkness."[164] In the time of judgment, all will be held accountable for their works "when the booke of the conscience is opened, and all are Judged out of it."[165] Fell elsewhere calls this book of the conscience "the Lambs booke of life," and it is clear in context that these two books are one and the same.[166]

At the center of this is Jesus Christ, who is the judge of the earth and of humanity. This is he "who is coming to Rule all Nations with his Rod of Iron, and to break to Pieces his Enemies . . . So that he is Lord of Heaven, and also of Earth, and he is coming to fulfill and perform his Noble Decrees; So that his will may be done on Earth as it is in heaven."[167] Although this seems fairly standard fare for a proclamation of God's coming judgment, Mother Fell's theology of the Light within complicates our interpretation of her meaning. It is thus difficult to determine exactly the type of judgment she intended. As we have seen in earlier sections, the Light has a present function of judging the consciences of those who turn toward it and walk in it. By the same token, Fell obviously envisioned a point in time beyond which salvation is not possible for those condemned by their life in the darkness. Here, as with previous sections, we can see how her eschatological slant on theological terms can prove cumbersome.

It is clear that Margaret Fell believed that an ongoing work of the Spirit of Christ was salvation unto perfection. Those who are in the Light have entered into a process where they submit perpetually to the judgment, guidance, and reproof of the Spirit as they continue toward perfection. Those who persevere and "who are faithfull unto the death" will receive "a crowne of life & immortality."[168] Those who are outside the Light dwell there in blindness, in part as an outworking of their own volition. And "this is the Condemnation, that Light is come into the world, and Men love Darkness rather than Light, because their deeds are evil."[169] As it is with those who choose to remain in the Light, those who have embraced the darkness are judged by their works and by their spiritual affiliation. They shall find, "that the Lord of the Vineyard is coming to look for Fruits, and will Reward every Man according to his Deeds."[170]

Those of us who reject the Light are under condemnation as our evil works are made manifest under divine scrutiny. The Light then becomes our source of damnation which "you can never flee from, but wherever you go, the Light, that is the condemnation of the World will pursue you, and that of God in your Consciences will be your Condemnation."[171] In our rejection of the Light we are unable to avail ourselves of the "baptism of repentance, which washeth away the filth of the flesh" and we will never "enter into the holy Citty; for nothinge that is unclean shall enter."[172]

In the time between the first appearance of the Light and the final judgment, the body of Christ proclaims the truth and fulfills a key role in the unfolding reign of Jesus Christ. In the theology of Margaret Fell, the body of Christ includes all those—and only those—who walk in obedience to the Light. This is the true church and the bride of Christ, which is constituted in God the Father of Jesus Christ.[173] According to Fell, "Christ Jesus hath given himself for his Church, and is the Head of the Church, even as a Husband to his Wife: So hath Christ loved his Church."[174] Jesus Christ is the foundation of the church, and the rock upon which the whole church is built. For Fell the church is the dwelling place of the Light, the holy temple of a righteous God. As we saw earlier, Mother Fell holds that "the Temple of God is holy, whose Temple are ye; and what, know ye not that your Bodies are the Temple of the Holy Ghost which is in you."[175] Thus her ecclesiology is oriented, like all else in her theology, toward the inward workings of the Light.

In Fell's theology, the essential qualities the church possesses are love, unity, and purity. She writes, "Therefore in that which is Pure and Eternal, which is one in all, which leads into Love and Unity, dwell and abide . . . And here is no strife and wrangling, yea, this leads to Purity and Holiness, without which none shall see the Lord; and to the Church of the First Born, which is in God, where he is one, and his Name one."[176] In more traditional, creedal language, Fell identifies the marks of the church as follows: the church is one, holy, and universal—but not apostolic as it is commonly understood. For Mother Fell, the concept of apostolicity would mean that we as followers of the Light share a common illumination with the apostles for, like them, we are filled with the Spirit of Jesus Christ and are taught by him.[177]

The central indication of the true church as it is manifest in local gatherings of the body is unity. In her most significant instructional epistles to early Quakers—those written and sent from 1653 to 1659—Mother Fell places a priority upon unity.[178] For example, in a 1654 letter she describes

> the Light, which is the Head of the whole body; in which Light, every particular, dwell and stand, and you shall see the whole Body full of Light: For this leads into Unity and Oneness, which is in the Body,

> though many Members. So my dear Hearts, in that which is the Light of the Whole Body, which leads into Unity, to that be subject and obedient, that you may be serviceable to the whole Body; and give freely up to the Service of the Head, which is one, and but one in all. Even So are ye called in one Hope of your Calling, where there is one Lord, one Faith, one Baptism, one God and Father of all, who is above all, and through all, and in you all.[179]

Unity is thus an essential attribute of the true church, because it is finally one body and one with Christ.

In Fell's theology, the idea that those who are in the Light are the body of Christ has both a literal and a metaphorical sense. As the Spirit of the Lord Jesus Christ is perfected in us, the prophetic promise of his coming in the flesh is fulfilled. In this sense we as a group (*corpus*) literally become the body of Christ incarnate, risen and rising. In this way, Jesus Christ has come and is coming again in the flesh. At the same time, the concept of the true church as a body with many parts serves as a guiding metaphor for a group of diverse persons who must work together through the leading of the Light. Mother Fell made frequent use of it in her early epistles to Quakers, and from an organizational standpoint one can see how this would serve them well. The early Quakers had few of the traditional Christian religious observances to lend structure to their religious and spiritual lives. Likewise, the strong emphasis upon the priesthood of all believers led the leadership style of meetings away from the more hierarchical structures that were the norm elsewhere. Meetings were now directed through individual leadings of the Spirit discerned through the leadings of the gathering as a whole. This expressed itself in a consensus style of group leadership for which the Pauline conception of the body of Christ was well suited.[180]

Within the body, with the wise counsel and discernment of likeminded believers, the individual is strengthened and perfected in the Light.[181] The significance of the Light within as represented in the gathering for meetings charged each one present with a weighty responsibility. For this reason Margaret writes to other Friends, "as unto dear and near Members of this Body, the Church, whereof Christ Jesus is the head, and hath given himself for it, that he might make it a Glorious Church, without Spot or Wrinkled."[182] In order to guard against sin, and to protect the true ministrations of God in their midst, Mother Fell cautions them to beware of strife and self-exaltation:

> Beware of Hastiness, or Forwardness, in speaking many Words, except it be from a pure Discerning, of a pure Moving; and that you discern what you speak from, and what ye speak to; and who speaks here, is a

Minister... So I warn you to be silent, and to wait low in the Silence, until the Word be committed to you to minister: And none to Strive for Mastery, but each to esteem other better than themselves.[183]

In her ecclesiology, Fell brings some balance to her soteriology, and what may appear to be an overly individualistic mechanics of salvation and perfection. In her theology, the comportment of Friends as members of the body is extremely important, for "in Love and Unity, in the pure Eternal Light, there is your Fellowship, there is your cleansing and washing."[184] In various ways, she encourages them to keep to the Light, "and consider one another, and provoke one another to Love and to good Works; not forsaking the Assembling of your selves, but exhorting one another."[185] By gathering for meeting, the Light "gatheres together into one all hearts who are faithfull & obeydient to it, where all is one in Christ Jesus."[186] In faithfully attending to the Light, Fell assures us we "will come to know the pure Law, the righteous Law of God, which is the School-Master until Christ."[187] Thus in Fell's theology, she pursues the idea that the one Spirit shared brings unity, not simply through the exercise of individual virtues such as patience or self control or charity, but through sharing alike the mind of Christ.

Fell's ecclesiology promotes more than just structural unity. Her understanding is that the body of Christ, sharing the same Spirit with Christ, is ultimately intended to function organically. Within the body its members are to be obedient to the Light, be serviceable to the measure of the gifts God has provided them, be mindful of one another, and to meet together regularly. This includes material support, so that the burden of hardship, persecution, and suffering may be borne equally by the whole of the body:

> For everyone in their measures, may be serviceable to the whole Body, in what is called for, and required; and who dwells in the Light, it makes subject to be serviceable to the Body. And now, that nothing may be kept back, but as you have received freely, so freely you may administer, in Obedience to the one Eternal Light; you may be serviceable to the whole Body, in what is called for, and required.[188]

It seems evident in this passage that Fell is not working toward the functional model of what we might colloquially call "a well-oiled machine." Instead she is again pursuing the idea that conscientious freedom exercised in obedience to the Light is essential for a healthy body.

Everyone who dwells in the Light has Christ as teacher within, and so walks with him, being taught directly. In this sense, the apostles and the Children of the Light have the same teacher, and have received the same revelation of God's truth in Christ Jesus.[189] Because of this, each person who is obedient to the Light functions as a minister when the Spirit of the Lord moves one to do so.[190] Margaret Fell accepted and taught the priesthood of all believers, provided the term believer is applied only to those who walk in the Light of Christ. True ministers of the gospel live a life of purity and charity, and do not seek pay for proclaiming the good news of the Light risen and rising. They seek to be obedient to the Light without regard to consequences.

The integrity of the church grows out of the unifying Spirit of Christ Jesus, which leads and guides in the Light, and from the obedience and humility of those who follow the Light in love. As we gather together and attend to the Light for the edification of our own souls and those with whom we are in fellowship, "my dear Brethren and Sisters, let Brotherly love continue . . . And so you come to the fulfilling of the Scriptures, in your measures, and the Practice of all the Saints in the Light, that ever went before."[191] The guidelines for living and dwelling in the Light mirror those which foster productive meetings, "For if you walk in the Light, and abide in the Light, which is Low and Meek, and wait in Silence and Faithfulness, and Obedience, wait Patiently and you shall have the Light of Life . . . And be still and low, that you may receive the teachings of the Lord; and learn of him, who is Low and Meek, and hearken diligently, and keep your Minds to the Light, that so your Souls may live."[192] Here is Margaret Fell's oft-repeated gentle caution given to preserve the health of the true church.

After reviewing her understanding of the marks of the church, it is equally important for our understanding of Fell's ecclesiology that we focus on those things that the church is not. Here again, Margaret Fell's eschatology determined the theological direction she took. With the coming of the Light, a new covenant has been established in which the laws of God are written on the heart and established in the human soul. This covenant fulfills the promises of Scripture, and so the law and covenants of all earlier dispensations (including the Old and New Testament periods) are brought to an end. This new covenant writes the law on the heart as the Light dwells in the human soul, the true temple of God. Therefore, the church is not found in the institutions or the structures built by human hands for the purpose of religion. Neither is it to be found in the gatherings initiated by the clergy acting in the name of Christ. These expressions of human spiritual need claim the name of Christ, but they do not lead to salvation. To Margaret Fell these expressions of faith and practice are merely the forms and rituals of religion, which claim Jesus Christ outwardly but do not profess him come again and made manifest in the flesh.

## The False Church, the Clergy, and the Judgment

As Margaret Fell's corpus of religious work expanded, so did her sense that the established church was mired in darkness. Further, she believed the long-standing practices of the church across the centuries had buried the true nature of salvation, and the "Ministry and Ministration has been lost and the Church, for which the Apostles suffered, hath been in the Wilderness."[193] The true church in essence ended with the apostles, after which the church entered a long period of apostasy. The traditions and vain imaginings of human beings brought the church into idolatry and kept her wandering in the desert. Thus Fell often devotes some portion of her text to addressing the errors and abuses of the professional clergy, who keep the people away from the true path of Christ, thus denying God the true inward worship that is his due. The many rituals and sacraments, the practices of the established or institutional church—by which we mean those Christian institutions opposed by Fell—focus upon the outward worship of God. However, these outward religious practices are not efficacious in any salvific way, and are in fact the yoke of bondage to darkness.[194]

According to Fell, "the Gospel, that hath been preached since the Apostacy, hath laid Oppression and Sufferings upon others, and they themselves have Ruled and Lorded over Peoples Consciences."[195] However the time has now come when "the Figures, and the Types, and the Shadows are ceased, the Lord God has departed out of them, and the Substance of them is come, the Holy Seed is risen, the Substance thereof."[196] Therefore the practices, forms, and rituals of the established church no longer serve any salvific function. Fell likens the practices of outward religion to "the Fig-leaves of your Profession" by which she means an inadequate covering that attempts to hide sin, but remains transparent to God.[197] These fig leaves include the manner of worship, the administration of the sacraments, and the handling of Scripture. Add to this an insistence upon the church tax and related tithe requirements, and the institutional church proves herself to be the false church.

Out of the darkness and blindness of their teachings, professional clergy deny the principle of the Light within, "and tell People, that they must look after them for Means and Ordinances; and so blind poor People, and keep them in Darkness and Ignorance."[198] Thus the teachings of the institutional church promote the spirit of darkness that has long reigned over the earth, and in such teaching the blind lead the blind. What Fell sought to have the clergy understand was that outward religious practices are not efficacious, for the genuine worship of God is that which is inward. This runs contrary to the established practice of a fallen people, who look to outward ritual in order to secure righteousness. But this outward focus toward Christ is an empty expression. It is religion that is form without content.[199]

This is a profession in words, says Margaret, a lifeless deception devoid of true life in the spirit, as she writes,

> You have the outward Writings and Declaration, which was spoken from another State and Condition than Ye are in; and these words ye take as your own when as ye are in another Condition, and of another Seed, than that which the Promise is to; it is not seeds, as to many, but to one Seed, which is Christ the Light, and Corner-stone, which the Builders refuse, and yet ye account it Railing to be called Thieves and Robbers, though ye have nothing [of Christ] but what you steal from others.[200]

Because they have rejected the Light within, both as an objective reality and as an inward experience, they have nothing of Jesus Christ in their worship or ritual.

Believing the path to Christ Jesus lay in the traditional teachings of the institutional church, the professional clergy and the professors (those who call themselves Christians but who are outside the Light) embrace their own condemnation. This is the gospel of Christ:

> Which ye blind Hypocrites profess, but know nothing of, farther than by Reading without you in the [dead] Letter. So ye make clean the outside, with an outward Profession, and a Form, and an Image and a Likeness . . . Though you profess a God and a Christ from Records without you, yet your Possession and Inheritance is of the Evil One.[201]

For this reason, Margaret Fell considers the hierarchy, clergy, and lay leadership of this false church "the blind Guides and Hypocrites in this, which Christ Jesus cried woe against."[202] This charge of hypocrisy stems from her observation that the established church clergy,

> say and Prophecy that he is come, and profess that that was he they Crucified, and ye profess he is risen again; and yet ye persecute and deny his testimony, which is risen and made manifest. Now see whether ye are not blind indeed, when as ye go about to oppose, deny and persecute that which ye your selves profess.[203]

Hypocrisy is evidenced in the fact that their proclamation of Jesus Christ, the affirmation of his lordship and the truth that he will come again, is made at the same time as they deny the true revelation of Christ made manifest and come again in the flesh.[204]

Initially, issues of the outward observances of Christian professors were Mother Fell's primary source of theological disagreement with the established church. She sought to proclaim the Light come again and to persuade them that the old forms were no longer necessary. However, her later works show a deeper antipathy for the clergy generally, and her theological opposition grew in keeping with the list of persecutions and outrages committed against religious nonconformists. This was especially true in the case of the Children of the Light, for here "doth the Lord suffer indeed in his Saints, by those that profess him in Words and deny his Power."[205] As the persecution of Friends increased, the depths to which the institutional church would stoop in order to suppress them became ever more apparent. Margaret Fell was outraged by the machinations of the political and religious leaders who set their caps against the Quakers, disrupting their worship, seizing their property, and imprisoning them without just cause.

Ultimately she articulates a number of theological objections to the idea of professional clergy, including those in the episcopacy. In her publication *A Touch-Stone: or A Tryal by the Scriptures, of the Priests, Bishops, and Ministers*, she writes:

> I am clearly convinced, and am assured, that the Bishops, as they are called, and those of their Order and Coat, or indeed any that have taken upon them that Function of the Clergy these many Hundred of Years, that they are not according unto Christ Jesus, nor unto his Disciples, not the Apostles, and the Saints in the Primitive Times, but are gone quite contrary, according to what the Scriptures of Truth hold forth.[206]

Fell's earliest theological disagreements along this line have to do with the forced maintenance of the established church and her clergy. This is wrong because it requires Quakers to support a ministry which they believed to be contrary to the teachings of Christ, and "which Ministry we could not Joyn with nor own. So we look upon it to be unjust to maintain them."[207]

She also objects to the idea of paid clergy, whom she called "hirelings." The idea that persons would be paid to minister ran contrary to her theology of ministry. In her 1660 work *A Declaration and an Information from Us the People of God Called Quakers*, she writes against them saying, "we receive nothing from, nor cannot trust our Souls under there Teaching, who Teach for Hire and Divine for Money . . . and they are maintained by Tithes, contrary to Christ and the Apostle's Doctrine, for Christ Jesus is the Everlasting Offering once for all."[208] She refers to the priests as hired hands who tend the flock, but are not willing to sacrifice for the sheep in the same way that the shepherd is.[209] Hirelings tend the sheep only because they are paid to. Adding insult to injury were the constraints placed upon people to worship in the manner the hirelings saw fit, and the threat of court for those who would not comply.[210]

Mother Fell also objects to clergy titles and the honors accorded them by those titles. She holds that the entire notion of titles and preferential treatment for one part of the body over another is contrary to the teachings of Scripture and Christ. Fell reminds them that Jesus called his apostles together and said, "Ye know that the Princes of the Gentiles exercise Dominion over them, and they that are great exercise Authority upon them, but it shall not be so among you."[211] Likewise, the titles given to Christ's servants in the Bible were those such as "our Brother, and Minister of God, and Fellow-Labourer in the Gospel of Christ" as opposed to those such as Lord-Bishop, your Lordship, and your Grace.[212] In keeping with this, Fell is critical of the estate, condition, and qualifications of the clergy, as well as their use of robes and vestments.

Margaret Fell, who was herself of rank and station, calls the clergy on their pride and haughtiness, which runs counter to Christ and the apostles, "who were Meek, Lowly, and Humble." The clergy also turn away from suffering for Christ, which goes against Christ's command that "if any Man will come after me, let him deny himself, and take up his Cross daily and follow me." Instead they are those who persecute and cause others to suffer for Christ's sake. They do not show an attitude of servanthood as demonstrated in instances such as Jesus washing the feet of his disciples; neither do they show love and compassion toward their brothers and sisters in the Lord. In this Margaret Fell reminds them that he "that saith he is in the Light, but hateth his Brother, in is Darkness."[213] She paints a portrait of vain ministers filled with pride and a desire for power. Their own comportment toward others is witness to their lack of qualification for the offices they hold.

The calling of clergy is also brought into question, because Fell believed that only the Holy Spirit ordained and empowered one for ministry. For this reason their call is "contrary to Christ and his Apostles, which was by Special Command, and Revelation in Christ Jesus," while the clergy receive their calling from human beings. Thus "it is truly manifested, that the order of their calling is not according to Christ."[214] Not surprisingly, Fell also challenges their doctrine with regard to their worship practices (which includes preaching). She writes, "The first thing that I accept against in Matter and Form of their Worship . . . is the taking a part or a portion of Scripture for a Text, and adding thereto their own Inventions, which they study in out of their own Brain; and also bring other Authors, who have done the like, many of them not Christian."[215] This may be contrasted with the efforts of Jesus and his followers who "to bring People to this Light and Spirit of the Lord within them, did Christ Jesus and all his Apostles endeavor, by their preaching." Thus the worship in the established church is not in accordance with the work of Christ.[216]

It also troubled Fell that preachers presented complicated sermons in which they attempted to be orators and wits, whereas the apostle Paul did not come preaching the wisdom of the world "because the Foolishness of God is wiser than Men . . . but God hath chosen the Foolish Things of the World to confound the Wise."[217] Likewise the clergy used the Book of Common Prayer, "also saying the Pater-Nosters and the Ave-Maries of the Papists."[218] Their lack of godly wisdom is also seen (or heard) in their use of chants and singing accompanied by instruments. More outrageous for Margaret was the time spent in universities, in "that which they call their Studying and their placing the very Foundation of their Call, and all their Practices in that function, in that which they call Learning; which thing we never find, neither in the Old Testament nor New."[219] Finally, she objects strenuously on theological grounds to the administration of church sacraments.

As we are well familiar with by now, Margaret Fell believed that the coming of the Light abolished the old covenants and laws and replaced them with Christ's eternal covenant and his law written on our hearts. This final covenant supercedes all that came before it, and the laws and rituals of the past are no longer valid. For Fell, this includes the sacraments. No outward washing in baptism, either of child or adult, is necessary. Neither is there any need for ordination or marriage formalized by Christian ritual. Confession and anointing are now spiritual rather than physical activities, and the Eucharist is replaced by the presence of Christ inwardly. She particularly denies the efficacy of any sacraments in which persons are compelled to participate or partake saying, "But what is their Supper or Dinner, that People can receive, when they have compelled them?"[220] Of these clergy practices, which Margaret Fell calls "the Traditions of Men," she writes,

> And this hath been the Doctrine of our Ages last past, the Tradition of Men, and Imaginations and Inventions of Men; By this they have holden up the Superiority, according as the Apostle faith, Having Mens Persons in Admiration because of Advantage, and so have Lorded over God's Heritage; and so have kept his People under the weight of Oppression, as the Scribes and Pharisees did; binding heavy Burthens grievous to be born; But this is contrary to Christ and his Apostles Doctrine and Example.[221]

In view of this, she urges Christian professors to examine the lives of their pastors and Priests of England and see whether what she says is true. She challenges them, "And now Reader do but consider, how these Teachers of the World live, and after what manner, and how they do oppress People for their Maintenance, and how they draw people from the Unction of the Holy One."[222] Likewise she encourages them, "Try them by the Scripture and you shall find them contrary to the Doctrine of Christ, and of the Apostles, and not to have received the Gifts which he gave to the Prophets, Apostles and Evangelists for the perfecting of the Saints, which all that ever were sent of God preached and prayed for."[223]

To those in the established church, from the episcopacy to the lowest church leader, she makes a variety of pleas and arguments against a profession of faith that claims Christ outwardly but does not know him inwardly. At times her arguments are gently put, and at others she is strident and rebuking, but she seems to have had a genuine concern for their salvation. Ultimately though, it comes down to this: "they who turn out from the Light, their Resurrection is to Condemnation . . . and this shall be witnessed for ever."[224] Fell would have all turn to the Light within, and leave behind the idolatry and dark ministrations of a decayed and impotent tradition. For this idol—built by the hands of human beings—cannot last when the Light "strikes at the feet of the Image: which the Disobedient part, which look'd out from the Eternal, and is shut out from God, the Will of Man hath set up," and which "is the Condemnation of the World."[225]

Judgment and destruction are the only things that await those who "witness against the Light, and plead for Sin, and for the Kingdom of Antichrist, which is of the World."[226] To Mother Fell, these are the deceivers and "false Prophets, which are entered into the World, who draw from the Light, which is the World's Condemnation."[227] They are ravening wolves clothed in sheep's clothing who seek to devour Christ's lambs and to impose burdens on the spiritually weary and weak. These are the blind guides of apostasy who "have long stood in their Forms; but never was there any Perfection, that the Power of Truth is made manifest, which will confound and break to pieces all their Forms."[228] These destroyers, who love the darkness and hate the Light are now "seen and known and made manifest to be the Deceivers, to be the False Prophets, and Antichrist; and with the Light that comes from Jesus they are Condemned, with the World, and turned from, by all the Children of the Light."[229]

## Conclusion

This review of Margaret Fell's theology has shown the weight and place of her realized eschatology in all of her theological work. A practical rather than systematic thinker, Fell nevertheless had an inner coherence to her theology which can be demonstrated through a careful reading of her tracts and letters. We have seen that a powerful realized eschatology, which she shared with other early Friends, runs throughout her theological thought, influencing her understanding of the Triune God, Christology, pneumatology, soteriology, ecclesiology, hamartiology, salvation history, and of course the temper of her times (which she understood to be the last days). In the chapters that follow, we shall turn to Fell's mission and ministry. We will show the central place of eschatology in her mission to the Jews, her defense of the spiritual equality of women in Christ, and her peace testimony.

# 4

## A Salutation to the Seed of Abraham
*Margaret Fell, Quaker Evangelism, and the Jews*

Early Friends' theology pulses with energy and urgency. Channeled through the social and religious context of the seventeenth century, the stern joy of Quaker proclamation melded with apocalyptic expectation to fit the tenor of the times. As a biblical prerequisite for Christ's return, the conversion of the Jews has a permanent place in the reckoning of Christian eschatology. Of course, wars, social unrest, disease, earthquakes, and other natural disasters also figure prominently in Christian end-times calculations, but they are much more flexible numerators in the equation. Weighting the vicissitudes of natural disaster and human desire is light duty compared to interpreting the destiny of an entire people through an end-times calculus. That so many have taken up this challenge is a marvel of its own kind. Given the tumultuous religious and political environment in which Margaret Fell lived and wrote, she surely encountered the question of the relationship between England and the Jews. Like most things in her time, the issue was both political and religious. The debate was shaped in large part by the concerns of the Protestant Reformation, and in a more general sense forced by the needs of a Christian faith that is bound historically and theologically to the Jewish people.

However, the social and religious anxiety that surrounded these last-times discussions was not limited to Christianized peoples. As we will see, the great Jewish Rabbi Menasseh ben Israel had his own reasons for accepting the king's invitation to England and the Whitehall Conference. There he entered public discourse on the state of world Jewry, believing in his own fashion that signs of the times pointed to the coming Jewish Messiah. In this sense, Menasseh ben Israel and Margaret Fell were part of the same historical discourse though there is no record that they ever met. What they shared was the belief that Jews should be readmitted to England and her territories, and that this would fulfill a requirement for the full reign of the Jewish Messiah. As a Quaker with a distinct theological perspective on the subject, Margaret Fell expressed solid interest in the readmission of the Jews to England. This is reflected in the four published pamphlets written by her and directed to the attention of the Jewish people. These four publications have earned Margaret Fell attention in publications aimed primarily at scholars outside the field of Quaker studies. The reasons for the interest are varied and at times have almost nothing to do with the woman herself.

Perhaps the most intriguing example of this is Margaret Fell's publication *A Loving Salutation to the Seed of Abraham*. It is probable that the Jewish philosopher Baruch Spinoza was the unnamed translator for the Hebrew version of this publication, which was then distributed abroad by Quaker missionaries. If Spinoza is the unnamed translator, then it would constitute Spinoza's first published work.[1] However, our purpose for considering these publications is to gain a better understanding of Margaret Fell's theology as it is revealed in her efforts toward Quaker evangelism of the Jewish people. To begin, we will consider a broad reconstruction of the context in which Fell articulated her religious and theological views, in this case on the issue of the Jews. In essence we are looking to capture those things that Margaret Fell could reasonably be expected to know and believe about the Jews and their place in the world of the seventeenth century. In so doing, we will see that the significance of the Jews for Fell and the early Quakers reflected not only their own theological perspective as Friends, but also the religious, political, and philosophical concerns which dominated England in the sixteenth and seventeenth centuries.

In attempting to reconstruct the context of her writings to the Jews, our first interest is in England's stance toward the Jewish people during the seventeenth century. We will look to evidence of attitudes that existed at the popular, scholarly, and political levels. From there we will briefly discuss the life of Rabbi Menasseh ben Israel, the leader of the Amsterdam Jewish community who came to England as an emissary to the 1655 Whitehall Conference. For Margaret Fell, as for many others, this visit was a sign of the last days, and to some degree it was made possible because of popular millenarian concerns in England. As we will see, ben Israel's identification as spokesman for the Jewish community in Amsterdam—and, by extension, Jews worldwide—was an expression of numerous western European concerns which emerged in part as a by-product of the Protestant Reformation. Not only were there eschatological implications for the visit of ben Israel, but Reformation influences also generated an interest in Hebrew studies as result of the emphasis placed upon reading Scripture in its original languages. Similarly, an idealized version of Judaism gleaned from the Old Testament and interpreted through Christianity found its way from the work of sixteenth- and seventeenth-century philosophers and sectarians into the minds of the general populace and millennialists.

## England and the Jews

Throughout the Middle Ages European Jews led a marginalized existence in Christian countries, where they were viewed with suspicion and distrust. As the objects of fear and hatred, they were the target of superstition, rumor, and allegations of the most fantastic sort. Although their economic presence was usually welcome, their social and religious existence was tentative and frequently under threat, for instance, when the assets or business interests of a Jewish community drew the covetous attention of those with political power.[2] Among the European populace generally, it was believed that Jews emitted a distinctive and unpleasant odor, and that Jewish hatred of Christ led them to poison Christians, their wells, and their animals. Jewish rituals were likewise viewed as diabolical activities involving practices such as desecration of the host and ritual murder of the innocents in sacrifice to Moloch. Stories of young children found hanging upside down as their blood was drained for Jewish religious rites were the stuff of popular myth.[3] These stories appear to have been perpetrated primarily by clergy, who often spread them from the pulpit.[4] Attempts by some religious thinkers to present a more reasoned view of Jewish practice and culture were met with vehement attacks from others in their own ranks.[5]

The degree to which these stories were successful in maintaining a culture of intentional misinformation is noted by Joshua Trachtenberg when he writes, "It is not necessary here to list accusations of this sort leveled at the Jews of the Middle Ages: suffice it to say that they were always in danger of answering for the death or disappearance of a child and that the danger materialized frequently in large-scale massacre and expulsion."[6] One such incident culminated in the Jews' expulsion from England at the close of the thirteenth century. There, a young boy was found drowned in an open cesspool located in the proximity of a Jewish wedding celebration. In the aftermath, several Jews in attendance were arrested and hanged after signing forced confessions. Though the death of the boy had no witnesses and was probably accidental, the event became the focus of public outrage and hysteria. This sense of panic and anger was fueled by a widespread belief, already discussed, that Jews murdered Christian children in secret religious rituals. That such misconceptions would prevail among the common folk is probably not surprising, unlettered and little traveled as they often were. However, it is important to remember the credibility that such beliefs enjoyed among the upper echelons of English society. In this case, the event was so widely discussed that it caught the attention of Edward I, who on July 18, 1295, signed a royal writ ordering the expulsion of Jews from English Shores.[7] Any Jew remaining in England after November 1 was subject to the penalty of death.

In the years between the expulsion of Jews in 1295 and the Whitehall Conference of 1655, there was understandably no identifiable Jewish presence in England. In this absence, Christianity was the unchallenged interpreter of Old Testament theology and practice, and became the primary lens through which its teachings were viewed. For much of this period Jewish language and custom were largely lost to the realm, save for the popular caricatures present in works such as William Shakespeare's *The Merchant of Venice*.[8] However, by the sixteenth century the Protestant Reformation was beginning to have an impact on this situation. With its emphasis on the Bible as the authoritative guide for Christian faith and practice, the Reformation re-instilled an appreciation for the study of Scripture in the original languages. The study of Hebrew gained a renewed respectability in England, and it again found a place in the scholarly community. In 1524 Robert Wakefield published his *Oritatio de laudibus & utilitate trium linguarum*, which was the first work published in England to incorporate Hebrew typescript.[9] Wakefield was the first Hebrew Reader at Oxford, and his brother Thomas Wakefield was appointed the first Regius Professor of Hebrew at Cambridge University in 1540.[10]

This resurgence in Hebrew studies was of significant benefit in the translation of the Bible for the Authorized Version of 1611.[11] That the impact of Hebrew scholarship soon extended beyond the interests of the church is seen in the growth of European philo-Semitism, which was particularly strong in England. With its elevation of the Hebrew language and its idealization of Old Testament Judaism, philo-Semitism addressed the philosophical and social concerns of European thinkers through the glorification of the Creation Myth.[12] In this arena, the interest in the Hebrew language gained greater impetus by the intersection of three concerns. First, there was the desire for a philosophical language that expressed a precise correlation between words and things. Second, there was a search for a new "universal" language to serve as a supplemental vocabulary to compensate for the limitations of English and replace the now-outdated Latin. Third, there was a quest to uncover in the Hebrew language a *lingua humana*, an original language of humankind.

In this third instance, Hebrew was of particular interest because it was "the language before Babel, the very tongue that Adam spoke in the Garden of Eden before the Fall, [and] was endowed with divine and supernatural qualities . . . By the mid-seventeenth century, after much discussion, most Englishmen agreed that God spoke Hebrew."[13] This interest in a return to the Adamic language spoken at creation gained appeal as various attempts to construct a universal language fell under the weight of their own cumbersome structures. The romanticized notion that Adam named animals, and in naming created a language that expressed the direct correlation between word and object, caught the imaginations of major seventeenth-century philosophers and poets. Francis Bacon, John Milton, and John Donne are among the luminaries who weighed in on the merits of the Hebrew language. Implicit in this view was the opinion that Hebrew was the original human tongue, and the attendant identification of Old Testament Hebrew with that of the seventeenth century.[14]

Another result of the resurgence of English interest in the Hebrew language and Jewish practice can be seen in the work of seventeenth-century Christian Judaizers. The term refers to non-Jewish Christians who favored some form of return to Old Testament observances and religious practices.

Although the word "Judaizer" was often employed as a pejorative term for Protestants who advocated Saturday Sabbath, or some other practice that merely hinted of legalism, there were those who would aptly qualify for this description. By way of example we can look to the prominent English Judaizer John Traske. As we saw in chapter 2, Traske was an ordained Christian minister who blended heterodox teachings on the nature of election and redemption with Jewish dietary laws, Old Testament practices, and a strict observance of Mosaic law.[15] As one of the earliest and most prominent of the seventeenth-century Judaizers and Saturday Sabbatarians, John Traske captures the tension that surrounded Jews in seventeenth-century England.[16] Common sentiment held that Jews were children of a lesser covenant who had been rejected by God for their idolatrous behavior. As such, they were capable of the most uncivilized abominations against Christians. Their physical presence in England was punishable by death, and the mere intimation of "Jewish legalism" in Christian practice met with scorn and alarm. At the same time, the work of Christian Hebraists advanced Hebrew scholarship under the mandate of the Protestant Reformation. The rise of philo-Semitism and the idealization of Jewish religion and language found fertile ground there and combined to become an influential movement among England's educated classes. To this we must add the weight of millenarian speculation that hung heavy in the intellectual air, speculation which appealed to many philo-Semites as well as religious thinkers generally.[17]

As we saw in chapter 2, the Reformation also reinvigorated millenarian speculation in England. By the time of Margaret Fell, seventeenth-century English millenarian concerns both reflected and built upon the chiliastic preoccupations of other European countries in previous centuries.[18] Whatever the context, the Jewish people remained an essential component of the apocalyptic cipher that Christians contemplated as they awaited the second coming of Christ. With the rejection of Roman Catholic authority over the English Church, the perception that England was the first truly Christian nation on earth encouraged the notion that the second coming would take place within her shores. Of this time, Cecil Roth has written:

> It was widely believed that the millennium was approaching. The four kingdoms spoken of in the book of Daniel had passed away; the fifth and final monarchy was about to be established in the world, under the rule of the Messiah himself. Even the date of this was fixed—the messianic year, 1666. It was the general opinion that the gathering, and the conversion, of the tribes of Israel was to be the prelude to this marvelous consummation . . . Only the conversion of the Jews remained to be effected. It was obvious that every effort should be made to remove this last obstacle to the final deliverance.[19]

In light of this, many Christians began to look to the ingathering of the Jews as a necessary step in ushering in the thousand-year reign of Christ. In addition, speculation that the lost ten tribes of Israel had been found in the Americas and the messianic claims of Shabtai Sevi—the "Jewish false messiah"—added urgency to the discussion of Jewish readmission to England.[20]

Thus, while scholars such as John Lightfoot and Edward Pococke were influential in advancing Hebrew language studies, "Judaizers . . . notorious millenarians, polemical language theorists, and religious tolerationists pushed the Jewish question into a prominent position in the political arena."[21] The force of speculation and debate about Jewish readmission to England led Oliver Cromwell to appoint a commission of twenty-eight delegates to consider the question. With this, the journey to the Whitehall Conference of 1655 began. However, the question had been before the English people in print as early as 1608, in a publication by Thomas Draxe. The conversion was to be "the last generall signe & fore-runner of Christs second coming."[22] These Early works calling for the readmission of the Jews were usually based upon some argument for religious tolerance. The culmination of this period can be seen in Edward Nicholas' 1650 *Apology for the honourable nation of the Jews*, which enjoyed wide circulation. There he argued that England should extend refuge as a prelude to the conversion of the Jewish people.

Nicholas reminded them that Jesus had not been killed by the Jewish people but by a select few Jews, and he cautioned that mistreatment of the Jews had the potential to remove England from God's favor.[23] By the time Nicholas' work was published, the practical question of Jewish immigration had already been under serious consideration within the halls of government for a few years, though nothing like consensus had emerged.[24] As is witnessed by Nicholas' *Apology*, a new line of reasoning had become prominent in publications on the Jewish question. Where earlier works advocating the readmission of the Jewish people to England argued on the grounds of religious toleration, later works proceeded from a more eschatological starting point.[25] "By 1650, a tradition of millenarian support for the Jews, and an appreciation of their place in the long-awaited cosmic drama had already been established."[26] This approach reflects a belief that the primary reason Jews had not yet converted to Christianity was that their experience was limited to observations of Roman Catholic practices.

The remedy for this was to bring Jews into England, where they would be exposed to the pure Christian faith, free of popish corruption.[27] Such an act would speed the Jews to a timely conversion and, by this, usher in the thousand-year reign of Christ. It was this thinking, encouraged by millenarian philo-Semites such as Samuel Hartlib, John Drurie, John Sadleer, and Henry Jessey, that brought Rabbi Menasseh ben Israel to England in 1655.[28] The rabbi had four stated goals for his visit to England. He sought "to obtain permission to have a synagogue, to ensure the complete dispersion of the Jews throughout the world, to bring wealth to England through Jewish merchants, and to find the same affection in the whole nation for his people as had been extended to himself by individual Englishmen."[29]

The visit of Menasseh ben Israel was the subject of wide speculation in Britain, and it was this visit which prompted Margaret Fell to publish her 1656 work *For Manasseth-ben-Israel: The Call of the Jews out of Babylon*. Unfortunately, the rabbi's presence in London as guest of the Lord

Protector did not bring him the success he sought, and only Cromwell himself appears to have favored immigration for the Jews.[30] One reason why ben Israel's proposals were rejected was the very reason why his visit had been greeted with anticipation. Put simply, Rabbi Menasseh asked permission to establish a synagogue. Christian leaders in favor of readmission as a means to the rapid conversion of the Jews wanted no part of a proposal that would allow Judaism to be legally reestablished in England.[31]

The failure of Menasseh ben Israel's proposals to garner clear public support led Oliver Cromwell to call the Whitehall Conference in order to discuss the conditions under which readmission of the Jews might take place. The conference began on the December 4, 1655, and ran through the eighteenth of that month.[32] The group that had gathered at the request of the Lord Protector was drawn from influential English theologians and merchants, and their opinions are likely a good representation of the sentiment in England at that time. According to Henry Jessey's *A Narrative of the late Proceedings at Whitehall* (1656), opinion was divided broadly into three camps.[33] The first view was that Jews should not be readmitted to England because this would have a negative economic impact. This was the position of merchants and a few clerics, whose stance seems to have been due to genuine fiscal concerns rather than any outright religious intolerance.[34] The second view favored readmission on a limited basis under carefully controlled circumstances. This was the choice of the majority of churchmen. The third view favored open immigration without restriction. This group was in the minority, though they apparently enjoyed the support of the Lord Protector.[35]

With the disappointment of the Whitehall Conference, the Jewish question lost much of its momentum as a political issue. However, with Cromwell's efforts, small numbers of Jews were allowed to immigrate, and by 1660 a small Jewish community had been established in London.[36] However, this did not bring an end to millenarian expectation, nor did it discourage individuals from publishing their various pleas to the Jews in efforts to win their conversion. Because of his status among Amsterdam Jews, Menasseh ben Israel continued to find himself at the center of English attention as millenarians, philo-Semites, and religious tolerationists—including Margaret Fell—addressed ben Israel in a second publication.[37] For Fell this reflects both her eschatological concerns and a related interest in the fledgling efforts of the Quaker mission in Amsterdam.[38]

## The Significance of Menasseh ben Israel

Given his significance in seventeenth-century England as well as his prominence as leader of the Amsterdam Jewish community, we now turn our attention more carefully to Rabbi Menasseh ben Israel. An attenuated treatment of ben Israel's life and eschatological expectation is useful to us here as a vehicle for conveying the long and complex history of the Amsterdam Jews to whom Margaret Fell sent her work. It will also give us a more contextual understanding of publications she wrote to them in hopes of their convincement in the Light. The Amsterdam community was an important focus of early Quaker missionary activity. It was here that Menasseh ben Israel ministered to a congregation comprised mainly of Marranos. These were the descendents of those Jews who migrated to Spain and Portugal in the wake of their thirteenth-century expulsion from England. However, Spain excluded Jews in 1492, at which time Spanish Jews were forced to accept Christian baptism or to leave the country and abandon their property and business interests. Portugal followed their example five years later.

Those Jews who chose to remain in Spain fell into two categories: *Conversos* who embraced Roman Catholicism, and *Marranos*, which is Spanish for "swine." One of the three women doctors of the Catholic Church, Teresa of Avila, was the daughter of Conversos. Ben Israel was the son of Marranos, those who practiced public Christianity and private Judaism. To Jews, these forced converts were known as the *Anusim*, meaning "Compelled Ones." Although the Anusim adopted Spanish or Portuguese names for public use, they retained Jewish names and practices as much as possible in private.[39] These crypto-Jews were unable to practice Judaism publicly, but they were able to travel throughout Europe with greater ease, where their identity as Spaniards or Portuguese carried with it the assumption they were Roman Catholic.[40] However, even the increased freedom of crypto-Jews was offset by perils.

As Christians, Marranos risked greater prosecution if their Jewish practices were discovered. As Jews they were of minor interest to the Inquisition, but as Christians caught in Jewish practices they would have to endure the most intense inquisitional ire.[41] One such Marrano family affected by the Inquisition was that of Manuel Dias Soeiro, known more commonly as Menasseh ben Israel. He was born in Madeira in 1604, into a family of Portuguese crypto-Jews originally from Lisbon. After immigrating to Spain from Lisbon, Menasseh's father Joseph drew the attention of the Spanish Inquisition, and he was arrested and forcibly "reconciled" with the Christian church. Twice arrested, he was tortured and had his property seized, and so took the family to the Madeira Islands. From there the destitute family emigrated to Amsterdam when Menasseh ben Israel was still a young boy.

In Amsterdam they found greater freedom of expression and acceptance in the growing Jewish population there. By the end of the sixteenth century, something like a "Dutch Jerusalem" existed in Amsterdam, even though Jews did not enjoy unrestricted citizenship until 1796. When Holland freed herself from the rule of Spain and the power of the Roman Catholic Church at the close of the sixteenth century, Amsterdam quickly became the destination of choice for many Marranos living in Spain and Portugal. Here ben Israel found his place at last. A talented and articulate young man, Menasseh ben Israel wrote his first book at seventeen, and achieved early and lasting fame as a theological writer and speaker.[42] He became a rabbi early in life and began serving the Jewish community in Amsterdam. Ben Israel was friend to, and correspondent with, many influential thinkers of his day, and he has the distinction of having had his portrait rendered by the artist Rembrandt during the period the artist resided in Amsterdam's *Jodenbreestraat*, or Jewish quarter. Historian Richard H. Popkin described ben Israel as "an amazing figure for his time. He was involved with Christian thinkers all over Europe, and boasted of the voluminous correspondence he carried on with people in France, England, Germany, Italy and elsewhere."[43] His prominence in the Amsterdam community eventually placed him in the position of spokesperson for Jews generally. As Cecil Roth notes, "Savants and statesmen, both at home and abroad (including many in England) were in the habit of consulting him on matters of Jewish scholarship. He had thus become a representative figure in Gentile eyes, and considered himself qualified to speak to those in authority on behalf of his people as a whole."[44] It was in this capacity that he became the central figure in the quest for readmission of Jews to England during the Whitehall Conference of 1655.

## Eschatologies Converge in England

Menasseh ben Israel's presence at the conference reflected his prominence in the Amsterdam community, but it also demonstrates his position at the intersection of English philosophical and theological interests of the seventeenth century. According to Henry Joel Cadbury, ben Israel "believed that the Holy Land would not be restored to the Jews until they spread into every inhabited part of the world, that the Messiah was soon to come, and that the North American Indians were the lost ten tribes.

The first of these beliefs explains his efforts for the admission of Jews into England, the second and third interested English Christians more generally."[45] These distinctives of Menasseh ben Israel's thought are present in Europe long before the seventeenth century. However, ben Israel's interest, taken in light of his position in Amsterdam, gave his thought special significance. It was the supposed discovery of the ten lost tribes of Israel in the Americas that brought these ideas into sharp focus for ben Israel, and generated intense interest in England. Those familiar with the work of the famous rabbi note that although he was intelligent and well read he was somewhat uncritical in his thinking, often accepting even the most fantastic tales with credulity.[46] Thus, the story of the ten lost tribes of Israel, long a source of speculation and conjecture, was of interest to him and he took the reports of them seriously. This particular flurry of interest in the lost Israelites originates in 1644, when a Marrano named Antonio de Montezinos presented himself before Menasseh ben Israel and other leaders of the Amsterdam synagogue.[47] The man claimed that he had traveled to South America, where he had encountered a tribe of Indians who recited the Shema (Deut 6:4-9) and practiced Jewish ceremonies. Montezinos believed them to be members of the lost tribe of Reuben. This report was significant for Menasseh ben Israel, who viewed the information in light of messianic prophesies.[48] As David Katz observes, "The search for the lost ten tribes of Israel provided the bridge to concrete action on behalf of readmission, for it was this debate that turned the attention of Rabbi Menasseh ben Israel to England."[49]

Apparently, the secondhand reports of Montezinos' story caused several in England to seek out the rabbi, and it was through the millenarian opinions of these correspondents that Menasseh read new significance into the story of the lost tribes. In his *Life of Menasseh ben Israel*, Cecil Roth writes, "He now began to connect in his mind the discovery of the remnant of the Ten Tribes with the messianic deliverance. This was to take place, according to the Bible, only when the dispersion of the Jews was complete."[50] As a result of the rabbi's growing interest in eschatological speculation he wrote his influential book *The Hope of Israel*. Published first in Spanish (Menasseh was of course a Spanish-speaking Jew), the work was enlarged and translated into Latin and appeared in England as the 1650 treatise *Spes Israelis*.[51] The work addressed recent reports that natives in the Americas were descendents of the lost tribes of Reuben and Levi.

The Latin work was dedicated to the English revolutionary government of the Cromwellian Interregnum, the Supreme Court of Parliament, whose favor and goodwill towards Jews was sought.[52] When Menasseh ben Israel weighed in on the controversy, the entire discussion changed in tenor and direction, giving "it a specific, polemical purpose toward Jewish readmission."[53] In England *Spes Israelis* enjoyed rapid success and was soon translated into English as *The Hope of Israel*. This success was due in part to the climate of the time, where the "main preoccupation of the time was religion; the most popular book the Bible; and it was about this that all other literature . . . revolved."[54] If the lost ten tribes had in fact been found in the Americas, a host of fascinating questions of biblical history and prophecy were ripe for the asking. Such questions—particularly those concerning fulfillment of prophecy—were now just as much a concern of Menasseh ben Israel as they were of millenarian English Christians.

In his correspondence with John Dury just prior to his publication of *Spes Israelis*, ben Israel sets forth the points he intended to make in the work. The rabbi believed that the ten tribes continued Jewish practices, and that they were scattered not only in the Americas, but around the world. He saw the Inquisition with its victims as an example of persecution that pointed toward the coming of the Messiah. Finally, ben Israel wrote, "I prove at large, that the day of the promised Messiah unto us doth draw neer, upon which occasion I explain many Prophecies."[55] Response to ben Israel's missive was mixed, but the work did succeed in moving the discussion of the readmission of the Jews to England from the theological into the political realm.[56] The question here is why messianic prophecies and the tale of the lost tribes would turn Menasseh ben Israel's attention to England? The answer in part has to do with the efforts of English evangelists to the Jews in Amsterdam.

Millenarian English philo-Semites in particular actively engaged the Jews in Holland, and developed an acquaintance with Menasseh ben Israel himself.[57] Through their apologetic efforts, the rabbi came to appreciate the effects of the Reformation on England. In this, "Their puritanical leanings, their hatred of images, their insistence upon the Old Testament, their attitude towards ancient Hebrew history as a prototype of their own, all tended to make them appear closer and more sympathetic to his own people."[58] The cumulative effect of his contact with English Christians in Amsterdam and abroad is seen in his letter to European Jews on the eve of his departure for England. There the rabbi wrote, "I have been informed by letters, and by faithful correspondents, that today the English nation is no longer our ancient enemy, but has changed the papistical religion and become excellently affected to our nation, as oppressed people whereof it has good hope."[59] However, Menasseh's interest in England had more to do with his acceptance of the lost tribes' existence in the Americas, and belief that England remained the one land in which Jews did not dwell. The idea that the Jewish people must be scattered into every country on earth was tied to prophesies concerning the appearance of the Messiah. For Menasseh ben Israel, this was tied to the dispersion of the holy people that Moses referred to in Deuteronomy 4:25-31, and 28:64-68.

The rabbi came to believe that this scattering of the Jews was necessary in order to usher in the arrival of the Messiah. England was the land that Jews must resettle in order that the promise of Daniel 12:7—"When they have made an end of breaking in pieces the power of the holy people, all these things shall be finished" (ASV)—would be fulfilled. Of this, Menasseh ben Israel wrote, "The opinion of many Christians and mine concurre herein; that we both believe that the restoring time of our Nation into their Native Country, is very near at hand . . . and therefore this remains only in my judgment before the Messiah come and restore our Nation, that first we must have our seat here [in England] likewise."[60] Unfortunately for the rabbi, the failure of the Whitehall Conference to decide in favor of Jewish immigration was not only the end of his messianic hopes, it also indirectly ended his life. Menasseh ben Israel had remained in London on his own meager funds after the conference in the hope that Cromwell would issue a positive answer on the question of Jewish readmission. The answer never came, and while he was waiting, his last surviving son Samuel (who had traveled with Menasseh to London) contracted a lingering illness. When Samuel died, the grieving rabbi was forced to borrow money and rely on charity in order to return home with his son's body. Menasseh ben Israel had barely landed in Holland when he himself became too weak to travel and in died in November 1657.

## Early Quakers and the Amsterdam Jews

Margaret Fell began her series of publications directed to the Jewish people in 1656, in the midst of the Cromwellian Interregnum. It was a time when Quaker missions had begun to carry their gospel of Christ's second coming as an inward, spiritual event to places such as the West Indies, North America, and Europe. One place of particular interest was Holland, which, because of its geographical location and its climate of prosperity and religious tolerance, had become home to a plurality of religious views. Quaker missions in Amsterdam were directed primarily toward the Jews, which places Friends evangelistic interests broadly in step with those of seventeenth-century England as a whole. In addition,

Amsterdam would have been of particular interest to Margaret Fell because it was the mission assignment of Quaker William Caton. Caton, who was taken into the home of Judge and Margaret Fell as a companion for their son George, converted to Friends' beliefs and remained faithful even after Margaret's son had rejected her teachings and quit the household for life in London.[61] Though appointed to work with Amsterdam Jews, William Caton knew no Hebrew. As we mention elsewhere, early Quakers were not scholars. They had a certain contempt for knowledge of Greek and Hebrew, or at least for the attitude which those possessing such knowledge had toward Scripture. The early Friends argued that the Spirit of God who revealed truth in Scripture is the same Spirit who teaches every person inwardly. Therefore, divine and eternal truth can be known experientially as well as it can through a reading of the Bible.

This said, Quakers did appreciate the rhetorical and persuasive power that studies in the original languages could lend in support of theological views. Also, they "believed in scripture authority, both as resident in the original in comparison with the English translation and as embodied in the signification of Hebrew words."[62] Thus, although biblical scholarship was not important for Quaker theology, they used it as an apologetic tool. This is especially true in the case of theologically trained scholars who converted to Quakerism. The best-known early Quaker scholar was Robert Barclay of Scotland, whose 1678 work *An Apology for the True Christian Divinity* remains a classic of Friends theology. Apart from Barclay, it seems the most proficient readers of ancient languages among early Quakers were continental converts. Among early Friends, the only known English university graduate was Samuel Fisher. Fisher read both Greek and Hebrew and, like William Caton, was active in the Amsterdam mission and in frequent contact with Margaret Fell.[63] Henry J. Cadbury presents strong evidence that George Fox had a proficiency in Hebrew, and owned a Hebrew Bible and Hebrew Lexicon.[64] Regarding the use of Hebrew by Friends he writes, "Of the occurrence of Hebrew words in Quaker writings, no complete list could be easily compiled. They are, however, used sparingly and often the same ones over and over again. The original language was quoted most often in areas of definite controversial subjects in which Friends wished to emphasize their own position."[65]

There is little evidence that Margaret Fell could read Hebrew. Although some records hold that Margaret's daughter Sarah Fell studied Hebrew, Quaker scholar Henry J. Cadbury does not think this likely.[66] This lack of familiarity with Hebrew made Fell dependent on the assistance of Friends such as Samuel Fisher in securing translation of her works into the language of the Jews. The lack of proficiency in language was only one of the difficulties encountered in the Quaker mission to Amsterdam Jews. One of the founding leaders of the Amsterdam mission was William Ames, a Quaker who spoke Dutch with fluency, but whose support for the heterodox James Nayler led him to be imprisoned and later exiled from Amsterdam.[67] Nayler, an early Quaker leader and friend to both Fell and Fox, had a falling out with many others in Friends leadership over his interpretation of Scripture. Though Nayler himself soon repented of his views, the affair had a significant impact on the work of the Quaker mission to the Amsterdam Jews for several reasons.

A number of pamphlets and tracts attacking the Quakers on the basis of Nayler's actions were also translated into Dutch and widely distributed in Holland soon after the affair.[68] This would have assuredly caught the attention of a people with strong interest in the Messiah, and who disagreed generally with Quaker eschatological positions. More importantly, the Nayler incident and the attendant damage it did to the Friends position would have been of particular interest to Menasseh ben Israel and his companions, who we know from earlier discussion was still in England hoping for a favorable intervention on their behalf from the Lord Protector. The fact that Cromwell declared Quakers to be an enemy of the state in response to the Nayler affair would have left quite an impression on the rabbi and his followers. We also know that some of Nayler's female followers appeared in Amsterdam soon after the Nayler trial and began disrupting Quaker meetings on a regular basis.[69]

### The Theology of Margaret Fell and the Conversion of the Jews

In the previous chapter, we looked closely at the religious work of Margaret Fell. There we saw that her theology is built around George Fox's eschatological concept of God the Light. In the Light, the promised second coming of Christ has arrived. This Light is present to some degree in the conscience of every person, and salvation is available to all who make themselves attentive and obedient to it. Participation in the kingdom of God begins when the Spirit of God takes up residence inwardly and establishes his presence there. Here the final, eternal covenant of God is established within us as his holy law is written upon our hearts. This new covenant does away with the need for outward rituals and rites, for the true temple of God is the human soul. Because this return of Christ is a universal "incarnation" of the Spirit within the soul or conscience of each person, it is the obligation of each person to remain low and humble before the Inward Light, where Christ teaches every person directly. It is this revelation that Quakers such as Margaret Fell sought to carry to the world, and they felt specially charged and commissioned to carry the good news of the Light to the whole of humanity. For early Quakers this was limited conceptually to Christians, Jews, and Muslims. For Fell, the offer of redemption in the Light was universally extended through the conscience of every individual.

It is this call that the Quaker missions sought to broadcast so that the prophecies concerning the coming of the Light might be fulfilled. At the same time, the close connection between the Jews and Christian prophecy remained within the early Quaker gospel, just as it was for English Christians generally. As Henry J. Cadbury has noted, "The first decade of Quakerism was a period of much English interest in Judaism."[70] Margaret Fell was in the full flower of her Quaker conversion during this time, which is reflected in the fact that she published four epistles specifically to the Jewish people, and two more that dealt with both Jews and Gentiles.[71] The first of these publications is the 1656 work *For Manasseth-ben-Israel: The Call of the Jews out of Babylon*.[72] This work was published shortly after the Whitehall Conference, and includes a reference to Menasseh ben Israel's presence in England. This was followed fairly quickly by *A Loving Salutation to the Seed of Abraham*, and the brief *Certain Queries to the Teachers and Rabbi's Among the Jews*, both of which were published later in 1656, or in 1657.[73] In this is a further articulation of the theological issues she addressed in her earlier 1656 letter, and all of these are included in her collected works. Her final epistle directed solely to the Jews is *A Call to the Seed of Israel*, published in 1668.

Margaret Fell's first publication directed to the Jews, her 1656 work *For Manasseth-ben-Israel: The Call of the Jews out of Babylon*, was published as millenarian speculation in England reached a fever pitch. One aspect of this was an intense interest in the question of Jewish readmission into England. Menasseh ben Israel, the rabbi for the Amsterdam Jewish community, had become the focal point for efforts in this direction. Numerous publications and volumes of correspondence were directed to his attention as he found himself identified as a spokesperson not just for the Amsterdam community but for all of Jewry. He was a visible representative of a very underrepresented population of European Jews, and as such was a regular addressee of open letters from anyone interested in Judaism generally. His position and his high-profile visit to London attracted the attention of religious thinkers including Margaret Fell, who sought to communicate the Quaker gospel to the Jews through him. Because of the significance that Margaret Fell would have attached to her first effort, it is a useful portal through which to explore her mind on what is surely one of the most interesting events in the seventeenth century.[74]

Looking at her first publication, it is helpful to consider the work in outline so that we can get a better sense of its structure. From there we will consider the theological ideas which Fell sought to communicate to the Jews. Our interest here is to discover how she viewed the Jews, and how she presented Quaker theological concepts in light of these perceptions. The goal is to draw on what we know of Margaret Fell's historical location in order to see what light that might shed on a reading of her work. In her 1656 letter *For Manasseth-ben-Israel: The Call of the Jews out of Babylon*, Fell addressed the presence of Menasseh ben Israel in England to attend the Whitehall Conference. Our encounter with the text actually begins with the title page, where we first encounter Margaret Fell's theological frame of reference for the work. As was the style of the time, the title page of a work such as this served as an announcement of content and a way of attracting the reader's attention. It also functioned as a précis for the work—a way of presenting an encapsulated message into the reader's mind, should the work be set aside without a full reading. For these reasons, title pages from this period are worth consideration as their own polyvalent cipher.

In the case of this publication, Fell's cover page begins "For Manasseth-Ben-Israel. The Call of the Jews out of Babylon, Which is Good Tidings to the Meek, Liberty to the Captives, and of opening of the Prison Doors."[75] The references to Isaiah are obviously eschatological, but does this tell us anything more, given what we have already discussed about Fell and her theology? In this case, we see that Margaret Fell squared up her audience before writing. Using only Old Testament references she invokes the messianic hopes conveyed there and introduces a phrase, the call of the Jews out of Babylon, as a point of connection between the two religious vocabularies. Babylon is the name given to Jewish captivity and scattering in Isaiah. For Fell this also identifies the realm of captivity as a spiritual one. From the outset, Margaret begins to shape the Old Testament Scriptures into a channel that empties at the feet of the Light. This calling together of the Jews is set within the biblical context of Isaiah 53:1, quoted by Fell as "who hath believed our Report, and to whom is the Arm of the Lord revealed."[76] Thus the calling of the Jewish people is good news, liberty, and freedom to those who accept her message. From there, she moves to Isaiah 65:1-2, a passage which, when placed in the context of Fell's title page, refers to God's calling of the Gentiles after the Jews have rejected him. Fell quotes it thus, "I am found of them that sought me, and I said behold me, behold me, unto a People that was not called by my

Name." The last of the three verses quoted on the opening page is Isaiah 53:3, which speaks of the Suffering Servant, "despised and rejected."

This periscope, and chapter 53 as a whole, have so often been read in Christian tradition as a description of Christ that the uninitiated could not be faulted for seeking these words in the New Testament rather than the Old. In the context of the opening page, the three verses let us know that the recalling of the Jews is of God, but is ultimately for the truly righteous, those Gentiles (Jews, Muslims, etc.) who believe in Messiah Jesus. This way of reading the front page as its own device should also take into account the experience we have as readers when we look to her Old Testament references to understand them in light of the chapter as a whole. First, Fell's connection between the gathering of the Jews out of exile as "good news to the oppressed . . ." leads us to consider Isaiah 61, the reference for that quotation, as a way of understanding her message. When we look to the passage itself, we find that Isaiah 61 is indeed about the good news of deliverance and the reestablishment of Israel. In a common application of Christian biblical texts, Fell follows this invocation of the messianic "promised land" imagery with a succession of Old Testament verses believed by Christians to refer to Messiah Jesus.

When we allow the second Scripture reference she uses to direct our participation in the argument, we open to Isaiah 53. Anyone familiar with the events of the Jesus narratives in the Gospels (which would have included Menasseh ben Israel, a Marrano Jew born in Portugal) would understand that Fell here means Jesus as God's chosen one. Next, Isaiah 65 opens to the story of a rebellious people who have reviled God and done evil. They must suffer the penalty, yet this chapter is also about the new heaven and new earth which will be remade. It seems fair to read this as Fell's attempt to connect the promise of Jewish restoration with this earlier image of the messianic figure who—despised and rejected—"bore the sin of many."[77] From there our attention is directed to Isaiah 65:1-2, "I am found of them that sought me not, and I said behold me, behold me, unto a people that was not called by my name."[78] Fell's intent here is to establish that God has now embraced a people not originally called his, which for her would be both Gentiles generally and Children of the Light specifically. At the end of her opening, Fell returns to Isaiah 53's Suffering Servant, the "Man of Sorrows." It may be that this also connected to her idea of George Fox as contemporary exemplar for Christ, but that is beyond the text.

From the discussion so far, we can see that Margaret Fell accepted the gathering of the Jews as an eschatological necessity, just as other Christians of her time did. She tried to draw their attention to the descriptions that point to a Messiah *already come* and *already rejected* and scorned. Her awareness that ben Israel was a Jew, and as such was seeking an unspecified messiah not yet arrived, made it necessary to include this in her interpretive argument. For the Jews to become a part of God's true kingdom, they must accept that Jesus is the Messiah. In this letter, Fell identifies the Jews as a people "who are scattered up and down the earth."[79] Her use of this image in a publication directed to the attention of Menasseh ben Israel suggests that she may have read his English publication *The Hope of Israel*. However, Fell is quick to point out that the plight of the Jews is due to their rebellion against God. They failed to follow the teaching that God sent them through Moses. As a result, God has fulfilled his warning that corruption will be followed by destruction. In support of this, Fell cites Deuteronomy 4:25-28, the passage also cited by ben Israel.[80] She bolsters this reading with supporting references and quotations from other Old Testament books.

Fell carries this into the present with the observation that the Jewish people were "Captive into Babylon where they carried, and cast out from the sight and presence of the Lord, and turned into Darkness, where you are."[81] Against this backdrop, Fell adopts an openly prophetic tone as she writes, "Therefore hear the word of the Lord, thou who art called Manasseth Ben Israel (who are come to this English Nation, with all the rest of thy brethren) which is a Land of gathering, where the Lord God is fulfilling his promise . . . this is fulfilling in our Day."[82] So Fell agreed with ben Israel that the scattering of the Jews was associated with the Messiah, and affirmed that she too saw eschatological significance to the readmission of the Jews to England. Of course, the esteemed rabbi viewed England as a prelude to the gathering of the Jews when they would be reestablished in Palestine by the (as yet unrevealed) Messiah. For Margaret Fell, England was the "land of gathering" itself.

In the event that Menasseh ben Israel should mistake her meaning in the above passage, she repeats it more plainly, writing, "And the Rod which Isaiah prophesied of, which should come forth out of the stem of Jesse (to wit the Messiah) . . . he assembles the outcastes of Israel, and gathers together the dispersed of Judah from the four corners of the Earth, and this is fulfilling in our day, in this Nation."[83] From here, Margaret Fell's theology becomes distinctly early Quaker. Once again using the book of Isaiah, she informs Menasseh ben Israel that the Jews must put aside their "vain oblations." Her position is that the outward observances of the law, which are religion in form only, have passed. True worship for Jews as for Gentiles takes place inwardly. Fell urges them to "hearken to the pure Law of God in your hearts," by which she intends the inward Light of Christ.[84] Quoting again from Isaiah, she explains, "The People that walked in darkness have seen a great light, they that dwell in the land of the shadow of death, upon them hath the Light shined."[85] This Light is the inward teacher of a new covenant, one in which God will write his word on the hearts of his people. According to Margaret Fell, the "new covenant is open to all, but for those who reject it, it brings the Day of Judgment" and she cautions them, "Therefore now, that ye may escape the overflowing Scourge, and be hid in the Day of the Lords' fierce Wrath; turn to the Lord God . . . For the tried Stone is risen, the sure Foundation, who lays Judgment to the Line."[86]

Confident of her reading, Margaret Fell urges them to examine the law and the testimony and test her claims. She assures them:

> Now if you will know the Way to Sion, turn your Faces thitherward, and turn your Mind to that of God . . . here you may see where the Lord will be worshipped, not in outward Temples, or outward Synagogues made with hands; But the time is come, that the Lord will be worshipped in Spirit, in the inward man. Therefore, cease from your outward Temples and Synagogues, for the day is come.[87]

The Jews were to turn to the truth that God has placed within them, and turn away from false security in their religious practices. She further urges, "Therefore Israel, arise and shine, for thy Light is come, and the Glory of the Lord is risen upon thee; . . . So this is the Day of Visitation: Awake, awake; stand up O Jerusalem."[88] From here, Fell sets out to reinterpret key Jewish observances by interpreting them as inward spiritual states. Circumcision is of the heart, as is the Sabbath rest.

To the degree that it is informative for early Quaker theological assumptions we note that although Margaret shared in many views common to her day, she did not single out Judaism or Jews for any unique human sins. Where terms of castigation are used, these come from the Jewish prophets themselves. Granted, this has been done in other Christian contexts against the Jews, and has brought them no end of undeserved suffering. But for Margaret Fell, this was employed as a persuasive element addressed to the Jewish people themselves. Her allegiance to the truth of biblical texts aligns with their position as the locus of authority for her conversation with the Jews. Again, Fell approached the Old Testament in a manner that demonstrated a great deal of reverence for the capacity of the Hebrew Bible to speak truth to its own people. She worked hard to exegete Old Testament passages in relation to Judaism's unique standing as God's chosen people, but this is done to point out two things of significance to her. First, within Judaism itself Jewish prophets have spoken to the rebellious history of their own people before

God. They have no special claim to righteousness or obedience to divine revelation. Second, they have been blind to the true revelation of the Messiah, and so look for him in the wrong places.

In this, Jews, Christians, or Muslims who do not seek out the Light are lost to religious truth. To see how straightforward this assertion is, a simple exercise is helpful. Simply substitute the term "Christ" for "Messiah" in reading her print offerings to the Jews. ("Christ" is of Greek derivation from *christos*, or anointed. This is an approximate translation of the Hebrew term *māshīaḥ*, or Messiah, for anointed.) Judaism—like all earlier and now "false" forms of religion—stands called to look inwardly for the Light of Messiah. This Light dwells within each human conscience, and as humans Jews partake fully in this opportunity. The failure of Judaism is the failure of all outward types of religion which have embraced dead forms and practices in place of the living God. Interpreting Hosea 2:11 in the contemporary context, she declares that the Lord has caused the celebrations of Feasts, New Moons, Sabbaths, and Solemn Feasts to end. He is weary of outward washings and observances, for, "The Sacrifices of God are a broken Spirit, a broken and a contrite heart, O God thou doest not despise" (Isa 51:17).[89]

The soteriological assurance of all people is found in the Inward Light which is Christ. He is the pure law. Drawing on Isaiah 56 she writes, "Therefore to this pure Law turn your minds, and wait, for this is he which brings salvation unto Jews and Gentiles: the Elect obtains deliverance. I will bring forth a seed out of Jacob, and out of Judah, an inheritor of my mountain. And mine Elect shall inherit it."[90] The essence of Fell's first address to the Jews can be summed up in this quotation:

> therefore to that Spirit of God, which calls your Minds within to turn, that so you may come to witness your Covenant new, which cannot be broken. And this is the Covenant which the Lord made with Abraham, and your Temple to be Spiritual, which is made of living Stones, Elect and Precious, and your Circumcision to be inward of the heart, in the spirit, and not in the Letter.[91]

From this first work directed at the Amsterdam Jews, we can see several things about Margaret Fell's approach. To begin, she addresses the Jewish community based on the authority of the Old Testament. In particular, Isaiah and Deuteronomy seem to have replaced the Quaker "mini-canon" of the Gospel of John, and First, Second, and Third John. Using Old Testament texts, she draws on Menasseh ben Israel's messianic reading of the Jewish scattering, but quickly proceeds to her own ends. Here, she explains the Quaker gospel to a community operating under the "old covenant."

She identifies the Jews as a scattered people. Although Margaret Fell's concern for the readmission of Jews to England reflected England's popular eschatological preoccupation, her published epistles distinguish themselves in their Quaker readings of the Old Testament that are largely the account of God's relationship with the Jews, his divinely chosen race.[92] Likewise, her use of the Old Testament in the epistles to the Jews displays a distinctive hermeneutic. Her reading of the text is dynamic and anchored solely in the prophetic present. She reads the ancient testament as a document without historic context, as if its meaning and prophesies were contemporary revelations written to address the seventeenth century alone. More importantly, Scripture is read through the lens of Quaker theology, with its particular Christology, eschatology, and hamartiology. One side note of interest here is that the publication is to the Amsterdam Jewish community, yet it is published in Hebrew. This hints at the growing literacy in the Hebrew language among the Amsterdam Jews, an effort to which Menasseh ben Israel had devoted himself. For earlier generations of Marrano Jews, the language of choice would have been Spanish or Portuguese.

As with any ancient didactic epistle, the letters of Margaret Fell to the Jews are best understood in their original cultural context. Knowledge of the cultural attitudes toward the Jews, the movements toward toleration, and the specific context of Menasseh ben Israel's visit to England all illuminate these specific theological texts from her pen. We discover that she was part of a general eschatological excitement concerning the restoration of Israel to England. Against the backdrop of European anti-Semitism, the openness to the Jews is striking.[93] Still, hers was not a lone philo-Semitic voice, but part of a minority of chiliastic enthusiasts who welcomed the return of the Jews to England for religious rather than merely commercial reasons. And yet, in a way typical of all her theological reflection, Fell takes the messianic expectations of ben Israel and others and turns them toward the Quaker way of the Inward Light. She sees England, not Palestine, as the place in which the Messiah will gather—and is gathering—his people. This gathering is spiritual and inward rather than external, legal, or institutional. For these reasons, Jews—as well as Protestants, Catholics, Muslims, Zoroastrians, and all others—are welcomed into the Light of the Messiah, when they turn from external religion to the inward truth.

# 5

## Living in the Last Days
*Women's Equality and Peace Testimony*

When asked to step forward and explain Friends practice or theology, Margaret Askew Fell Fox was always willing. Of all the areas where her religious writings have had an impact in her own time and ours, it is her contribution on women and pacifism that continues to generate the most widespread interest. Now it is time to extend an analysis of Fell's religious corpus to include her efforts toward establishing the spiritual equality of women and the Quaker peace testimony. As already presented, eschatology shaped Margaret Fell's theology more than any other area of doctrine. This chapter will expand an understanding of the influence her realized eschatology exerted on her theology by a closer consideration of Fell's positions on women's ministry and the peace testimony as they relate to her publications, *Women's Speaking Justified* and *A Declaration and an Information*. In these areas, Fell's realized eschatology was central to her views on the spiritual rights of women and on violence. Those views, which seemed so radical to others in her place and time, retain a similar effect on readers today.[1]

In the modern context there can be no doubt that Fell's most influential and well-known publication is her 1666 booklet *Women's Speaking Justified* (rev. 1667).[2] The modern movement for the equality of women and the development of feminist theory in general has sparked a renewed interest in the foremothers of feminist thought. Margaret Fell has been rediscovered, and her work reprinted and discussed, by scholars interested in the history of women in Christianity, of early modern England, or both.[3] These developments are surely welcome, and Fell's booklet on women and Scripture merits the attention it has received and more. She has a unique place among women of early Quakerism, as might be expected from a woman like Margaret Fell.

However, in most ways, Fell's ministry and approach were not unlike those of other women of religious significance in the sixteenth and seventeenth centuries in Europe. She was not alone, but stood in a tradition of women prophets and religious authors that began with the Renaissance.

The rebirth of classical learning and Christian humanism of the European Renaissance brought with it important opportunities for women in the West. The Christian humanism of the Renaissance was accompanied by a reevaluation of the status and potential of women by many religious scholars. The lay orientation and educational emphasis of this religious humanism also provided opportunities for women to learn, and to become artists, poets, classical scholars, and philosophers in their own right. The movement was, for the most part, limited to women of high social standing, and it took place in the larger context of a patriarchal culture which wanted women to be educated so that they might be better wives and mothers. Still, the Renaissance opened a door that many intelligent and learned women walked through. Their activities would lead society in ways that were quite new compared to the Middle Ages. Two well-known examples of sixteenth-century women who were scholars and important leaders of their people may be found in Elizabeth I of England and Marguerite, Queen of Navarre and sister to the king of France. These women were trained in the classics from a young age by their humanist parents, in keeping with the goals and aspirations of the Renaissance.

Some Renaissance scholars—both women and men—began to reexamine the status of women and to accept them as fully human individuals. This development took place against the backdrop of medieval theories in which women were deemed defective in a manner that rendered them less than fully human—that is, less than men. The tensions between the medieval and Renaissance social constructions of women sparked a literary debate throughout Europe, the so-called *querelle des femmes*. This debate (*querelle*) about the status of women took place in poetry, plays, and essays written by European humanists, often in Latin or French, during the late Medieval and Renaissance periods.[4] Both sides of the debate referred to biblical stories and texts, which is not surprising given that this was a Christian humanism in which the Bible was a normal and normative part of culture.[5]

Initially the humanist woman scholars of the sixteenth century came from the aristocracy, and were primarily the wives, daughters, and granddaughters of the privileged classes. One of the first publications in which a self-aware woman intentionally discussed the Scriptures from a female perspective and in defense of spiritual gender equality was that of Marie Dentière in 1539. Written from Geneva as an open letter to Queen Marguerite of Navarre from a classically trained humanist, preacher, and convert to Calvinism, the section entitled "Defense for Women" is a reflection on the teachings of Scripture. Here Dentière seeks to show women's equality in Christ and their fitness for the preaching ministry.[6] Women such as Marie Dentière were often tutored in the home, but gradually a few schools for ladies were founded in Europe. However, these schools educated only a very small percentage of girls, in part because the initial popularity of education for aristocratic girls in the sixteenth century did not last into the seventeenth. For example, a Catholic laywoman named Mary Ward (1585–1645) founded the Institute of the Blessed Virgin Mary (IBVM), thus realizing a lifelong dream. However, her efforts to educate girls in the classics were opposed by Catholics and Protestants alike.[7]

By the period of the Reformation in Europe, the spirit of the times had changed things for women in Europe for the better and the worse. The emphasis that many Protestants placed on the availability of Christian Scripture across a wider variety of social classes increased access to the Bible in vernacular translations, which made it more accessible to women as well as men. A woman did not have to be wellborn and educated in the classics to study Scripture productively. Likewise, the advent of the printing press in Europe made biblical text itself available to a degree inconceivable prior to Johann Gutenberg and his innovations in printing technique. At the same time, the elevation of Scripture as an authority for Christian teaching and practice—and the biblical primitivism it brought to Protestant exegesis—made the subordination of women more clear-cut with regard to the offices of the church. However, the literalistic manner in which unsophisticated readers tended to interpret the Bible was balanced to some degree by the Protestant belief that through the text each person had access to the final authority for Christian faith and practice: the word of God. One result of these dynamics was the possibility that the Bible could be read and fruitfully interpreted by any believer. This increasingly popular notion that the biblical text could and should be read by everyone also reflected the strong influence of Martin Luther's teaching on the role of individual believers in the ministry of the church. Radical Reformationists, with their prophetic message and sectarian views, embraced Luther's teaching on the priesthood of all believers, a key element of the Protestant Reformation, and in some cases even extended it to women.[8]

Looking back to earlier discussions in this volume, the years leading to the English Civil War were marked by a mood of apocalyptic expectation, and numerous eschatological sects and figures arose during the civil war and Interregnum. During this time, both women and men took up a public and symbolic prophetic office in England, acting out radical prophetic roles which often brought them persecution, imprisonment, torture, or even martyrdom.[9] Historian Phyllis Mack has identified approximately three hundred known women prophets and preachers who wrote during that particular period in England.[10] The most published Englishwoman of the seventeenth century was just such a radical apocalyptic prophet: Lady Eleanor Davies.[11] The wealthy daughter of an Earl, Davies heard the prophet Daniel speaking to her in 1625, and despite certain obstacles she became a well-known woman prophet. Author of some sixty tracts—including a commentary on Daniel in which she accurately predicted the death of Charles I—she was able to publish her works in London and Amsterdam, though usually at her own expense. These publications and her prophetic vocation brought her into social conflict with both church and Crown. She was eventually imprisoned. During one of her imprisonments, she spoke with an angel for an hour in her cell, and afterward she was condemned as a lunatic. Released two years later, she lived to see her prophecy fulfilled with the beheading of the king in 1649. She was buried with honor in the family chapel in 1652.

Most of the women prophets in English religion during this time were not related to the Crown, as Lady Eleanor was, but were of much more humble origins. The most successful group to accept women as preachers and prophets were the Friends, and here one finds the farmer's wife Elizabeth Hooton (1600–1672).[12] A wife and the mother of five children, as well as a missionary, preacher, and prophet, Hooton was the first person known to be convinced by George Fox. She devoted the rest of her life to the cause of the Light. As a result, she suffered imprisonment, hardship, and long periods away from her family. She died in the West Indies in 1672 while on a mission with Fox and ten other Quakers.[13]

Conversely, Margaret Fell is situated in the line of women such as Marie Dentière, and midway between the two social extremes represented by women in the radical prophetic movements of the seventeenth century. Like Dentière, she defended spiritual gender equality in publication, although Fell was certainly no flower of the Renaissance. She was not a humanist, but did apparently receive some private education while still in her father's home. Also, Fell did not know the classical languages, although she did know a smattering of words and phrases in Latin.[14]

Her path to leadership in religion was not by way of education, nor did she move forward under the influence of Renaissance ideals. Margaret

Fell was, like many others in her time and place, a woman prophet. This role of prophet was the primary path open to women leaders in religion during Fell's time. She shared this and other similarities with both Lady Eleanor Davies and Elizabeth Hooton. Like Davies, Fell was a member of the gentry who published her works in London and Amsterdam, sometimes at her own expense. These publications brought her problems with authorities of the Crown, which resulted in imprisonment. Thankfully, Fell was not committed to an asylum. At the same time she mirrors Hooton insomuch as she was a native of northern England who lived the life of a wife and the mother of five children in a rural household. Like Hooton, Fell was also an early convert of George Fox.

### Margaret Fell and the Justification of Women's Speaking

Of the various sects and religious groups that arose in England during this period, Quakers were not only the most successful and long-lived, they were also the most accepting of women in spiritual leadership.[15] Henry J. Cadbury has argued that Fox's theology made him receptive and sympathetic to the ministry of women, and this may well have been why so many joined the new movement of Friends.[16] In more recent scholarship, Christine Trevett and Cathleen Wilcox have demonstrated the importance of women to the theology, practice, and organization of early Friends.[17] Especially important was the fact that Fox not only allowed women to organize in their own meetings, but he defended this practice several times in published tracts and letters.[18] In this way, they were going beyond the profile of the isolated woman prophet who could be understood in eschatological terms to be simply a "mouthpiece of the Spirit." It is therefore particularly interesting that Bonnelyn Young Kunze has recently demonstrated the centrality of Fell and her daughters in establishing the separate Women's Meetings.

Though noteworthy Quaker women such as Margaret Fell and Elizabeth Hooton ministered in the public arena, the majority of early women Friends exercised their calling in the context of the "Women's Meetings."[19] These meetings, which were officially organized in the summer of 1671, were envisioned by both Fox and Fell as the women's institutional counterpart to the Monthly and Quarterly Men's Meetings already in existence.[20] Margaret Fell played a prominent role in the formation of the Women's Meetings, a fact noted by historian Bonnelyn Young Kunze who writes, "one of Margaret's greatest single accomplishments in her Quaker career was her pivotal work in establishment of separate women's meetings which she commenced shortly after she was released from Lancaster prison."[21] The primary business of these meetings was the visitation of the sick, the elderly, and the imprisoned Friends. Additionally, the meetings collected funds and organized assistance for the support of the poor, widows, and orphans.

Although the Women's Meetings did not extend throughout all of England, they did take place in several countries abroad. In London the Women's Meetings bore the broadest range of responsibilities from the outset, reflecting the pressing needs encountered in a complex urban area. These included "the education of children, the employment and apprenticeship of young women Friends, the proper care of marriages, and the consistent refusal to pay tithes."[22] This vast network of leadership and support, directed entirely by women, had a lasting effect on the rituals and practices of the Quakers. As Quaker historian Elisabeth Potts Brown has demonstrated, "Margaret Fell and early women supporters of the movement . . . settled questions of the religious life such as marriage practices, the care of the sick and poor, and community responsibilities . . . in terms favorable to women's participation and leadership."[23]

As noted earlier, Margaret Fell's Quaker pedigree as one who had endured imprisonment and praemunire for her religious beliefs was well established. By this point she was also the wife of George Fox and the visible representative of Quaker women and of Fox himself. In this role Mother Fell was often the target of those factions which opposed women in church leadership meetings. From the outset, the Women's Meetings met with resistance and criticism, proving almost as controversial as the activity of preaching by women. This criticism was strongest among Friends, for while it is true that the Quaker tradition has always placed an emphasis upon the spiritual equality of Friends, "there has not been quite the same serene development . . . where the work of organization and discipline has been concerned."[24] To be fair, there were several reasons for this resistance, including the presence of anti-organizational sentiments held by former "Ranters" who had become prominent among the Friends.[25] Additional resistance surfaced among Quaker men who objected to scrutiny by the Women's Meetings prior to marriage, as well as those who resented the pressure that the meetings exerted on those who paid the tithe in an attempt to avoid persecution.[26]

There was, however, a more significant factor in the opposition to Women's Meetings. An undercurrent of antipathy toward women's preaching followed the infamous Nayler affair, and the participation of women in James Nayler's unfortunate "triumphal entry" into Bristol fueled a distrust of women's leadership in general.[27] As Ruth A. Tucker and Walter Liefeld have noted, "despite the fact that these women were involved in the traditional female activities involving deeds of charity, the very fact that they were meeting without the supervision of a man drew heavy criticism."[28] This controversy, which centered around the Westmorland Friends leaders John Story and John Wilkenson, engendered a split in the fellowship and left Margaret Fell—now wife of George Fox—at the center of the northern tempest.[29] However, she was not targeted merely because she was the wife of Fox and was working to institute his reorganization of the Society of Friends.[30] She was the vocal woman leader who ten years earlier had written the historically significant *Women's Speaking Justified*.

## *Women's Speaking Justified*

Margaret Fell's *Women's Speaking Justified* was one of the publications written and circulated during Fell's first imprisonment in Lancaster Castle from 1664 to 1668. During this period—which was her most productive period of theological work generally—she wrote eleven of the selections reprinted after her death in her *Works* (*A Brief Collection*). During her long imprisonment in Lancaster Castle she engaged in theological debate with other nonconformists, held Friends Meetings in the jail, and had the time away from the duties of organizing the Friends movement at Swarthmoor Hall to devote to serious study of the whole of Scripture and to focus more directly upon her writing.[31] From here Mother Fell published her largest book, the 1667 *The Standard of the Lord Revealed*, to serve as a kind of summary of the Scriptures intended for the education of Friends.

Her time spent in discourse and debate with other imprisoned religious nonconformists helped further clarify her theological disagreements with Christian Protestants outside the Church of England, and the results of that exercise may be seen in her 1667 *A Touch-stone or a Tryal by Scripture*. There she expanded her condemnation of clergy practices to include those from religious groups outside of the Church of England. In this same year, her 1666 publication *Women's Speaking Justified* proved important enough to be reprinted again in an expanded form. Though this work has been referred to as "the Magna Carta for Quaker Women," it was not in fact written specifically for Friends.[32] This work is a survey of the scriptural teachings concerning women, with the purpose of defending on theological grounds the right of women to "speak," that is, to preach and prophesy. She writes that the purpose of the tract is to "lay down how God Himself manifested His will and mind concerning women and unto women."[33]

The arguments which Fell sets forth in *Women's Speaking Justified* represent the maturity of her theological reflection and exegetical skill brought to bear on ideas she held from early in her Quaker conversion. Her eschatological views were part and parcel of her convincement in the Light, and the coming of Jesus Christ the Light made manifest provided the revelatory lens through which Scripture was interpreted. This expressed itself in an early defense of women speaking in the church that appears in an unpublished letter written barely two years after her 1652 convincement. There she argues, "If thou will but seriously Consider thou wilt see thy blindness, & ignorance of God, & of his truth; for verily the living God thou art Ignorant of: and yet thou takes the Apostles words, and faith, that he forbids a woman to speak in the Church, but thou knows not the life and Substance which was in him: for he knew the woman Clothed with the son, & the woman that sits upon the many waters, which thou dost not, nor cannot put a difference betwixt the precious & and vile."[34] The women to whom Fell refers appear in the book of Revelation, and she would make reference to the same figures in *Women's Speaking Justified* twelve years later.

This early letter is evidence not only that Fell had long experience in the defense of women preaching, but also that end-times rhetoric is present in her arguments from the beginning. Thus the publication of *Women's Speaking Justified* represents the fruition of long reflection within the context of the larger Quaker movement and its eschatological fervor, prophetic ministry, and spiritual leadership by women among the Friends. Her work follows a line of reasoning seen in the ideas of Richard Farnsworth and affirmed by George Fox in his 1656 *The Woman Learning in Silence*.[35] At the same time, Fell's publication advanced George Fox's underdeveloped arguments in favor of women preaching, and influenced his later publication *This is an Encouragement to All Womens-Meetings*.[36] Her long experience with Friends theology concerning women's ministry, as well as her time spent in debate and study of Scripture during her imprisonment in Lancaster Castle, informed her strategy for the structure and presentation of her arguments in *Women's Speaking Justified*.

One significant decision along these lines is found in her handling of the Pauline corpus. While the main objections to women's ministry came from the epistles of Paul, Fell wisely refocuses the discussion early and so reduces the impact of the Pauline material. Rather than jump right into Paul, Fell writes that these texts will be treated "when we come to them in their course and order."[37] Approaching the biblical texts in order from Genesis to Revelation, she takes pains to see these texts in their larger canonical and salvation-historical context, as well as the larger literary context in which they occur. Another important choice is seen in the two-pronged challenge her work presents to those who would silence women in the assembly of believers. In Mother Fell's arguments for a woman's right to preach and teach in the church she makes effective use of Scripture and draws heavily upon her eschatology and the Quaker teachings on the Light. She first argues in favor of a woman's right to teach and preach from a biblical standpoint, beginning with Adam and Eve in perfection. From there she leans increasingly upon her eschatological perspective as the basis for a second line of argument.

The second line of Margaret Fell's defense in *Women's Speaking Justified* addresses the so-called "biblical prohibition" against women's public ministry. Here she proves herself an able exegete with a strong command of Quaker theology. In the opening discussion in *Women's Speaking Justified*, Fell acknowledges the objections raised against women speaking in the Church, based upon 1 Corinthians 14 and 1 Timothy 2. She sagely places these verses in the larger context of male and female as *imago Dei*; she presents a portrait of "pre-Fall" Adam and Eve, living together as equals before God as the appropriate biblical model for Christian practice. Using Genesis 1, she reestablishes the condition of humanity before the serpent's deceit and the introduction of sin. For Margaret Fell, the Genesis account is normative.

At this point the more eschatological aspects of Fell's arguments move forward in priority. In the last days, according to Scripture, God will pour out his spirit upon all flesh. Here, says the prophet Joel, "your sons and daughters shall prophesy" (Joel 2:28), and Isaiah prophesies, saying, "all your children shall be taught of the Lord, and great shall be the peace of thy children" (Isa 54:13 KJV). This eschatological slant, with women speaking the word of God in keeping with biblical prophecy, carried an urgency which Fell believed would be compelling to all Christians regardless of their predisposition to the issue of women's leadership. Within this context, George Fox's teaching on the Inward Light takes on even greater force, for the Light becomes not only an inward salvific presence, but an outward fulfillment of the "promise of the Father."[38]

In early Quaker theology, one of the effects of the return of Christ in the last days was to restore the full image in both the male and the female, who hearken to the "seed" of Christ within.[39] Of this Fell writes, "Here God joins them together in his own Image, and makes no such distinctions and differences as men do . . . And God hath put no such difference between the Male and Female as men would make."[40] Having set forth the appropriate model for man and woman in the divine image, Fell acknowledges that it is woman who gave man the fruit of the tree to eat. However, she does not relinquish the interpretive control of Scripture here, but points instead to Genesis 3:13 and the truthfulness of the woman's response to God. In this context Fell highlights Genesis 3:15. This is a key text for both Fox and Fell, which speaks of the seed (or children) of Eve being in conflict with the seed of the serpent. This is not read as a curse on women, but rather as a prophetic witness that woman is the agent of God in the serpent's defeat.

The seed of the serpent will bruise his heel, but the seed of Eve will crush the head of the seed of the serpent. Christians have long understood the seed of Eve here to refer to Christ, and the seed of the serpent to be the children of the devil (see Romas 16:20). This crushing of the serpent's head comes through woman in the birth of Christ. On this basis Fell argues,

> Let this word of the Lord, which was from the beginning, stop the mouths of all that oppose women's speaking in the power of the Lord, for He has put enmity between the woman and the serpent, and if the seed of the woman speak not, the seed of the serpent speaks. For God has put enmity between the two seed.[41]

Like many other apocalyptic authors before her—including Fox—Fell divides humanity and history into two camps: the children of Light and the children of darkness. Those who seek to stop the mouths of women who "speak in the power of the Lord" must therefore be working for Satan. This eschatological dualism continues in some measure throughout the rest of her tract.

Fell draws a connection between the seed and the church with Christ, and focuses attention to the various ways the church is portrayed in feminine imagery. Christ is husband to the church, his bride, which is also the heavenly woman of Revelation 12, and in this is the ultimate reflection of the spiritual value of women. Having set forth powerful images of the work of God through woman, Fell adopts a more polemical tone, writing:

> Thus may prove that the Church of Christ is a woman, and those that speak against the Womans speaking, and speak against the Church of Christ, and the Seed of woman, which seed is Christ; that is to say, Those that speak against the Power of the Lord, and the Spirit of the Lord Speaking in a woman, simply, by reason of her Sex, or because she is a Woman, not regarding the Seed, and Spirit, and Power that speaks in her, such speak against Christ, and his Church.[42]

She pays particular attention to the positive attitude that Jesus had toward women, and provides further examples.

After establishing the presence of the feminine nature in the imagery of the church, Margaret Fell cites examples of women entrusted with the gospel. She looks to the Samaritan woman at the well, Martha at the resurrection of Lazarus, the woman anointing the feet of Jesus, and others who are brought to the fore. Even more important in Fell's argument are the women who ministered to Jesus as he traveled to his death, where "we see that Jesus owned the Love and Grace that appeared in Women, and did not despise it."[43] Fell places an emphasis upon the fact that they (not the men) were witnesses of his crucifixion and the first to proclaim the good news of the risen Christ:

> Mark this, you that despise and oppose the message of the Lord God that He sends by women: what would have become of the redemption of the whole body of mankind, if it had not cause to believe the message that the Lord Jesus sent by these women, of and concerning His resurrection?[44]

It is once again the Lord Jesus who empowers the women to speak and to carry the message from him to the other believers.

With the positive role of women established in both the Old and New Testaments, Fell again turns to the 1 Corinthians and 1 Timothy texts. Her rebuttal is based upon an examination of Scripture and of church practices which directly contradict an anti-woman interpretation of these so-called "hard sayings" of Paul. In response to the demand to silence women in church, Fell notes instances where such interpretation leaves Paul blatantly contradicting his own writings in other passages. This is problematic because "God is not the Author of Confusion, but of Peace."[45] She assumes that to accept contradiction without any attempt to establish some harmony of Pauline purpose is indicative of some more sinister force at work.[46] It is obvious that Fell finds this a powerful argument in favor of her position. In further support of her contention that the command to silence targets a special audience, Fell identifies several groups of women for whom the Pauline injunction to women would not apply. Widows and unmarried women, for instance, would have a difficult time learning from their husbands at home.

This given, Fell argues that 1 Corinthians and 1 Timothy do not reflect Paul's attempt to silence all women, but rather address only a particular group of women in particular categories. Thus with respect to the letters of Paul, in those places where he calls for women to be silent in church, Fell interprets these as women who have listened to the snake (devil), who are worldly and sinful. She argues that Paul "speaks of women that were under the law and in that transgression as Eve was."[47] These women, indeed, must be quiet. But the women who are filled with the Spirit—and are thus one with Christ their spiritual head—must speak, for the head speaks through them. Fell chides, "What is all this to women speaking who have the everlasting gospel to preach, upon whom the promise of the Lord is fulfilled and His Spirit poured upon them according to His Word."[48] Here she is making reference to Acts 2:16-21, where Peter refers to the prophecy of Joel 2:28-32 where, as noted above, in the last days God will pour out his Spirit upon women and men, young and old.

Mother Fell believed, as did all early Quakers, that they were living in the last days, and therefore the Spirit had fully come upon both women and men. The old things had passed away and therefore—as she explains in reference to I Timothy 2:8-15—what is all this "to such as have the power and Spirit of the Lord Jesus poured upon them, and have the message of the Lord Jesus given unto them?"[49] She argues instead that—taken in its larger context—Paul was writing about "undecent and unreverent women," that is, women who have followed the devil rather than Christ.[50] She explicitly identifies these women with the "undecent" women of 1 Timothy 2, who were likewise arrayed in rich finery. Fell holds that "this is the woman that has been speaking and usurping authority for many hundred years together."[51]

Fell contrasts this with the heavenly woman of Revelation 12, who is the church and the bride of Christ. This eschatological dualism lies behind her central argument: that the women who must be silent in church are the followers of Satan, while the women who must preach and prophesy are in Christ, and full of his Spirit. As she puts things in her concluding paragraph, "Christ is the head of the church, the true woman, which is His wife. In it do daughters prophesy, who are above the Pope and his wife, and atop of them." This becomes more explicit when Fell discusses the "great whore, Babylon" from the book of Revelation. As noted in chapter 3, Margaret Fell generally uses the name Babylon in an eschatologically symbolic manner to refer to the kingdom of darkness. This includes the papacy, rather than being the wife of the pope. However, in this context she obviously associates the pope with the antichrist of Revelation, and his wife is Babylon, the false church that follows after the beast in the last days.

Fell's realized eschatology is key to her argument in two ways. First, because Christ has now come in these last days, the Spirit is poured out on men and women. Thus, men and women can and should prophesy in his name. Second, there is a strong eschatological dualism that runs through her argument. The time has now come for the ultimate conflict between good and evil, Babylon and Jerusalem, the church and the antichrist, the ministers of darkness and the Children of the Light. The woman that must be silent in the true church is the great whore, Babylon, the bride of the pope (antichrist). But the bride of Christ, whose head and bridegroom is the Lord Jesus, can and will speak in his name. What is missing is any reference, in name at least, to the Light.

In her excellent study *Theology and Women's Ministry in Seventeenth-Century English Quakerism*, Catherine Wilcox has called attention to this relative absence of language about the Light, not only in Fell's work, but in Quaker tracts generally.[52] She argues that it is not because of the universal, Inward Light that the early Quakers promoted women in ministry, but rather because Christ has come to restore the original image of God and the unity between man and woman before the fall. Wilcox is right to call attention to this interesting aspect of early Quaker theology. Against the easy assumption that the universal Light was the basis for women's right to speak, she demonstrates that it is rather Christ and the Spirit who provide the theological rationale in early Quaker writings. She certainly demonstrates the main thesis of her work, that it is in "the eschatological beliefs of the early Friends that the explanation of their radical attitude towards the ministry of women is to be sought."[53]

But is there another possible explanation for the relative absence of Light terminology in *Women's Speaking Justified* when compared to Fell's other work? As already noted, Margaret Fell's application and presentation of biblical texts changes to reflect her purpose and target audience. As these change, so does her approach to biblical citations. That may provide an alternative to Wilcox's position, for in the case of *Women's Speaking Justified* this is likely a matter of good rhetorical positioning and the underlying polemical context. Why does Fell not speak more of the Light in this text? It is entirely plausible to assume that she does so intentionally out of an awareness of her conversation partners and her desire to be persuasive.

Added support for this interpretation comes from the time of the work's publication. As mentioned previously, Fell's long imprisonment in Lancaster Castle brought her into contact with other incarcerated nonconformists. She became more conversant with the wider views of English Protestants, and her sensitivity to the significance of Scripture for most Protestants made her an even more able apologist. In giving a detailed defense based upon the biblical texts she was also constrained by her rhetorical need to use traditional language and her exegetical efforts reflect this, as do the actual content of the passages she used. The biblical texts she works with almost always speak either of God (as in the image of God), the Spirit (as in Joel 2 and Acts 2), or Christ (as in Ephesians 5), as opposed to the Light. But if this is the case, why did Fell choose here to exclude the passage concerning the universal Light in John 1:9, which she elsewhere takes to refer to all people, women and men?

An explanation for the absence of this passage in *Women's Speaking Justified* has to do with a problem Fell would have encountered in the common English translation. In the King James (or Authorized) Version, this verse reads, "That was the true Light, which lighteth every man that cometh into the world." Without the background of a humanist or the training to read the text in Greek, Fell could not know that the word "man" or "person" in the original Greek text is inclusive, not gender-specific. Only modern gender-accurate English Bibles make this plain in translation (in the New Revised Standard Version, it reads, "The true light, which enlightens everyone, was coming into the world."). So the only verse where Light might have been used to support the ministry of women was blocked for Fell in her time by Bible translations done by and for men.

While it is true that Christ, the Spirit, and eschatology are key to Fell's argument for women's preaching and prophesying, this does not mean that the Light is unimportant. As already shown in considering her doctrine of the Trinity, for Fell the Light is equivalent to the present work of Christ and to the Holy Spirit.[54] In emphasizing the lack of language about the Light in their defense of women in ministry, Wilcox may be making a distinction in the study of early Quakerism that is in the end of little theological importance. The Light simply *is* the present work of Christ and of the Spirit, and vice versa. Wilcox is certainly correct that the Light in early Quaker theology was not "a philosophical concept or mystical experience," but rather the work of Christ.[55] No doubt some part of the development of the Light as a philosophical concept that expresses a truth about the divine nature is attributable to its complex yet casual usage in the work of early Friends. However the later preference for a generic "religious" or "spiritual" reading of Quaker theology concerning the Light also reflects developments and attitudes within the broader Society of Friends itself.[56]

Perhaps a final historical caution is appropriate when considering the arguments of Fell and the early Quakers in support of the spiritual equality of women. While the need to recover something of women's contributions to history has placed us face to face with these early Quaker women, it is easy to overestimate the degree of freedom they benefited from and defended in print. In particular, Fell was not a feminist. More to the point, her eschatological preoccupation along with her low opinion of university education would have made it hard for her to grasp the many strengths and merits of feminist theory. The liberty in the Spirit she defended was limited both temporally and socially.[57] As historians like Phyllis Mack have observed, there were strict social limits on women even among the Quakers, who "anchored themselves to the specific social position into which they were born and raised while allowing themselves to be possessed by forces that rendered that position temporarily null and void."[58]

As public prophets and handmaidens of the Lord, these women did break social stereotypes for their sex. In other ways, however, they were much more typical seventeenth-century Englishwomen. Phyllis Mack concludes that "the proposed arena of Quaker women's authority was completely hedged in, not only by moral injunctions that stressed service rather than self-expression but by outward social barriers."[59] What is more, over time the eschatological fervor of the exciting days of civil war and Interregnum waned, and women Friends did not act out their prophetic calling in the streets of English cities. The Women's Meetings, too, were slowly subordinated to the Men's Meetings, and absorbed into a more androcentric national organization.[60] As Christian Trevett observes at the end of her study of Quaker women in the seventeenth century, the "the tenet about the spiritual equality of the sexes, which had been held among Quakers from the outset, retained enough of its vigor to ensure that the worst excesses of other churches were avoided" among the Friends.[61]

### The Early Friends and the Public Peace Testimony

Having considered the eschatological underpinnings for Fell's understanding of the spiritual equality of women, we turn to the centrality of her realized eschatology for the Quaker peace testimony in her theology. A central text for consideration is Fell's important 1660 work *A Declaration and an Information from Us, the People Called Quakers, to the Present Governors, The King and Both Houses of Parliament, and All Whom It May Concern*. As with previous discussions, no claim is made here that Fell was the sole instigator of this peace testimony, or that her position here was original within the Quaker context. Instead, we want to look at the document and its context to understand what it says about Mother Fell and her own theology. This begins with a brief consideration of the articulation of the Friends' peace testimony as it emerged among early Quakers.

Christians have long had a conflicted attitude toward violence and war.[62] Despite the fact that some early Christian writers were against believers joining the army, a consistent pacifism is not to be found in any group or church until the fifteenth century and the Radical Reformation. The Anabaptist movement, particularly as it took shape under Mennonite founder Menno Simons (1496–1561), embraced pacifism as a biblical mandate given by Jesus Christ and therefore one intended to be observed by all believers. Although Anabaptist ideas were present in England from the first days of Quakerism, it seems unlikely that the early Quakers developed their theology with an eye toward Anabaptist teaching. The earliest attitudes of the Quakers toward war were not uniform. As Quaker historian Marilyn Baldwin Weddle has written, "Not only did many early Quakers continue to serve in the military, but others encouraged Cromwell in foreign military adventures and later enlisted in militias and cooperated with the restored Rump Parliament in military activity at home."[63]

With regard to George Fox, he refused an appointment to serve in Cromwell's army in 1651, even though it would have provided him freedom from the Derby jail.[64] However, while this reflected his own theological and moral stance in the situation, we know that Fox did not make nonviolence a bedrock teaching on par with something like the proscription against oaths of any kind.[65] No universal prohibition of war or Quakers joining the army is found during the earliest period of Quaker writings. Likewise, we do know that Fox was himself aware of convinced Quakers in military service, and did not seem to doubt the legitimacy of their convincement based on their occupation.[66] Hugh Barbour has identified the first consistently pacifist theological tract published by a Quaker as James Nayler's 1657 *The Lamb's War* (rev. 1658).[67] Nayler, who was the central figure in the infamous "triumphal entry" into Bristol in a consciously eschatological imitation of the entry of Christ into Jerusalem, wrote it from prison.

Nayler was arrested, imprisoned, and brutally punished for this extreme act of identification with Christ, and he was repudiated by the main leaders of the Friends, including Fox and Fell.[68] Yet prior to his ill-fated actions in Bristol—which certainly brought problems for all Friends—Nayler was among the best-known and most influential Quaker leaders.[69] Rosemary Moore states that the earliest Quaker leadership "consisted in the first place of Fox as general organizer, then Fell as administrator in charge of finance, and thirdly of Nayler as the chief publicist."[70] It was in prison, therefore, after a long time of successful ministry among Friends, that Nayler wrote *The Lamb's War*. It was printed anonymously, and an expanded version appeared the next year. The text is highly apocalyptic, with phrases drawn from Daniel and Revelation.

The thesis is clearly laid out: followers of Christ must do no violence to the bodies of others. Nayler holds, "What Their Weapons Are: as they war not against men's persons, so their weapons are not carnal nor hurtful to any of the creation."[71]

The main point of the work is to make clear the fixed chasm between the workings of the dark and the Light, between Satan, the god of this world, and the Son of God, who is the Lamb. Nayler writes, "Now against this evil seed, and its whole work brought forth in that nature [i.e., evil], does the Lamb make war to take vengeance of his enemies."[72] With words like this, he echoes the strong millenarian and apocalyptic language of the early Quakers. The powerful eschatological dualism of this apocalyptic viewpoint divides everything and everyone into two camps. In one camp are those who follow Satan and war against the Lamb. In the other camp are those who follow Christ in the Lamb's War. But what kind of war is this? Quakers had long insisted that this war was "spiritual," but the militant imagery of the Lamb's War vocabulary was problematic in defending such a position. Nayler made it clear that the Lamb's War was not a physical battle with carnal weapons and ultimately God's peace would spread over all the earth.

Reading accounts of James Nayler's harsh treatment as punishment for blasphemy leaves no doubt that his experience of physical defeat, punishment, and imprisonment must have exerted a strong influence on his theological reflection in prison. However, it is an exaggeration to claim, as W. Alan Cole did in an oft-quoted phrase, that "pacifism was not a characteristic of the early Quakers: it was forced upon them by the hostility of the outside world."[73] This opinion needs some qualification. Pacifism is implicit in the realized eschatology of early Friends, and some hints in this direction already existed in the teachings of Fox. Their strong eschatological dualism gave them a basis for rejecting the worldly manner of warfare in the Lamb's War. It may well be that only after their experience of persecution and violence, and the general disappointment of the Protectorate, they came to a consistent rejection of "carnal" weapons of violence for all those on the side of the Light of Christ. The weapons of carnality, they therefore leave to the followers of Satan.

## Margaret Fell and the 1660 Peace Testimony

The next topic for analysis is the peace testimony of Margaret Fell, and the 1660 *A Declaration and an Information from Us, the People Called Quakers*. Neither Fell nor Fox made any consistent and public statement of pacifism until *A Declaration and an Information*. This tract, published some six months before the more famous one written by George Fox and others, sets forth the basic principles of Quakerism for the newly crowned King Charles II. It is in fact the first published statement of the Quaker peace testimony, but was eclipsed by the later statement among Quakers and Quaker historians until recent times.[74] Still, there is no doubt that Fell worked closely with Fox and that she was devoted to him and trusted by him. Whatever theological views Fell held concerning nonviolence, it is likely they were shaped by the teachings of Fox. This said, Margaret Fell had her own history with the question, thus warranting an approach to the text as a trustworthy expression of her theological views.

For her part, Margaret Fell refers to the Quakers as a nonviolent people as early as 1653 when she writes to Justice John Archer, "know that though thou hast exercised thy cruelty upon a harmless people, that will offer violence to no man, nor wrong any man."[75] This is the first time one finds her defense in extant material, but it comes shortly after her convincement by Fox, and seven years before the publication of *A Declaration*. At that time Fell was confident enough in the connection between Quakers and nonviolence that she would attest to it in a letter written to one of her husband's peers. This is helpful when considered in view of how soon after her convincement George Fox entrusted Fell with the power to speak for the Children of the Light. In an unpublished letter written in 1679 she recalled the early days of her convincement, when the clergy in the north of England became alarmed at the growth of the movement and wrote members of Parliament.

George Fox was an itinerant preacher who carried his message throughout England and abroad. In those early days especially, Fox was often on the move as he followed the leading of the Light. Of this time Mother Fell later wrote:

> the preists, & professors in our parts began to write against us: and G:F: [George Fox] being gon out of the Countrey, Frst [first] brought things to mee, & I answered them. And I was but Young in the truth yet I had a perfect & a pure Testimony of god in my heart, for god & his Truth. And I believe I Could that day have Layd down my Life for it. And I was very zeallous in itt.[76]

Against this backdrop arises the possibility that Fell's letter to Justice Archer reflected her recent deputation by Fox, who himself delivered the letter to Archer. Her reference to her early perfect and pure testimony of God is at least some evidence that Fox and Fell were in agreement on the issue of nonviolence. Thus, in a manner similar to the example given in the proceeding section on Fell's *Women's Speaking Justified*, early evidence of her theological perspectives from unpublished letters is later borne out in her publication.

Fell published *A Declaration* in 1660. As discussed in chapter 1, this year was the end of a watershed period for her personal and religious life. Her husband had died nearly two years before, and his death in many ways represents a transition between her first and second lives. She was at the apex of her personal freedom and power early in her widowhood while she was still protected by the status of her late husband, yet free of the constraints that his interests and career obligations exercised on her. At home at Swarthmoor Hall, Margaret Fell was at the center of the comings and goings of her daughters, servants, and other members of the Friends community. However, her activities as a Quaker were now much more troubling to her well-heeled neighbors, who found them inappropriate for a widow of her high station. Thus, when George Fox came for an extended visit in May 1660, he was arrested on a pretext and jailed at Lancaster Castle, where he would remain until September. A month after his imprisonment, Margaret Fell traveled to London with her daughter, and there delivered her peace testimony to King Charles II.[77]

The importance of this document should not be underestimated. Coming just a month after Charles II returned to England, it was the first published articulation of the Quaker peace testimony. This work, which precedes George Fox's *Declaration from the Harmless and Innocent People of God called Quakers, Against All Plotters and Fighters in the World* by a period of six months, is a careful attempt to explain those Friends beliefs and practices which were the grounds for much of their religious persecution. As already noted earlier in this work, it was important for Quakers to explain themselves to their new ruler in London, with the hope that he might bring religious toleration to England and freedom to imprisoned Friends. The document was published with names of thirteen other weighty Friends, including George Fox and William Caton, and a postscript by Fell.

The circumstances surrounding the writing and publication reveal something of Mother Fell, affirming previous arguments offered in support of her standing, her abilities, and her importance to the early Quaker movement. For our purposes here, briefly note two points of interest. First, the 1660 peace testimony was delivered to the newly crowned King Charles II by Margaret Fell in person. She was one of the few Friends who possessed the necessary social connections in conjunction with the requisite skills to articulate the Quaker position. As T. H. S. Wallace rightly observes, "Margaret's *Declaration and Information from the People Called Quakers* . . . reflects her key position among early Friends and her stature as one of the individuals best suited to represent them before, and negotiate with, the government."[78] Second, Fell continues to be invested with the right to speak on behalf of the people called Quakers. Her authority is witnessed by the thirteen Quaker leaders who "in the unity of the Spirit and members of Christ, do subscribe and witness the truth of this and in behalf of those in the same unity."[79]

The names of the thirteen witnesses are followed with an addendum in which Margaret herself forcefully declares, "And now I am here to answer what can be objected against us on behalf of many thousands . . . and to give an account of the hope that is in me to everyone who asks according to scripture; [I] who was moved of the Lord . . . to come two hundred miles to lay these things before you, who to the will of the Lord am committed."[80] Fell was in London to gain audience with the king, and she stood alone ready to defend the cause of Quakers on the basis of Scripture. The force of her postscript bears witness that she was no passive courier or mouthpiece for someone else's message. Fell delivered this publication directly into the hands of the king, and it begins immediately with a sober account of the suffering of Quakers. Fell writes, we "are the people of God called Quakers, who are hated and despised and everywhere spoken against as people not fit to live."[81]

She explains Friends' religious beliefs and practices, noting those that had been used as cause to fine and imprison Quakers under cover of law. She describes the illegal search, seizure, and arrest without just cause, and appeals to the legal rights that should be theirs as freeborn citizens of England. In the text she informs them,

> We do not desire any Liberty that may justly offend any one's conscience, but the liberty we do desire is that we may keep our consciences clear and void of offense towards God and towards men, and that we may enjoy our civil rights and liberties of subjects, as freeborn Englishmen.[82]

Her argument against paying tithes also appears to reflect a "quid pro quo" contractual analogy when she writes, "we look upon it to be unjust to maintain them. We receive nothing from nor trust our souls under their teaching."[83] From this it appears that Fell had gained some insight into English law in her twenty-six years of marriage to a barrister who often defended Quakers from abuse under that law. However, legal issues were not Fell's concern, so much as they were offered in evidence of the unjust persecution the Friends had long endured.

Concerning this persecution, Margaret Fell obviously understood their suffering to be the work of Satan, for she writes, "he that is born of the flesh persecutes him that is born of the Spirit," and again, "the Old

Enemy what has continually appeared against us."[84] Her interpretive framework of eschatological dualism is employed from the outset. From her perspective, those the Quakers have preached against have been followers of Satan: priests, preachers, and other religious leaders, though she does not indict the government itself. She identifies Friends as peaceful and law-abiding citizens. Then Fell turns to her realized eschatology: "Now if [all] would turn to this witness in their own consciences, this would keep from oppressing and persecuting of others without cause, for God is coming to teach His people Himself, by His own Light and Spirit."[85] Therefore, "No people can retain God in their knowledge, and worship Him as God, but first they must come to that of God in them."[86]

Near the end of this establishment of Quaker principles, Fell and the other weighty Friends (including Fox) make a clear statement of pacifist principles:

> We are a people that follow after those things that make for peace, love and unity. It is our desire that others' feet may walk in the same. [We] do deny and bear our testimony against all strife, wars, and contentions that come from the lusts that war in their members, that war against the soul, which we wait for, and watch for in all people. [We] love and desire the good of all.[87]

Notice that this is a statement of principle against all strife and war made on behalf of those who are followers of the Light. The Quaker message was a spiritual one, addressed to the soul, and they "wait for, and watch for in all people" a positive response to the Light. Violence and war make this impossible.

Margaret Fell's 1660 *A Declaration and Information* is a clear statement of the Quaker peace testimony, and the first one published by the early Friends leadership.[88] While the text is not as clearly eschatological as is the disgraced Nayler's essay *The Lamb's War*, there are strong hints of the eschatological in it. We see the familiar standards of her theology raised: God has now come in these last days to teach his people himself. This end-times return of Christ as the Light shining in the conscience of all people is a key part of Fell's eschatological theology. Here too is the sharply defined apocalyptic dualism of good and evil, light and darkness, woven into her text. Mother Fell makes it clear that the spiritual nature of the Lamb's War prohibits the Quakers from employing the same instruments and weapons as the children of darkness. Although something along these lines was long in the mind of Fox with respect to his own practice, it had not yet been publicly articulated as a pacifist principle for all the Friends of truth.

However, with these earlier points made clear to all, Fell makes it clear that the Friends' desire to exercise liberty of conscience to publish the truth abroad freely and without hindrance from religious or political powers. Now that the Spirit and Light of Christ have come in these last days, what is important is the spiritual battle for the soul of every woman and man, not carnal and worldly strife, war, and lust. Fell's presentation is formed within a theological frame of reference, though something like the argument she makes to the king could have been done on the basis of reason and philosophy, rather than spirituality, eschatology, and Christology. As a matter of historical fact, however, Fell's reasons were not based in Enlightenment rationality, but in the fervor of Quaker eschatology. This notion of the return of Christ in the Light is the concept within which the early Quakers worked out their peace testimony. As Ben Pink Dandelion remarks in the introduction to a recent volume *Heaven on Earth: Quakers and the Second Coming*:

> Central to early Friends' belief that they were working within God time was the present sense of the Second Coming of Christ, as outlined in Scripture, and the bringing of heaven on earth. God's time, the realm of the mythic and the eternal was coming to replace historical time to bring about the end of history and the beginning of a transformed humanity.[89]

# Concluding Remarks

Having traced the life of Margaret Fell within the broader portrait of the early Society of Friends and drawing her contributions more carefully out of the shadow of neglect and obscurity, it becomes clear just why her enigmatic historical persona is both intriguing and worthy of close study. Early on this particular exercise looked to the life of Margaret Askew Fell Fox (1614–1702) as a way of creating context for interpreting her contributions to the Quaker movement. Evidence of her significance and the worthiness of scholarly efforts directed toward her was apparent from the start. The attempt to grasp something of Margaret Fell has taken place on two levels. Placing her more carefully in her own social, political, and religious contexts led to a close look at her own writings to fully underscore the fact that she did, in truth, have an articulated theology that she owned and taught. The purpose of this first tack was to allow the subtle shifts in her writings to move us closer to her own charted course. Given her belief that religious truth flows from the experience of the divine life in human life, it is only right to consider the ways in which her human situation may have shaped her presentation of divine revelation.

Fell was not simply an author of texts, but wrote her works in the ebb and flow of exciting times in English history and religion. This makes it worthwhile to see her theological work in the larger context of her life. Toward this end a portion of this study is an overview of her life and ministry. We discovered that Margaret was central to the organizational, social, and financial structure of the early Quaker movement. She was rightly understood to be the "nursing mother" of Friends, and her home at Swarthmoor Hall was an important base of operations. These conclusions are not based on affection for Mother Fell per se, but by a desire to use all the tools available to understand her as an author and religious thinker. Another portion of this investigation focused upon her published writings, especially her main tracts and pamphlets. These writings are in many ways as removed from our time as we are from the author herself.

The time in which she wrote, and the urgency she felt for proclamation, show that she would have identified more with the Apostle Paul or St. Francis than with contemporary authors. Margaret Fell's commitment to the message of Christ's return was steadfast and energetic. It even can be argued that when using the word "convincement" to refer to Margaret's own experience, one is tempted to write it in capital letters. Another key point is the centrality of eschatology and millennialism for English religion in general during Fell's lifetime, and chapter 2 explored briefly the development of these ideas from the time of Henry VIII to the period of the civil war. Sampling a number of sects and movements displayed the effect this had on political and theological thought in the aftermath of the war and the establishment of Cromwell's Protectorate. This places the Society of Friends in the context of a larger number of religious movements that drew powerful religious inspiration from their apocalyptic expectations. Fox and the early Quakers were distinguished by the spiritual and realized nature of their eschatological faith. In keeping with the basic principles of Fox, it was in this theological context that Fell's own theology developed.

The scholarly significance of this piece is such that an exposition of Margaret Fell's theology is possible when an emphasis is made upon her social context. The idea was to keep the chapter structure as unadorned as feasible and to articulate her theology in her own words where possible. Approaching Mother Fell as a theologian in her own right is the heart of this study. Underlying this is the reality that while others may disagree with a particular reading of Fell's religious works, there is little argument that she herself authored them and stood ready to defend them. Therefore, in summary form we set forth the basic shape of her theology, with special attention to her eschatology. Her theology is broadly Christian and held many of the same key terms and themes one would find in Puritan or Independent authors of her time. Yet there were distinctive elements. Like the other Quakers of her day, she held that Christ had come fully in the Light, shining in the conscience of all people.

Although her views on the character of the second coming changed somewhat after the return of the king in 1660, they retained an obvious and consistent realized eschatology. More controversial perhaps is the assertion that Margaret conceived of the Light as the Triune Godhead expressed as Father, Son, and Spirit. We saw that she viewed the Light as the source for all divine revelation to the world across time. The second coming of Christ has begun and he is come again in the flesh, as his truth rises in the hearts and minds of those who dwell in the Light. He is now revealed in the eternal spirit of Christ who is come among us as a teacher and guide, ending all outward laws and covenants and replacing them with a new law, written inwardly on the heart. It is here, in the inwardly cleansed self that Christ makes his habitation, and our bodies become the temple and dwelling place of God. Those who still look for the coming of Christ in clouds of glory are looking in the wrong direction, toward outward things. Margaret Fell insisted that these outward things include the sacraments, the paying of tithes, the swearing of oaths of any kind, rank showing deference, or other honor from the hand of man. Old forms no longer play any salvific role.

The witness to the coming of Jesus Christ in the flesh has been missed because it is revealed inwardly by turning toward the Light and that made manifest of God within. The day of his coming has arrived and continues to arrive, and now we have come to the time of prophetic fulfillment where we are taught directly by Jesus Christ himself and judged by the Light. Having seen the nature of her realized eschatology, we then have a purchase from which to understand the whole of her ministry, especially her mission to the Jews, her justification of the spiritual equality of women, and her defense of the Quaker peace testimony. For this reason, our attention focused on her attempts to evangelize to the Jews, an enterprise in which many other Friends led the way. This again brought forward a focus on the place of the Light in her eschatology and in her soteriology. Considered in that context was the tragedy of Rabbi Menasseh ben Israel and the Whitehall Conference, leading to a better sense of the role that the return of the Jews to England played in Margaret's conception of the last days.

Looking back at her work on behalf of the ministry of women in the church, the centrality of eschatology for her most famous theological work *Women's Speaking Justified* was made more apparent. By consulting material from her early, unpublished writings we saw that germinal ideas found there appear in a more considered and mature form in her publications. This was true in her 1666 work on women speaking and also in her neglected 1660 publication *A Declaration and an Information*, the first published statement of the Quaker principle of nonviolence. Like Fox and other Friends, Fell's understanding of war and peace was based upon a fundamental, apocalyptic dualism between spiritual forces: Light and darkness, Christ and Satan. Even in this area, then, eschatology played an essential role in the gradual development of the peace testimony about early Quaker theology and experience.

Driven by her belief in the Light of Christ, she worked for peace in an age of violence. She reached out to the Jewish community, believing that the Light was shining on a new day for Israel as well as for England, a nation that had long ago expelled the Jews. In a time of structured gender roles and patriarchal assumptions, Mother Fell wrote in defense of women's religious equality. Unlike many Christian groups, the early Friends accepted the important ministry of women in their midst, and none was more important in those early days than Margaret Fell. In all of these exceptional works, Fell was motivated by a deep eschatological conviction. The Light was dawning, and Christ had now arisen again in the flesh. In the power of the Spirit, Fell and her fellow Quakers understood themselves to be ushering a new age, an age of peace, righteousness, and universal joy. In other works by other scholars, the personal strengths and failings of the Mother of Quakerism will no doubt be explored from similar but distinct perspectives which differ from mine.

The scope of this project was to become acquainted with Margaret Fell insofar as she is displayed as a practical theologian. Most of what scholars today would wish to know about Fell she herself chose to leave unsaid. What, if anything, did Margaret learn from her individual life experiences? Did her own wealth teach her about sacrifice and life in the Light? Did her class and social status, by virtue of which others reflexively estimated her and deferred to her, give her any insight into the nature and necessity of humility for salvation? Is it possible that in the course of her long partnership in marriage to a man of influence and legal authority that she had developed a greater sensitivity to the difference between legality and justice? Could it be that the deaths of her "unconvinced" husband, just and faithful, and son, angry and treacherous, and both deeply loved, add anything to her understanding of the salvific Light? These kinds of questions are interesting in a personal way, but cannot be answered from the evidence. What is quite clear is that for Fell, life, experience, and theology were not separate domains; they all combined in her understanding of God, the coming of Christ, and the revelation that was her measure in the Light.

Yet for all that remains unanswered and unsung, she did leave a solid body of religious writings which tell something of who wrote them and why, and of her understanding of the truth of God. There are many ways of approaching the Mother of Quakerism, and many modern concerns, which cause interest in her life and work. The approach of this work has been theological, and has endeavored to do some justice to her own drive to explain the truth and light of Christ in theological terms. In those terms, and over the course of this study, her realized eschatology has provided a key to understanding the vibrant center of her theology and ministry in the Light.

# Notes

### INTRODUCTION

1. A word here about usage of the name Religious Society of Friends to apply to early Quakers. There is a modern preference for the term Quaker in reference to all things that pertain to the Society. Early Quakers knew the term in its derogatory sense yet took it as a badge of honor. In this sense the name of Quaker represents a victory for the movement in that it successfully subverted the dominant paradigm which sought to shame believers with pejorative language. At the same time, the earliest Friends had a preference their own: Children of Light. This title disappeared from common usage within Margaret Fell's own long lifetime, and it was probably intentional. Both strike me as more poetic than the more official Religious Society of Friends, but I appreciate its practicality. Though the name has been identified in use as early as 1665, it is likely the term only grafted onto common usage later than that. This makes its use a bit anachronistic as a choice, but not completely without some historical connection. My primary reason for using the simple form, Society of Friends, is that it captures the occasional and casual reference we see used during the life of Margaret Fell. Ideally I would use only the term Friends because it is simple, elegant, and theologically loaded for bear, just as she was.

2. The Society of Friends, *The Life of Margaret Fox, Wife of George Fox, Compiled From Her Own Narrative, and Other Sources, With a Selection From Her Epistles, Etc.* (Philadelphia: Association of Friends for the Diffusion of Religion and Useful Knowledge, 1859), iv.

3. Maria Webb, *The Fells of Swarthmoor Hall and their Friends*, 2nd ed. (Philadelphia: H. Longstreth, 1884).

4. Helen G. Crosfield, *Margaret Fox of Swarthmoor Hall* (London: Headley Brothers, 1913).

5   Isabel Ross, *Margaret Fell: Mother of Quakerism* (London: Longmans, 1949), iii–iv.
6   Bonnelyn Young Kunze, *Margaret Fell and the Rise of Quakerism* (Stanford: Stanford University Press, 1994), 198.
7   Kunze, 202.
8   Kunze, 284 n. 11.
9   William C. Braithwaite, *The Beginnings of Quakerism*, 2nd ed. (Cambridge: Cambridge University Press, 1955), 307.
10  Thomas Camm, "Testimony Concerning our Dear and Honoured Friend Margaret Fox," in *Works*, A3–6.
11  Thomas Edwards, *Gangraena*, 3 parts in 1 volume (1646; repr., Exeter: University of Exeter Press, 1977).
12  "An Epistle to the Reader," prefaced to her important tract, *A True Testimony* (1660), as printed in Wallace, 16. The volume edited by Wallace contains a number of the works of Fell, in modern English, with helpful introductions by the editor.
13  One of the many tracts and publications that greeted the rabbi publicly was Margaret Fell's *For Manasseth-ben-Israel: The Call of the Jews out of Babylon*, which appeared in 1656.

## Chapter 1

1   Nicholas Morgan, *Lancashire Quakers and the Establishment, 1760–1830* (Halifax, UK: Ryburn Academic, 1993), 14.
2   There are numerous explanations for this within the practices of the first generations of Friends themselves. Members of the Society of Friends were discouraged from arrogance, pride, and vanity so that they might remain appropriately humble before the Light of Christ. Upon reviewing the extant material from the pen of early Quakers, it is clear that they gave little import to their daily experiences except where those served to illustrate divine grace and provision, or as evidence of the oppression and persecutions of Friends by others. Their interest in biography as such was limited primarily to "testimonies" of faithful Friends and focused upon events they held to be of religious significance. Introspective theological autobiography along the lines of Augustine's *Confessions* held little value for early Friends. As will be apparent in later chapters, this preference for testimony over biography also reflects the eschatological presuppositions of early Friends, as well as their emphasis upon evangelistic and proselytizing activities.
3   As a result, the single autobiography of Margaret Fell's early years is the source for most subsequent account of her life. See "A Relation of Margaret Fell," Wallace, 105–14; also in *Works*, 1–15.
4   The best study of the life of Fell is still Ross, *Margaret Fell*. This should be supplemented by the more recent study by Kunze, *Margaret Fell*, and by the *Letters* (*Undaunted Zeal*). For Fell's own autobiographical notes, "A

Relation of Margaret Fell," see the first fifteen pages of her *Works*; also in Wallace, 105–14.
5  *Works*, 1.
6  In his book *Literacy and the Social Order: Reading and Writing in Tudor and Stuart England*, David Cressy has calculated that in some areas literacy (the ability to sign your name) among women was a low as 11 percent (Cambridge: Cambridge University Press, 1980), 119–21.
7  Morgan, 14.
8  John Punshon, "The End of (Quaker) History? Some Reflections on the Process," in *The Creation of Quaker Theory: Insider Perspectives*, ed. Ben Pink Dandelion (Aldershot: Ashgate Press, 2004), 32.
9  *Letters*, 106–10.
10  *Letters*, 194.
11  For information on Thomas Fell, see T. M. [Thomas Mounsey], *A Brief Account of Thomas Fell of Swarthmore Hall* (Manchester, UK: Wm. Irwin, 1846); Webb, *The Fells of Swarthmoor Hall*; Ross, 3–5, 115–24; Kunze, 29–37; Richard G. Bailey, "Research Note on Judge Thomas Fell," *Journal of the Friends' Historical Society* 57 (1994): 1–5.
12  Bailey, 4.
13  Judge Fell's will also offers us a glimpse into his political connections, as he left a small legacy to his friend John Bradshawe. Bradshawe succeeded Thomas Fell as chancellor and is most notable in history for presiding at the trial of Charles I, which ultimately resulted in the king's death by beheading. An account of Thomas Fell's last will and testament can be found (among other places) in appendix 10 of Ross' work, *Margaret Fell: Mother of Quakerism*.
14  Hugh Barbour, *The Quakers in Puritan England* (New Haven: Yale University Press, 1964), 93–94.
15  See, e.g., Thomas Camm's testimony in *Works*, A4.
16  Trevett, *Women and Quakerism in the Seventeenth Century* (New York: Ebor Press, 1991), 211–12.
17  Kunze, 231.
18  Now found in *Letters*, 428–33.
19  William Lampitt, an experienced preacher with Baptist leanings, had attended Oxford and served in the New Model Army. H. Larry Ingle, *First Among Friends: George Fox and the Creation of Quakerism* (Oxford: Oxford University Press, 1994), 86.
20  Ingle, 86.
21  *Letters*, 430.
22  Ross, 11–12.
23  Margaret Fell continued to battle Justice Sawrey throughout his life, with the conflict extending to the next generation, and the ongoing animosity is obvious in extant correspondence. In a letter before his death by drowning, Fell wrote him, "the seed of the woman shall bruise the serpents head,

examine and try whether the serpent be not head in thee." In the context, Fell confronts Sawrey for "malice towards my childe, my friends and family," and warns him "looke into thy family . . . a family of lyers, tattlers, tale bearers, false accusers . . . lovers of pleasures more than lovers of God." *Letters*, 13–15.

24  As we consider the implications of this line of reasoning, we are faced with even more questions. For example, since Margaret Fell and George Fox are the sources for our only firsthand accounts of the events at Ulverston, why did their accounts portray George Fox as the dominant figure in the story? No doubt both Fell and Fox would have been aware of the social realities of the situation. How then do we account for all the historical evidence in a manner that also affirms the integrity of our firsthand narratives? One possible explanation is that Fox and Fell were telling all the truth that mattered to them and the Quaker community. Looking back across the years and recounting events in Ulverston, they were repeating a story that may have been told and retold in the context of Friends gatherings. It was their story: the story of Margaret and George's first meeting, of her convincement, of the confounding of hireling priests, of the Truth of Fox's message, and, ultimately, of the power of God.

25  Ross, 11.

26  This northern foundation provided some of early Quakerism's most dynamic and hearty leadership, and the movement thrives there still. However, the locus of Friends' organization and leadership shifted south in the wake of the decimated the post-Restoration persecution. See Morgan, *Lancashire*; also Bruce G. Blackwood, *The Lancashire Gentry and the Great Rebellion, 1640–1660* (Manchester, UK: Manchester University Press, 1978).

27  *Letters*, 430.

28  As George Fox himself noted in his preface to the journal of William Caton, "Judge Fell . . . stood up nobly for us and the Truth, and our adversaries were confounded; so that he was a wall for God's people against them." William Caton, *A Journal of the Life of Will. Caton* (London, 1689), iv.

29  Margaret Fell's first trip to London as a Quaker occurred after Thomas Fell's death in 1658. See Ross, 125.

30  Those interested in a more detailed outline of these events will find an excellent resource in Kunze, x–xvii.

31  Kunze, 21.

32  Morgan, 65.

33  *Letters*, 430–32.

34  In a preface to one of Margaret Fell's letters written from London, Elsa F. Glines notes that Margaret once brushed aside "a report in the Country concerning my Stay." Her unusual behavior of staying so long in London aroused gossip. *Letters*, 328.

35  Bear in mind Christine Trevett's observation that sixteenth-century Friends "were not producing great academic or pastoral theology and

little which was very good theology . . . They concentrated on a small number of things." *Women and Quakerism*, 51.
36 Thomas Camm in *Works*, A3–6.
37 Thomas Camm in *Works*, A3–6.
38 Kunze, 191.
39 Ross, 382.
40 Thomas Camm in *Works*, A4.
41 Fell, "A Relation of Margaret Fell," *Works*, 2; and Wallace, 106.
42 *Works*, 2.
43 For information on the Seeker movement, see Rufus M. Jones, *Studies in Mystical Religion* (London: Macmillan, 1909); Rufus M. Jones, *Mysticism and Democracy in the English Commonwealth* (Cambridge, Mass.: Harvard University Press, 1932); and Douglas Gwyn, *Seekers Found*.
44 Phyllis Mack, *Visionary Women: Ecstatic Prophecy in Seventeenth-Century England* (Berkeley: University of California Press, 1992), 147.
45 Oliver Cromwell, quoted in Douglas Gwyn, *Seekers Found* (Wallingford, Pa.: Pendle Hill, 2000), 183.
46 Edwards, *Gangraena*.
47 Edwards, *Gangraena*, Part I, 28.
48 Gwyn, *Seekers Found*, 235.
49 Gwyn, *Seekers Found*, 235.
50 Fell, *An Epistle of M.F.'s to the World, Priests and People, concerning the Light; and for all People to Try their Teachers by the Scriptures* (1654), in *Works*, 60.
51 Gwyn, *Seekers Found*, 51.
52 The Seekers' domain was the inward, spiritual experience of the individual believer. The worship practices of Seekers modeled those later associated with Quaker gatherings, particularly the waiting in silence and thoughtful contemplation. Although many Seekers eventually joined the Society of Friends, some form of organized Seeker gatherings continued for another hundred years or so.
53 *Works*, 2.
54 Gwyn, 56.
55 "The Testimony of Margaret Fox Concerning Her Late Husband . . .," in Wallace, 116.
56 Wallace, 132.
57 *Works*, 2.
58 "The Testimony of Margaret Fox Concerning Her Late Husband . . .," in Wallace, 116 (emphasis added).
59 Margaret Fell was a gentleman's daughter who had inherited property and married well. Her father, John Askew, "was bred after the best way and manner of persons of his rank in his day" and she was sophisticated to a degree in keeping with this. *Works*, 1. She was also a mother of eight children and the mistress of a large household who managed servants and land.

60 George Fox, *The Journal of George Fox*, ed. John L. Nickalls (Cambridge: Cambridge University Press, 1952), 1.
61 Early Quakers Richard Farnsworth and James Nayler both visited the Fell house shortly after her convincement by Fox. *Works*, 2.
62 Gwyn, *Seekers Found*, 220.
63 Fox, *Journal*, ed. Nickalls, 36–37.
64 Fox, *Journal*, ed. Nickalls, 34–35.
65 *Works*, 2.
66 For accounts of the early Friends see Elfrida Vipont, *George Fox and the Valiant Sixty* (London: Hamilton, 1975); and Ernest E. Taylor, *The Valiant Sixty* (London: Bannisdale Press, 1947).
67 The place of George Fox as *the* founder of the Society of Friends was not secure until the 1660s, after the Quaker leadership had been decimated in post-Restoration persecution.
68 Trevett, *Women and Quakerism*, 214–15.
69 Morgan, 14.
70 Morgan, 68.
71 Now found in *Letters*, 35–39, 113–21, 140–43, 222–23.
72 *Letters*, 36.
73 *Letters*, 38.
74 *Letters*, 38.
75 *Letters*, 141–42.
76 *Letters*, 13–15.
77 *Letters*, 14.
78 *Works*, 60–67; *Letters*, 90–106.
79 *False Prophets, Antichrists, Deceivers Which are in the World* . . . (London: Giles Calvert, 1655). This pamphlet is not found in her *Works*, but the substance of it is found in *An Epistle of M.F.'s to the World, Priests, and People* (1654), in *Works*, 60–68.
80 *An Epistle of M.F.'s to the World*, in *Works*, 61. These practical theological themes appear repeatedly in Fell's later works.
81 *An Epistle of M.F.'s to the World*, in *Works*, 61, 65.
82 *Works*, 90–91.
83 Ross, 89.
84 Ross, 89–95.
85 The first two of these works is found in her *Works*, 125–51. *Some Ranter Principles Answered* is not found in her *Works*, but is reprinted in Wallace, 85–96.
86 Ingle, 196.
87 Morgan, 15.
88 Margaret Fell, *To the General Councel and Officers of the Army* . . . (London: Th. Simmons, 1659), 1.
89 See Morgan, 67; and Ingle, 191.
90 Wallace, 49; *Works*, 202.

91  *Works*, 218–19.
92  Wallace, 19; *Works*, 237.
93  Wallace, 26.
94  *Works*, 226.
95  Morgan, 68.
96  "A Relation," Wallace, 107; *Works*, 4.
97  Michael J. St. Clair, *Millenarian Movements in Historical Context* (New York: Garland, 1992), 193.
98  Bernard S. Capp, *The Fifth Monarchy Men: A Study in Seventeenth-Century English Millenarianism* (London: Macmillan, 1972), 199–200.
99  Morgan, 15.
100  Kunze, 42; Ross 129–43; William C. Braithwaite, *The Second Period of Quakerism*, 2nd ed. (Cambridge: Cambridge University Press, 1955), 9–12.
101  *Works*, 7, 277–78.
102  Fell recounted an event in which her son-in-law Daniel Abraham had met Judge William Kirby on the road. He gave an unfriendly warning to pass along to Margaret advising them to hold no more meetings or she would again be brought before the court. Abraham offered the standard Quaker reply: we must have meetings while we have lives. According to Fell, "Then William Kirby said, we will not take your lives, but whilst you have anything [else] we will take it." From Society of Friends, *The Life of Margaret Fox*, 60.
103  *Works*, 304–24.
104  *Works*, 311.
105  This summary is in fact her longest published book: *The Standard of the Lord Revealed* (London, 1667). It is not included in her *Works*, and is a kind of summation of major biblical texts rather than a theological work by Fell in her own voice.
106  Ross, 177–78, 191.
107  *Works*, 327–29; *Letters*, 390–94.
108  Abstracted in her *Works*, 19. For the full text of this letter see *Letters*, 278–88.
109  *Letters*, 288.
110  *Works*, 299.
111  See, e.g., *Works*, 299–303; *Letters*, 386–90.
112  *Works*, 467–91.
113  *Works*, 492–508.
114  Ross, 89–97.
115  Christopher Hill, *The Experience of Defeat: Milton and Some Contemporaries* (New York: Viking, 1984), 166.
116  Morgan, 15.
117  Mother Fell again took up a leadership role in the Weekly Meeting in her home, and among the Quakers in Lancaster.

118 Ross, 205–15; Fell, "A Relation," *Works*, 7–8.
119 Fox, *Journal*, ed. Nickalls, 554.
120 "The Testimony of Margaret Fell Concerning Her Late Husband," Wallace, 121.
121 With their wedding they sought to defuse criticism, and Fox took the further step of refusing to profit by Fell's wealth. Swarthmoor passed on to her children, and Fox supported himself by his own means.
122 Ross, 218.
123 Braithwaite, *Second Period*, 263. This letter was disliked by Friends, and seems not to have survived in manuscript form; but a printed version survives in a book written by one of their critics (cited in Braithwaite, *Second Period*, 263 n. 1). Fox gives a similar account in his *Journal*, ed. Nickalls, 557.
124 *Letters*, 73–76; see 76–83 for an example.
125 See, e.g., Morgan, 15; "The Testimony of Margaret Fell Concerning Her Late Husband," Wallace, 121.
126 Braithwaite, *Second Period*, 290–325.
127 For more about George Fell, see Kunze, 49–53; and Ross, 220–25.
128 Kunze, 53.
129 Norman Penney, "George Fell and the Story of Swarthmoor Hall," *Journal of the Friends' Historical Society* [3 parts] 29 (1932): 51–61; 30 (1933): 28–39; and 31 (1934): 27–35; and Alfred W. Braithwaite, "The Mystery of Swarthmoor Hall," *Journal of the Friends' Historical Society* 51 (1965): 22–29.
130 Kunze, 51.
131 Kunze, 51.
132 Kunze, 52–53.
133 Braithwaite, *Second Period*, 265.
134 "A Relation," Wallace, 111.
135 On the origin of the Women's Meetings in London, see William Beck and T. F. Ball, *The London Friends' Meetings* (London: Kitto, 1869), 344–50; Braithwaite, *Second Period*, 271–75, 286–88.
136 Kunze, 157.
137 On the Women's Meetings, see Ross, 283–302; Kunze, 143–68; and Ingle, 252–53.
138 Ross, 302.
139 Ross, 247–57; Fox, *Journal*, ed. Nickalls, 673–706.
140 Trevett, *Women and Quakerism*, 212–13.
141 *Works*, 510.
142 *Works*, 528.
143 See, e.g., the letter printed in Ross, 311–12.
144 Ross, 310–13.
145 Ross, 314–16.
146 Ross, 319–20.

147 Fell, "A Relation," Wallace, 111–13.
148 Morgan, 68.
149 Ross, 327–29.
150 Braithwaite, *Second Period*, 170–75.
151 Braithwaite, *Second Period*, 98–125.
152 H. J. Cadbury, in Fox, *Journal*, ed. Nickalls, 751–54; see also Ross, 330–32.
153 Fell, "The Testimony of Margaret Fell Concerning Her Late Husband," found in every multi-volume edition of Fox's *Journal*; and Fell, "A Relation," found in her *Works*, 1–5; also in Wallace, 105–24.
154 Morgan, 70.
155 Morgan, 70.
156 *Works*, 531; see also Morgan, 68.

## Chapter 2

1  As William C. Braithwaite has rightly observed, it is premature to speak of the Society of Friends as existing in the 1650s. His earliest evidence of the name itself is from a document in 1665. However, we are looking to the early activities of Quakers as a developmental step in the emergence of the Society of Friends. Braithwaite, *Beginnings*, 307.
2  Caton, *Life* (1689), chap. 3.
3  N. Jones, "Negotiating the Reformation," in *Religion and the English People 1500–1640: New Voices, New Perspectives*, ed. Eric Josef Carlson (Kirksville, Mo.: Thomas Jefferson University Press, 1998), 273.
4  Barry Reay, "Radicalism and Religion in the English Reformation: An Introduction," in *Radical Religion in the English Revolution*, ed. J. F. McGregor and B. Reay (Oxford: Oxford University Press, 1984), 3.
5  Howard Shaw, *The Levellers* (New York: Harper & Row, 1968), 8.
6  A. L. Morton, *The World of the Ranters: Religious Radicalism in the English Reformation* (London: Lawrence & Wishart, 1970), 10.
7  Bernard McGinn, ed., *The Encyclopedia of Apocalypticism*, vol. 2, *Apocalypticism in Western History and Culture* (New York: Continuum, 1998), 36.
8  Walter Klaassen, *Living at the End of the Ages: Apocalyptic Expectation in the Radical Reformation* (Lanham, Md.: University Press of America, 1992), 1.
9  William Haller, "John Foxe and the Puritan Revolution," in Richard Foster Jones, *The Seventeenth Century: Studies in the History of English Thought and Literature from Bacon to Pope* (Stanford: Stanford University Press, 1951), 62.
10 John M. Headley, *Luther's View of Church History* (New Haven: Yale University Press, 1963), 32; see also 195–96.
11 Joy Gilsdorf, *The Puritan Apocalypse: New England Eschatology in the Seventeenth Century* (New York: Garland, 1989), 15.
12 Christopher Hill, *Antichrist in Seventeenth-Century England* (Oxford: Oxford University Press, 1971), 160.

13  In the introduction to his commentary and in its marginal notes, Bale places himself firmly within a long tradition of exegesis of the book of Revelation. With some exceptions, he most frequently cites either contemporary reformed scholars or medieval heretics. Paul Christianson, *Reformers and Babylon: English Apocalyptic Visions from the Reformation to the Eve of the Civil War* (Toronto: University of Toronto Press, 1978), 15.
14  Christianson, 94.
15  Christianson, 6.
16  Isaac Newton, *Chronology of Ancient Kingdoms Amended* (London, 1728); and the modern critical edition, *Isaac Newton's Observations on the Prophecies of Daniel and the Apocalypse of St. John*, ed. S. J. Barnett with introduction by Mary E. Mills (Lewiston, N.Y.: Edwin Mellen, 1999).
17  F. Manuel, *The Religion of Isaac Newton* (Oxford: Oxford University Press, 1974), 8.
18  Indeed, this identification of pope with antichrist became so prevalent that in a 1581 tract dedicated to the Earl of Leicester, John Field observed that "to prove the Pope Antichrist" was in fact "needless, considering how it is a beaten argument in every book." John Field, *A Caveat for Parson Howlet* (1581), cited in Hill, *Antichrist*, 18.
19  According to Christopher Hill, "Foxe's great Acts and Monuments, given the widest possible circulation through its use as propaganda by the Elizabethan government, depicted Englishmen throughout the centuries battling against Antichrist, especially since the days of Wyclif." *Antichrist*, 12.
20  The full title of the work is *The Acts and Monuments of Matters Most Special and memorable, happening in the Church, with an Universal Historie of the Same. Wherein is set forth at large the whole race and course of the Church, from the Primitive age to these later times of ours, with the bloudy times, horrible troubles, and great persecutions against the Martyrs of Christ, sought and wrought as well by heathen Emperors, as now lately practiced by Romish Prelates, especially in this Realme of England and Scotland. Now againe as it was recoginesed, perused, and recommended to the studious Reader, by the Author, Mr. John Foxe.*
21  Haller, "John Foxe," 64.
22  Foxe scholar David Loades observes, "The *Acts and Monuments* also created a sense of shared national experience, which was actually enhanced by the events of Elizabeth's long reign . . . The papal bull *Regnans in Excelsis*, issued shortly after the 1570 edition, not only appeared to confirm Foxe's demonization of the papacy, but also intensified the identification of the English Church with the Crown and the realm." *John Foxe and the English Reformation* (Hants, UK: Scholar Press, 1997), 4.
23  Carl Bridenbaugh, *Vexed and Troubled Englishmen, 1590–1642* (Oxford: Oxford University Press, 1967), 279.
24  Christianson, 93.
25  Bryan W. Ball, *A Great Expectation: Eschatological Thought in English Protestantism to 1660* (Leiden: E. J. Brill, 1975), 1.

26 There were other contributors to premillenialist eschatology, including John Napier, Arthur Dent, and Thomas Brightman. According to Ball, "Joseph Mede (or Mead), an Anglican loyal to Episcopal principles, stands out among this early group, if not among all expositors in the seventeenth century, for his colossal contributions to prophetic interpretation." Ball, *A Great Expectation*, 59 n. 16.
27 R. G. Clouse, "The Rebirth of Millenarianism," in *Puritans, the Millennium and the Future of Israel: Puritan Eschatology 1600 to 1660*, ed. Peter Toon (London: J. Clarke, 1970), 56.
28 Ball, *A Great Expectation*, 58.
29 Christianson, 124.
30 V. Norskov Olsen, *John Foxe and the Elizabethan Church* (Berkeley: University of California Press, 1973), 32–36.
31 Barnett, in Newton, 7.
32 P. G. Rogers, *The Fifth Monarchy Men* (Oxford: Oxford University Press, 1966), 6.
33 Christianson, 5.
34 Barnett, in Newton, 9.
35 Ball, *A Great Expectation*, 75.
36 Ball, *A Great Expectation*, 2.
37 Hill, *Antichrist*, 131.
38 This distinction between Magisterial Reformers and Radical Reformers appears in the work of other scholars, but the earliest appearance I have found is in the work of V. Norskov Olsen.
39 Olsen, 84–85.
40 Olsen, 33–34.
41 C. J. Clement, *Religious Radicalism in England, 1535–1565* (Carlisle, UK: Paternoster Press), 2.
42 David S. Katz, *Sabbath and Sectarianism in Seventeenth-Century England* (Leiden: E. J. Brill, 1988), 4–6.
43 George H. Williams traces the Sabbatarian movement to a "Judaizing movement which in the late fifteenth century seized all of Christianity" with important centers of influence in Eastern Europe. "Protestants in the Ukraine During the Period of the Polish-Lithuanian Commonwealth," *Harvard Ukrainian Studies* 2 (1978): 41–72; quoting 46. Cf. Bryan W. Ball, *The Seventh-Day Men: Sabbatarians and Sabbatarianism in England and Wales, 1600–1800* (Oxford: Oxford University Press, 1994), 20–21.
44 Heiko A. Oberman, *The Roots of Anti-Semitism in the Age of Renaissance and Reformation*, trans. J. I. Porter (Philadelphia: Fortress, 1984), 47–50. Luther's initial response to Sabbatarians in 1538 shows that his attitude toward the Jews in general had "in fact hardened, presaging the vitriolics to come." Oberman, 48.
45 See, e.g., Clyde C. Smith, "Laodicea, Canons of," in *The New International Dictionary of the Christian Church*, ed. J. D. Douglas (Grand Rapids: Zondervan, 1978), 578.

46 Ball, *Seventh-Day Men*, 27–30.
47 Ball, *Seventh-Day Men*, 83–85.
48 See, e.g., Peter Toon, "The Latter Glory," in Toon, *Puritans*, 23.
49 Daniel Liechty, *Sabbatarianism in the Sixteenth Century: A Page in the History of the Radical Reformers* (Berrien Springs, Mich.: Andrews University Press, 1993), 4–7.
50 Katz, *Sabbath*, 16.
51 Ball, *Seventh-Day Men*, 22.
52 Ball, *Seventh-Day Men*, 47.
53 Reay, "Radicalism and Religion," 5.
54 Ball, *A Great Expectation*, 58.
55 Hill, *Antichrist*, 107–11.
56 Christianson, 246–48.
57 Reay, "Radicalism and Religion," 1–2.
58 It is of course granted that the initial cohesion and success of the New Model Army was due as much to professional leadership and good wages as to any particular religious agenda. Kenneth Morgan, ed., *The Oxford Illustrated History of Britain* (Oxford: Oxford University Press, 1984), 318.
59 Ian Gentles, *The New Model Army in England, Ireland and Scotland, 1645–1653* (Oxford: Blackwell, 1992), 11.
60 Gentles, 115.
61 Barnett, in Newton, 8.
62 Gentles, 115.
63 Gentles, 119.
64 Douglas Gwyn, *Apocalypse of the Word: The Life and Message of George Fox (1624–1691)* (Richmond, Ind.: Friends United Press, 1984), 14–15.
65 Mills, in Newton, iv.
66 Henry Holorenshaw, *The Levellers and the English Revolution* (New York: H. Fertig, 1971), 14–17.
67 Brian Manning, "The Levellers and Religion," in McGregor and Reay, 65.
68 H. N. Brailsford, *The Levellers and the English Revolution* (Stanford: Stanford University Press, 1961), 523–40.
69 Manning, 67.
70 D. B. Robertson, *The Religious Foundations of Leveller Democracy* (New York: King's Crown Press, 1951), 13. In addition to Lilburne's influence, Richard Overton, William Walwyn, and John Wildman articulated the Leveller position in germinal publications. Christianson, 90.
71 Fenner Brockway, *Britain's First Socialists. The Levellers, Agitators and Diggers of the English Revolution* (London: Quartet Books, 1980), 25.
72 Brailsford, 10–11.
73 Jones, *Mysticism*, 154.
74 Holorenshaw, 72–73.
75 J. Frank, *The Levellers: A History of the Writings of Three Seventeenth-Century Social Democrats: John Lilburne, Richard Overton, William Walwyn* (Cambridge, Mass.: Harvard University Press, 1955), 221.

76 Frank, 231.
77 Bernard S. Capp, "The Fifth Monarchists and Popular Millenarianism," in McGregor and Reay, 165.
78 Capp, "Fifth Monarchists," 170.
79 Ball, *A Great Expectation*, 10.
80 Hill, *Antichrist*, 120.
81 Rogers, 39.
82 Rogers, 84–85.
83 Capp, "Fifth Monarchists," 89.
84 Morton, 18.
85 Ingle, 46.
86 Reay, "Quakers and the English Revolution," in McGregor and Reay, 20.
87 Hugh Barbour and Arthur Roberts, eds., *Early Quaker Writings, 1650–1700* (Grand Rapids: Eerdmans, 1973), 47–55.
88 Barbour and Roberts, 58.
89 Fox, *Journal*, ed. Nickalls, 71.
90 Fox, *Journal*, ed. Nickalls, 121.
91 Gwyn, *Apocalypse*, passim.
92 *Letters*, 32.
93 George Fox, *The Works of George Fox* (Philadelphia: M. T. C. Gould, 1831), 3:251 and 7:157; see also Gwyn, *Apocalypse*, 206.
94 Fox, *Newes coming up out of the North, Sounding towards the South* (London, 1654).
95 Reay, "Quakerism and Society," in McGregor and Reay, 164.
96 This tract is reprinted in Barbour and Roberts, 102–166; quote on 106f.
97 See Reay, "Quakerism," and especially his book, *The Quakers and the English Revolution* (New York: St. Martin's Press, 1985).
98 Reay, "Quakerism," 153.
99 Fox, *Journal*, ed. Nickalls, 400.
100 William Dewsbury, *A True Prophecy* (1655), reprinted in Barbour and Roberts, 95.
101 Capp, "Fifth Monarchists," 165.
102 Catherine M. Wilcox, *Theology and Women's Ministry in Seventeenth-Century English Quakerism: Handmaids of the Lord* (Lewiston, N.Y.: Edwin Mellen, 1995), 12.
103 In Barbour and Roberts, 115.
104 Fox, *Journal*, ed. Nickalls, 204.
105 Fox, *Journal*, ed. Nickalls, 205.
106 This is true in two large collections of early Quaker writings: Barbour and Roberts, *Early Quaker Writings*; and Mary Garman, ed., *Hidden in Plain Sight: Quaker Women's Writings, 1650–1700* (Wallingford, Pa.: Pendle Hill, 1996).
107 Ingle, 190.
108 Quaker missionaries spread the Light of Truth from England to the rest of

## Chapter 3

1. Fell, *A Touch-stone: or Tryal by the Scriptures of the Priests, Bishops and Ministers*, in *Works*, 19.
2. To illustrate: Fell's early letters and publications, especially those aimed at Oliver Cromwell and Parliament, proved problematic when the English monarchy was restored with Charles II (1660). In response, she wrote private and public letters such as the 1660 *A Declaration and an Information from Us the People of God Called Quakers, to the Present Governors, the King, and Both Houses of Parliament, and to All Whom it May Concern*, which she published after first presenting it in person to the newly restored King Charles. We discuss this tract more fully in chap. 5, below.
3. *Letters*, 431.
4. For an overview of the concept of a moral conscience in the West, see Michael Despland, "Conscience," in *The Encyclopedia of Religion*, ed. M. Eliade (New York: Free Press, 1990), 4:45–52. See also Michael G. Baylor, *Action and Person: Conscience in Late Scholasticism and the Young Luther* (Leiden: E. J. Brill, 1977), 22–29. For the importance of conscience in the age of Fell, see Kevin T. Kelly, *Conscience: Dictator or Guide? A Study in Seventeenth-Century English Moral Theology* (London: G. Chapman, 1967); and Edward G. Andrew, *Conscience and Its Critics: Protestant Conscience, Enlightenment Reason and Modern Subjectivity* (Toronto: University of Toronto Press, 2001).
5. One of the most popular references to "conscience" in contemporary culture is found in Walt Disney's animated version of *Pinocchio*. There, a cricket named Jiminy is appointed as a conscience for the wooden boy. Jiminy sings the song "Give a Little Whistle," with the famous refrain "and always let your conscience be your guide."
6. J. M. Gundry-Volf, "Conscience," in *Dictionary of Paul and his Letters*, ed. G. F. Hawthorne, et al. (Downers Grove, Ill.: InterVarsity, 1993), 154.
7. For the role of conscience in Luther and Calvin, see Baylor, *Action and Person*; Randall C. Zachman, *The Assurance of Faith: Conscience in the Theology of Martin Luther and John Calvin* (Minneapolis: Fortress, 1993).
8. "Luther at the Diet of Worms," in *Luther's Works: American Edition*, eds. J. Pelikan, et al. (St. Louis: Concordia Publishing House and Philadelphia: Fortress, 1955–1986), 32:112.
9. *Luther's Works*, 33:49.
10. *Letters*, 35–38.
11. *Works*, 15.
12. *Works*, 19.
13. *Works*, 531.
14. "People having lived in the Darkness, out of the Knowledge of the Light; it

was such a new Doctrine to them, that there was a mighty War in People's Minds against it." *Diverse Epistles of M. Fell to Friends*, in *Works*, 46. For a study of the Light in the theology of Robert Barclay, see Leif Eeg-Olofsson, *The Conception of the Inner Light in Robert Barclay's Theology* (Lund: C. W. K. Gleerup, 1954). For the Light in the thought of Fox, see Gwyn, *Apocalypse*, 60–91.
15 *Works*, 270.
16 *Works*, 196.
17 *Works*, 275. For another approach: "friends of God, who are in the Unity of Faith, and in the Spirit of Grace," to whom she writes "in the Name and Power of Jesus Christ." *Works*, 196.
18 E.g., God the Father is "the God and Father of our Lord and Savior Jesus Christ." *Works*, 52.
19 *Works*, 92.
20 Kunze, 203.
21 *Letters*, 131.
22 *Works*, 252.
23 *Works*, 48.
24 *Works*, 195–96.
25 *Works*, 52, 151.
26 *Works*, 47, 74, 95. Elsewhere she speaks of "God, who created all things by Jesus Christ." *Works*, 194–95.
27 *Works*, 74–75.
28 *Works*, 69.
29 *Works*, 315.
30 In order to properly apprehend the divine we may "read and Examine by the Light of Jesus in every particular, how ye stand in the presence of God concerning these things." *Works*, 198.
31 *Works*, 53.
32 *Works*, 46–47.
33 *Works*, 74.
34 *Works*, 135.
35 *Works*, 238–39.
36 *Works*, 200.
37 *Works*, 199.
38 *Works*, 254.
39 *Works*, 309; see also 257.
40 *Works*, 422.
41 *Works*, 79.
42 *Works*, 91–92.
43 *Works*, 270.
44 *Works*, 65.
45 *Works*, 238.
46 *Works*, 354.

47  *Works*, 199.
48  *Letters*, 37.
49  *Works*, 86.
50  *Works*, 200.
51  *Letters*, 200–201.
52  *Works*, 238.
53  *Works*, 196.
54  *Works*, 221.
55  *Works*, 65.
56  *Works*, 221.
57  *Works*, 74; see also 78, 79.
58  Wallace, 24.
59  *Works*, 224.
60  See, e.g., her 1660 *A Declaration and an Information*, in *Works*, 202–11.
61  An example of this is seen in Fell's 1656 tract, *For Manasseth-ben-Israel*, in *Works*, 101–24.
62  As, e.g., in *A Touch-Stone: or A Tryal by the Scriptures*, in *Works*, 351–466.
63  *An Epistle to the World Priests, and People*, in *Works*, 61. See also 64.
64  "[A]nd he is that true Light, that lighteth every Man that cometh into the World, John 1.9." *Works*, 144.
65  *Tryal of the False Prophets*, in *Works*, 148.
66  *To all the Professors of the World*, in *Works*, 79.
67  *Works*, 501.
68  *Works*, 48–49.
69  *Works*, 74.
70  *Works*, 248.
71  *Works*, 312.
72  *Works*, 294.
73  *Works*, 215.
74  See, e.g., *Works*, 20–21.
75  *Works*, 77.
76  *Works*, 77.
77  *Works*, 49.
78  *Works*, 79–80.
79  *Works*, 200.
80  *Works*, 216.
81  *Works*, 70–71.
82  *Works*, 83.
83  *Works*, 95.
84  *Works*, 496.
85  *An Epistle to Friends*, in *Works*, 273.
86  *Works*, 294.
87  *Works*, 294–95.
88  *Works*, 200.

89  *Works*, 60.
90  *Works*, 268.
91  *Works*, 49.
92  *Works*, 133–34.
93  *Letters*, 61.
94  *Works*, 221.
95  *Works*, 96.
96  *Works*, 54.
97  "Now the free Grace of the everlasting God is offered to you this Day; and therefore return to the Pure Light . . . and by that let your Minds be guided up to God, who is Light." *Works*, 115.
98  *Works*, 207.
99  *Works*, 95.
100 *Works*, 115.
101 In the unpublished letter to James Cave, composed about 1665, Fell writes against election as an act of God before eternity. *Letters*, 159.
102 *Works*, 221.
103 *Works*, 63.
104 *Works*, 309; also 257.
105 *Works*, 159.
106 *Works*, 94.
107 *Works*, 96.
108 *Works*, 98.
109 *Works*, 416.
110 *Works*, 417.
111 *Works*, 295.
112 *Works*, 295.
113 *Works*, 533.
114 *Works*, 66.
115 *Works*, 92.
116 *Works*, 44.
117 *Letters*, 181.
118 *Works*, 194; also *Letters*, 220.
119 *Works*, 67–68.
120 *Works*, 67.
121 *Works*, 67 (emphasis in original).
122 *Works*, 417.
123 See, e.g., *Works*, 66, 129.
124 *Works*, 309, 257.
125 *Works*, 87.
126 *Works*, 48.
127 *Works*, 48.
128 "Even the Day which the Serpent in the beginning veiled and clouded with darkness throughout his temptation, and drawing Adam and Eve

into disobedience to the Command of God in the beginning, and so beguiled them, by which they and all their posterity, in that fallen state, have brought upon them ever since the heavy Displeasure and Wrath of Almighty God." *Works*, 511.
129 Fell writes, "if ye hate the Light, and turn from the Light, the Light is your condemnation." *Works*, 85.
130 *Works*, 295.
131 *Works*, 154.
132 *Works*, 72.
133 *Works*, 149.
134 *Works*, 56.
135 *Works*, 268.
136 *Letters*, 124.
137 *Works*, 52.
138 *Works*, 33.
139 *Works*, 203.
140 *Works*, 203.
141 *To the Jewish and Hebrew Nation*, in *Works*, 117.
142 "Let it enter into thy Consideration, the sad and perilous Days, that this Age is fallen into, even into those last Days that Christ and his Apostles foresaw, and foretold of, which are the last Days." *Works*, 352.
143 *Works*, 33–34.
144 *Letters*, 266.
145 *Works*, 149.
146 *Letters*, 200.
147 *Letters*, 202.
148 *Letters*, 200–201, which also includes a (somewhat humorous) reference to those "who looks for a Christ yet to come," those she had called antichrist. They in turn asked, "What will you Quakers doe who saith Christ within you, when Christ comes in the Clouds?"
149 See chap. 2, above.
150 See chap. 2, above.
151 *Works*, 105.
152 *Works*, 124; compare with 98.
153 *Works*, 46.
154 *Works*, 58–59.
155 *Works*, 124.
156 *Letters*, 79.
157 *Works*, 124; see also 295.
158 See *Works*, 43, 60; see also *Letters*, 29.
159 *Works*, 66.
160 *Works*, 63–64.
161 *Works*, 44.
162 *Works*, 60.

163 *Works*, 140; see also 88.
164 *Works*, 53.
165 *Letters*, 63.
166 *Letters*, 124.
167 *Works*, 299.
168 "An Epistle to Friends" (1661), *Works*, 272.
169 *Works*, 35.
170 *Works*, 44.
171 *Works*, 48.
172 *Letters*, 58–59.
173 *Works*, 126.
174 *Works*, 318.
175 *Works*, 248.
176 *Works*, 56.
177 *Works*, 126.
178 *Works*, 57.
179 *Works*, 57; see also 71.
180 For a most creative and insightful presentation of the similarities between the concerns and ministry of the early Church and early Quaker theology, see Ben Pink Dandelion, Douglas Gwyn, and Timothy Peat, *Heaven On Earth: Quakers and the Second Coming* (Birmingham, UK: Woodbrooke College, 1998).
181 *Works*, 96.
182 *Works*, 294.
183 *Works*, 55.
184 *Works*, 96.
185 *Works*, 96.
186 *Letters*, 124.
187 *Works*, 49.
188 *Works*, 57.
189 *Works*, 396.
190 *Works*, 55.
191 *Works*, 58–59.
192 *Works*, 48.
193 *Works*, 61.
194 *Works*, 294.
195 *Works*, 419.
196 *Works*, 124.
197 *Works*, 82.
198 *Works*, 61.
199 *A Tryal of the False Prophets*, in *Works*, 145.
200 *To all the Professors of the World* (1656), in *Works*, 85.
201 *Works*, 87.
202 *Works*, 86.

203  *Works*, 87.
204  *Works*, 87.
205  *Works*, 44.
206  *Works*, 358.
207  *Works*, 203.
208  *Works*, 203.
209  *Works*, 78.
210  *Works*, 403.
211  *Works*, 360.
212  *Works*, 361.
213  *Works*, 364.
214  *Works*, 368.
215  *Works*, 375.
216  *Works*, 370.
217  *Works*, 381.
218  *Works*, 388.
219  *Works*, 390.
220  *Works*, 406.
221  *Works*, 355.
222  *Works*, 355.
223  *Works*, 150.
224  *Works*, 73.
225  *Works*, 60.
226  *Works*, 62.
227  *Works*, 62.
228  *Works*, 44.
229  *Works*, 62–63.

## Chapter 4

1  For further discussion see Richard H. Popkin's introduction to Fell, *Spinoza's Earliest Publication?: The Hebrew Translation of Margaret Fell's "A Loving Salutation to the Seed of Abraham among the Jews"*, eds. R. H. Popkin and M. A. Signer (Assen: Van Gorcum, 1987).

2  James W. Parkes, *The Jew in the Medieval Community: A Study of His Political and Economic Situation* (New York: Hermon, 1976), 251–52.

3  Joshua Trachtenberg, *The Devil and the Jews: The Medieval Conception of the Jew and its Relation to Modern Anti-Semitism* (Philadelphia: Jewish Publication Society of America, 1961), 97–139.

4  Trachtenberg, 124.

5  "For instance, right now there is this superficially learned children's preacher with the hoof of the golden calf in his flank, who presumes to defend the bloodthirsty Jews, saying that it is not true and plausible that they murder Christian children or use their blood, to the mockery and ridicule of the

authorities and all of Christendom . . ." Johannes Eck, *Ains Judenbuechlins Verlegung* (1524), fol. A Ivr, cited in Oberman, *Roots*, 17.
6 Trachtenberg, 125.
7 Toon, 115.
8 Parkes, ix.
9 Published by Wynkyn de Worde in 1524. See the English translation, *On the Three Languages [1524]* (Binghamton, N.Y.: Renaissance Society of America, 1989).
10 David Katz, *Philo-Semitism and the Readmission of the Jews to England, 1603–1655* (Oxford: Clarendon, 1982), 10. See further the introduction to the English translation of Wakefield, *On the Three Languages*.
11 See David Daiches, *The King James Version of the English Bible* (Chicago: University of Chicago Press, 1941).
12 Katz, 145.
13 Katz, 41.
14 As David Katz notes, "most early modern Englishmen, and the majority of scholars across Europe, believed that Adam and Eve spoke Hebrew in the Garden of Eden, and that this modern language was substantially the same as the one used by modern-day Jews." *Philo-Semitism*, 60.
15 Cecil Roth, *A History of the Jews in England* (Oxford: Oxford University Press, 1941), 149.
16 Roth, *A History of the Jews in England*, 149.
17 In his *History of the Jews in England*, Cecil Roth contends that, "The religious developments of the seventeenth century brought to their climax an unmistakable Philo-Semitic tendency in certain English circles," 148.
18 Richard H. Popkin demonstrates convincingly that the millenarian expectations sparked by the prophecies of Joachim de Fiore lay behind the expulsion of the Jews from Spain in 1492. This was also the driving force behind Archbishop Francisco Ximines de Cisneros' Inquisition activities. Popkin, "Jewish Christians and Christian Jews in Spain, 1492 and After," *Judaism* 41 (1992): 248–67.
19 Cecil Roth, *A Life of Menasseh Ben Israel: Rabbi, Printer, and Diplomat* (New York: Arno, 1975), 195.
20 For a discussion of Shabtai Sevi (or Sabbattai Zewi) see, e.g., Appendix III: "Eschatological Expectations Concerning the Conversion of the Jews in the Netherlands During the Seventeenth Century," in Toon, *Puritans*.
21 Katz, 44.
22 Thomas Draxe, *The Worldes Resurrection, Or the generall Calling of the Jews* . . . (London, 1608), 51, 88–91, 94. This was followed by L. Busher, *Religions Peace, or, a Plea for Liberty of Conscience* (London, 1615).
23 Toon, 116–17.
24 Toon, 116.
25 Toon, 117.
26 Katz, *Philo-Semitism*, 44, 103.

27  Popkin, "Some Aspects of Jewish-Christian Theological Interchanges in Holland and England, 1640–1700," in *Jewish-Christian Relations in the Seventeenth Century: Studies and Documents*, eds. J. van den Berg and Ernestine G. E. van der Wall (Dordrecht: Kluwer, 1988), 4–5.

28  For insight into their efforts see Ernestine G. E. van der Wall's "The Amsterdam Millenarian Petrus Serrarius (1600–1669) and the Anglo-Dutch Circle of Philo Judaists," in van den Berg and van der Wall, 73–94.

29  See Menasseh ben Israel's letter to European Jewry on the eve of his journey to England, cited in Toon, 112.

30  Roth observes, "It is impossible to fathom the entire complex of reasons that drove Cromwell himself in this direction, but the intensity of his personal interest in the question of the readmission of the Jews is certain." *History of the Jews in England*, 158.

31  Toon, 122.

32  Some of the most helpful analysis of the Whitehall Conference of 1655 may be found in Cecil Roth's *History of the Jews in England*, 149–72.

33  See Ernestine G. E. van der Wall's "A Philo-Semitic Millenarian on the Reconciliation of Jews and Christians: Henry Jessey and His 'The Glory and Salvation,'" in *Sceptics, Millenarians and Jews*, eds. David Katz and Jonathan I. Israel (Leiden: E. J. Brill, 1990), 161–84.

34  See H. D. Traill and J. S. Mann, eds., *Social England* (London: Cassell, 1953), 383.

35  Contrary to the widest opinion, David Katz points out that at the time of Whitehall there was speculation that Cromwell rejected the readmission of the Jews because their delegation had researched Cromwell's lineage to determine if he was himself of the Davidic line, and might therefore be the Messiah. In this line of reasoning, the resettlement was rejected to enable Cromwell to save a damaged reputation. See Katz, *The Jews in the History of England, 1485–1850* (Oxford: Clarendon, 1994), 207.

36  Roth argues that this gradual settlement worked in the best interest of the Jews in England in the long term, because it left no legislation which could later be overturned after the Restoration, and also avoided the formation of Jewish ghettos and, with them, the possibilities for persecution on the level of other European countries. *History of the Jews in England*, 171–72.

37  *A Loving Salutation to the Seed of Abraham* and the brief *Certain Queries to the Teachers and Rabbi's Among the Jews* were both published later in 1656, or in 1657.

38  See Kunze, particularly chap. 11, "Fell's Work to Convert the Jews."

39  Roth, *Menasseh*, 5.

40  For a chronological overview of this process in Portugal, see Roth's *Menasseh*, particularly chap. 1, "The Marrano Background."

41  See Roth, *Menasseh*, chap. 4, sec. 9, "Protection From the Inquisition."

42  Roth, *Menasseh*, 26–27.

43  Popkin, "Some Aspects," 5.

44  Roth, *History of the Jews in England*, 154.

45 Henry Joel Cadbury, "Hebraica and the Jews," in *Children of Light*, ed. Howard Brinton (New York: Macmillan, 1938), 156.
46 Roth, *Menasseh*, 38–39.
47 Roth, *Menasseh*, 183.
48 Cadbury, "Hebraica," 157.
49 Katz, *Philo-Semitism*, 5.
50 Roth, *Menasseh*, 185.
51 Toon, 118–19.
52 Roth, *Menasseh*, 187–89.
53 Katz, *Philo-Semitism*, 141
54 Roth, *Menasseh*, 190.
55 Menasseh ben Israel's letter to John Dury, quoted in Roth, *Menasseh*, 186.
56 The most noteworthy contribution in this vein was penned by Sir Edward Spencer. Published in London in 1650, the work was entitled *An Epistle to the learned Manasse ben Israel, in answer to his, dedicated to the Parliament*. Here as a Member of Parliament, Spenser sought to respond to the rabbi in publication, including in his discussion the question of resettlement of the Jews in England. See Roth, *Menasseh*, 193.
57 Popkin, "Some Aspects," passim.
58 Roth, *Menasseh*, 188.
59 For a translation of this letter in full, see Roth, *Menasseh*, 226.
60 Menassah ben Israel, quoted in Kunze, 211.
61 Popkin, *Spinoza's Earliest Publication*, 5.
62 Cadbury, "Hebraica," 135.
63 In addition to his work in Amsterdam, Fisher traveled with fellow Quaker scholar John Stubbs on a mission to convert the pope in Rome and the sultan in Constantinople. Popkin, *Spinoza's Earliest Publication*, 4–5.
64 Cadbury, "Hebraica," 147.
65 Cadbury, "Hebraica," 148.
66 Cadbury, "Hebraica," 140.
67 Popkin, *Spinoza's Earliest Publication*, 5.
68 Ross, 149.
69 Popkin, *Spinoza's Earliest Publication*, 5.
70 Cadbury, "Hebraica," 157.
71 Fell's 1664 *A Call to the Universal Seed of God* and her 1677 *The Daughter of Zion Awakened* are included by Isabel Ross in her discussion of Fell's epistles to the Jews (Ross, 89–97). Though these do include the Jewish people in their target audience, they are not written to the Jewish community alone. Bonnelyn Young Kunze does not include them for this reason.
72 Kunze lists *The Call of the Jews Out of Babylon* as Fell's first epistle to the Jewish people.
73 There is a possibility that these were published in 1656, though the 1657 date seems more likely. The standard work by Isabel Ross does not include the *Queries* as a separate publication. Kunze, 286.

74 On the surface it is unlikely that her work would have received his attention. Hers was not the only publication to address him, and it likely would not have been of particular interest to him given his own focus. At the same time, the Quakers were already active in a missionary context during his time in Holland and they made a concentrated effort to translate their material into Hebrew. Ben Israel himself ran the first Hebrew press in Holland, and so it is possible that he was aware of translated letters published for his attention. What we do know is that Fell took the attempt to communicate seriously, and for our purposes that is most relevant.

75 A loose quotation of Isaiah 61:1.

76 Fell, *For Manasseth-ben-Israel*, in *Works*, 101.

77 Isaiah 53:12.

78 Fell's translation. A more nuanced translation of the Isaiah 65 passages would not avail itself as easily of this reading. In the context of chapter 65, the verses are clearly directed to Israel, and speak of her unwillingness to seek God.

79 Fell, *For Manasseth-ben-Israel*, in *Works*, 102.

80 For some reason, Fell misidentifies her quotations from Deuteronomy 4:25-26 as being verses 18-19, though she correctly identifies the majority of the passage.

81 Fell, *For Manasseth-ben-Israel*, in *Works*, 104.

82 Fell, *For Manasseth-ben-Israel*, in *Works*, 104.

83 Fell, *For Manasseth-ben-Israel*, in *Works*, 104.

84 Fell, *For Manasseth-ben-Israel*, in *Works*, 106.

85 Isaiah 9:2; Fell, *For Manasseth-ben-Israel*, in *Works*, 107.

86 Fell, *For Manasseth-ben-Israel*, in *Works*, 109.

87 Fell, *For Manasseth-ben-Israel*, in *Works*, 117.

88 Fell, *For Manasseth-ben-Israel*, in *Works*, 110.

89 Fell, *For Manasseth-ben-Israel*, in *Works*, 120–21.

90 Fell, *For Manasseth-ben-Israel*, in *Works*, 109.

91 Fell, *For Manasseth-ben-Israel*, in *Works*, 123.

92 This appropriation of Jewish religious beliefs and the perceived connection with Jewish destiny are based primarily on the Bible, which has also been the source of many negative stereotypes of Jewish people. The image of Jews as disobedient and often idolatrous servants of God runs through the Old Testament. The New Testament gospels present Jewish religious leaders as the killers of Christ, and as whitewashed tombs that look clean on the outside but are filled with death on the inside.

93 Heiko A. Oberman argues in his work *The Roots of Anti-Semitism in the Age of Renaissance and Reformation* that, "Strictly speaking, 'anti-Semitism' did not exist prior to the race theory of the nineteenth century. Nevertheless, there are events, attitudes, or statements which long before the rise of the concept come very close to the reality of anti-Semitism"; xi.

## Chapter 5

1. See, e.g., Dandelion, Gwyn, and Peat, 217–19.
2. Cited by its most popular modern reprint, in Wallace; and also from her *Works*. According to the OCLC "WorldCat" database the Wallace edition is found in more libraries than any other reprint.
3. For an example of a survey of women in Christianity that touches upon Fell, see Ruth A. Tucker and Walter Liefeld, *Daughters of the Church: Women and Ministry from New Testament Times to the Present* (Grand Rapids: Zondervan, 1987); and for a survey of women in early modern English history, see Sara H. Mendelson and Patricia Crawford, *Women in Early Modern England, 1550–1720* (Oxford: Oxford University Press, 1998). See further Retha M. Warnicke, *Women of the English Renaissance and Reformation* (Westport, Conn.: Greenwood Press, 1983). For books that place Fell in the broad context of English religion, see Patricia Crawford, *Women and Religion in England, 1500–1720* (London: Routledge, 1993) and Mack, *Visionary Women*.
4. On this *querelle*, see Gisela Bock, *Women in European History* (Oxford: Blackwell, 2002).
5. For this debate and the larger Renaissance context, see Jane Dempsey Douglass, *Women, Freedom, and Calvin* (Philadelphia: Westminster, 1985), chap. 4.
6. For an extract in English, see Thomas Head, "Marie Dentière," in *Women Writers of the Renaissance and Reformation*, ed. Katharina M. Wilson (Athens: University of Georgia Press, 1987). See further Douglass, *Women*, 102–5.
7. For more on Ward, see Warnicke, chap. 9.
8. See Joyce L. Irwin, *Womanhood in Radical Protestantism, 1527–1675* (Lewiston, N.Y.: Edwin Mellen, 1975) and Hilary Hinds, *God's Englishwomen: Seventeenth-Century Radical Sectarian Writing and Feminist Criticism* (Manchester, UK: Manchester University Press, 1996).
9. See Mack, *Visionary Women*; and Stevie Davies, *Unbridled Spirits: Women of the English Revolution, 1640–1660* (London: Women's Press, 1998).
10. Mack, *Visionary Women*, 1.
11. She is also known by her maiden name (Audley) and her second married name, Douglas. See the modern collection of her writings, *The Prophetic Writings of Lady Eleanor Davies*, ed. Esther Cope (Oxford: Oxford University Press, 1995). See further Esther Cope, *Handmaid of the Holy Spirit: Dame Eleanor Davies* (Ann Arbor: University of Michigan Press, 1992).
12. See Emily Manners, *Elizabeth Hooton: First Quaker Woman Preacher (1600–1672)* (London: Headley Brothers, 1914).
13. Trevett, *Women and Quakerism*, 22. One of Hooton's last acts was to petition the king for the release of Margaret Fell.
14. These she most probably learned in the course of her husband's work as a judge.

15  Mack, *Visionary Women*, 1.
16  H. J. Cadbury, "George Fox and Women's Liberation," *Friends' Quarterly* 18 (1974): 370–76.
17  Trevett, *Women and Quakerism*; idem, *Quaker Women Prophets in England and Wales, 1650–1700* (Lewiston, N.Y.: Edward Mellen, 2000); Wilcox, *Theology*.
18  See the tract by Fox, *The Woman Learning in Silence* (1656), found in his *Gospel Truth Demonstrated in a Collection of Doctrinal Books* (London: T. Sowle, 1708), 77–82; and his open letter defending Women's Meetings, *An Epistle to All the People of the Earth*, repr. *Gospel Truth*, 91–102. Both are reprinted in Fox, *The Works of George Fox*, vol. 4.
19  The precursors to the Women's Meetings took place in London beginning in 1656 or 1657, largely in response to the needs of the poor and sick who attended Friends Meetings in search of assistance. The most significant of these meetings, known as the "Box Meeting," gathered together funds and resources for the support of the poor and those Friends suffering religious persecution. According to Isabel Ross, the Box Meeting has an unbroken record of minutes from the year 1671. Ross, 284.
20  Though George Fox is traditionally credited as the instigator of the Women's Meetings, Kunze makes a strong case for Margaret Fell as the primary force behind these gatherings. Kunze writes, "In light of the evidence on early women's meetings, it seems reasonable to suggest the hypothesis that the record neglects to assess the full impact of Fell's role in relation to Fox. George Fox was an itinerant, charismatic preacher who spent most of his adult life wandering about England and America, while Margaret Fell maintained her home base at Swarthmoor and hammered out, year in and year out, with her daughters and neighborhood Quaker women, an organization format that worked on a practical level and that borrowed from the experience and organization of the London Quaker Women's Meetings. It is reasonable to suggest that it was in keeping with Fell's personality, wealth, permanence of place, and organization skills learned in the domestic sphere, that she, and not Fox, was the main ideologue and instigator of the women's meeting outside London." Kunze, 167.
21  Kunze, 21.
22  Ross, 285.
23  Elisabeth Potts Brown and Susan Mosher Stuard, eds., *Witnesses for Change: Quaker Women Over Three Centuries* (New Brunswick, N.J.: Rutgers University Press, 1989), 15.
24  Ross, 282.
25  Barbour, *The Quakers in Puritan England*, 119–22.
26  Ross, 285.
27  Nayler's "triumphal entry" into Bristol and his subsequent imprisonment and trial did a great deal of damage to the movement. Not only was the event seized upon by Friends opponents, but some of Nayler's followers continued to draw attention to themselves by disrupting various Friends

meetings in England and abroad. See, for example, the mention of Ann Cargill, one of Nayler's followers who "went to Holland breaking up one Quaker meeting after another," in Popkin, *Spinoza's Earliest Publication*, 230.
28 Tucker and Liefeld, 230.
29 Kunze, 147–51.
30 Penn, in Ross, 288.
31 Ross, 177–78, 191.
32 Ross, 283.
33 Wallace, 61; *Works*, 331.
34 *Letters*, 59.
35 *The Woman Learning in Silence*, in *The Works of George Fox*, 4:109. Fell's work also follows a similar line of reasoning put forth by Richard Farnsworth in 1655. Kunze, 154.
36 See David J. Latt's introduction to his edition of *Womens Speaking Justified, Proved, and Allowed by the Scriptures, etc.* [1667], ed. David J. Latt, Augustan Reprint No. 194. (Los Angeles: Clarke Memorial Library, UCLA, 1979).
37 Wallace, 61; *Works*, 331.
38 Wallace, 61; *Works*, 331.
39 Wilcox emphasizes this aspect of their theology in her study (*Theology and Women's Ministry*).
40 Wallace, 62; *Works*, 332.
41 Wallace, 64; *Works*, 332.
42 Wallace, 67; *Works*, 337.
43 Wallace, 66; *Works*, 335.
44 Wallace, 67; *Works*, 337.
45 Wallace, 68; *Works*, 338.
46 Wallace, 69; *Works*, 340.
47 Wallace, 68; *Works*, 338.
48 Wallace, 68; *Works*, 338.
49 Wallace, 69; *Works*, 339.
50 Wallace, 69; *Works*, 340.
51 Wallace, 70; *Works*, 341.
52 Wilcox, passim.
53 Wilcox, 235.
54 See chap. 3, above.
55 Wilcox, 28. For a Christological reading of the Light in the theology of George Fox, see Gwyn, *Apocalypse*, chap. 3 and 4.
56 See, e.g., Ben Pink Dandelion's "Fresh Light, Dimmer Hopes," in Dandelion, Gwyn, and Peat, 159–66.
57 Here I reference the influential Quaker historian Hugh Barbour:
> The writings of the first Friends have been for three centuries a treasury of personal religious experiences and dramatic narratives. In our time, converted evangelicals, secular radicals, ethical reformers and modern

mystics have each seen early Friends in their own image. All these groups share a central concern for Friends' intense and joyful directness of experience and ethical commitment and creativity, but each group sees in original Quakerism what corresponds to its members' own experiences of radically inward worship and apocalyptic social change. Yet we do not "create Quaker History," but, according to our varied abilities, we listen sensitively to whatever people partly different from ourselves tell us in their own languages about their events, ideas and experiences, trying to share them as we write about them. Barbour, "Sixty Years in Early Quaker History," in *The Creation of Quaker Theory: Insider Perspectives*, ed. Dandelion, 19.

58  Mack, 239.
59  Mack, 301.
60  Wilcox notes these changes in the final chapter of her book (chap. 6). See also Mack, 265–402; Trevett, *Women and Quakerism*, 130–31.
61  Trevett, *Women and Quakerism*, 130–31.
62  For an historical overview of war and peace in Christian thought, see Roland H. Bainton, *Christian Attitudes Toward War and Peace* (New York: Abingdon, 1960).
63  Meredith Baldwin Weddle, *Walking in the Way of Peace: Quaker Pacifism in the Seventeenth Century* (Oxford: Oxford University Press, 2001), 57.
64  Hugh Barbour and J. W. Frost, *The Quakers* (New York: Greenwood Press, 1988), 45.
65  He claimed, "I lived in the virtue of that life and power that took away the occasion of all wars." Fox, *Journal*, ed. Nickalls, 65. See further Weddle, 40–43; Barbour and Frost, 45–46.
66  E.g., Fox wrote to William Penn in 1674 asking him to look after a young army officer of the aristocracy who had become a convinced Friend. Weddle, 59.
67  Barbour and Frost, 45. See the reprint in Barbour and Roberts, *Early Quaker Writings*, 102–16.
68  For more about James Nayler and his "fall," see Braithwaite, *Beginnings*, 271–88; and more recently, Rosemary Moore, *The Light in Their Consciences: The Early Quakers in Britain, 1646–1666* (University Park: Pennsylvania State University Press, 2000), chap. 3; and especially Loepold Damrosch, *The Sorrows of the Quaker Jesus: James Nayler and the Puritan Crackdown on the Free Spirit* (Cambridge, Mass.: Harvard University Press, 1996).
69  E.g., the close relationship between Nayler and the Fell family generally is evidenced by the greetings of Judge Fell conveyed to Nayler via Fell's letter. The letter was later published in *Works*, 51–53; but the section concerning Judge Fell is missing from that and was found only in the Spence (now in the published *Letters*, 25).

70  Moore, 35.
71  Barbour and Roberts, 106.
72  Barbour and Roberts, 105.
73  W. Alan Cole, "The Quakers and the English Revolution," *Past and Present* 10 (1956): 42.
74  H. Larry Ingle's claim that Fox in fact "composed the first public version of what would become known among his followers as the 'Peace Testimony'" in a letter to Oliver Cromwell in 1654, is flawed (*First Among Friends*, 121). First of all, this was never a public document. This letter was never published, and thus was not "public" in any real sense (it remained in manuscript form until 1911). What is more, it is a declaration of Fox's intention, not a statement of principle for Quakers. This much is clear even from Ingle's summary of the letter (121–22); see the modern publication of it in George Fox, *The Journal of George Fox*, ed. Norman Penney (Cambridge: Cambridge University Press, 1911), 1:161–62.
75  From an unpublished letter to John Archer, *Letters*, 49.
76  *Letters*, 431.
77  As T. H. S. Wallace notes, "she began the arduous journey to London . . . to foster good will with the new government and to seek a remedy for the persecution of Quakers throughout the nation. She could not foresee that she was entering upon one of the most active and significant decades of her ministry, a decade that would see the initial success of her mission, followed by some of the most distressing persecution of friends." Wallace, 44.
78  Wallace, 44.
79  Wallace, 55; *Works*, 210.
80  Wallace, 55; *Works*, 210.
81  Wallace, 49; *Works*, 202.
82  Wallace, 51; *Works*, 205.
83  Wallace, 49–50; *Works*, 203.
84  Wallace, 49; *Works*, 202.
85  Wallace, 52; *Works*, 203.
86  Wallace, 53; *Works*, 207.
87  Wallace, 54; *Works*, 208–209 (brackets in original).
88  As Tucker and Liefeld have noted, Fell "was an outstanding apologist for the movement during the early years, and her policy positions became an integral part of Quaker belief." *Daughters of the Church*, 230.
89  Dandelion, Gwyn, and Peat, 1.

# Bibliography

## Works by Margaret Fell

### Published

*A Brief Collection of Remarkable Passages and Occurrences Relating to the Birth, Education, Life, Conversion, Travels, Services, and Deep Sufferings of That Ancient, Eminent, and Faithful Servant of the Lord, Margaret Fell, But By Her Second Marriage, Margaret Fox.* London: J. Sowle, 1710.

*False Prophets, Antichrists, Deceivers Which are in the World . . .* London: Giles Calvert, 1655.

*A Sincere and Constant Love.* Edited by T. H. S. Wallace. Richmond, Ind.: Friends United Press, 1992.

*Some Ranter Principles Answered.* London, 1656. Also reprinted in Wallace, 85–96.

*Spinoza's Earliest Publication?: The Hebrew Translation of Margaret Fell's "A Loving Salutation to the Seed of Abraham among the Jews, wherever they are scattered up and down upon the Face of the Earth."* Edited by Richard H. Popkin and Michael A. Signer. Assen: Van Gorcum, 1987.

*The Standard of the Lord Revealed.* London, 1667.

*To the General Councel and Officers of the Army . . .* London: Th. Simmons, 1659.

*Undaunted Zeal: The Letters of Margaret Fell.* Edited by Elsa F. Glines. Richmond, Ind.: Friends United Press, 2003.

*Womens Speaking Justified, Proved, and Allowed by the Scriptures, etc.* [1667]. Edited by David J. Latt. Augustan Reprint No. 194. Los Angeles: Clarke Memorial Library, UCLA, 1979.

### Unpublished Manuscripts

Spence Manuscripts. 3 volumes. Friends House Library, London.

## Other Works Cited

Adler, Michael. *Jews of Medieval England.* London: Jewish Historical Society of England, 1939.

Andrew, Edward G. *Conscience and Its Critics: Protestant Conscience, Enlightenment Reason and Modern Subjectivity.* Toronto: University of Toronto Press, 2001.

Ash, James. "Oh No, It's Not the Scriptures." *Quaker History* 63 (1974): 97–107.

Austin, M. R. "Bible and Event in the *Journal* of George Fox." *Journal of Theological Studies* n.s., 32 (1991): 82–100.

Aylmer, G. E., ed. *The Levellers in the English Revolution.* London: Thames and Hudson, 1975.

———, ed. *The Interregnum: The Quest for Settlement, 1646–1660.* Hamden, Conn.: Shoestring Press, 1972.

Bacon, Francis. *The Works of Francis Bacon.* Edited by James Spedding, Robert Ellis, and Douglas Heath. London: Longman, 1974.

Bacon, Margaret Hope. *Mothers of Feminism: The Story of Quaker Women in America.* San Francisco: Harper & Row, 1986.

Bailey, Richard G. "Research Note on Judge Thomas Fell (1598–1658)." *Journal of the Friends' Historical Society* 57 (1994): 1–5.

Bainton, Roland H. *Christian Attitudes Toward War and Peace.* New York: Abingdon, 1960.

Ball, Bryan W. *A Great Expectation: Eschatological Thought in English Protestantism to 1660.* Leiden: E. J. Brill, 1975.

———. *The Seventh-Day Men: Sabbatarians and Sabbatarianism in England and Wales 1600–1800.* Oxford: Oxford University Press, 1994.

Barbour, Hugh. *The Quakers in Puritan England.* New Haven: Yale University Press, 1964.

———, and J. W. Frost. *The Quakers.* New York: Greenwood Press, 1988.

———, and Arthur Roberts, eds. *Early Quaker Writings, 1650–1700.* Grand Rapids: Eerdmans, 1973.

Baylor, Michael G. *Action and Person: Conscience in Late Scholasticism and the Young Luther.* Leiden: E. J. Brill, 1977.

Beck, William, and T. F. Ball, *The London Friends' Meetings.* London: Kitto, 1869.

Beuken, Wim, Seán Freyne, and Anton Weiler, eds. *Messianism Through History.* London: SCM Press, 1993.

Blackwood, Bruce G. *The Lancashire Gentry and the Great Rebellion, 1640–660.* Manchester, UK: Manchester University Press, 1978.

Bock, Gisela. *Women in European History.* Oxford: Blackwell, 2002.

Brailsford, H. N. *The Levellers and the English Revolution.* Stanford: Stanford University Press, 1961.

Braithwaite, Alfred W. "The Mystery of Swarthmoor Hall," *Journal of the Friends' Historical Society* 51 (1965): 22–29.
Braithwaite, William C. *The Beginnings of Quakerism*. 2nd ed. Cambridge: Cambridge University Press, 1955.
———. *The Second Period of Quakerism*. 2nd ed. Cambridge: Cambridge University Press, 1955.
Bridenbaugh, Carl. *Vexed and Troubled Englishmen, 1590–1642*. Oxford: Oxford University Press, 1967.
Brinton, Howard H., ed. *Children of Light*. New York: Macmillan, 1938.
Brockway, Fenner. *Britain's First Socialists: The Levellers, Agitators and Diggers of the English Revolution*. London: Quartet Books, 1980.
Brown, Elisabeth Potts, and Susan Mosher Stuard, eds. *Witnesses for Change: Quaker Women Over Three Centuries*. New Brunswick, N.J.: Rutgers University Press, 1989.
Brown, Louise Fargo. *The Political Activities of the Baptists and Fifth Monarchy Men in England During the Interregnum*. New York: Burt Franklin, 1911.
Busher, L. *Religions Peace, or, a Plea for Liberty of Conscience*. London, 1615.
Cadbury, H. J. "George Fox and Women's Liberation." *Friends' Quarterly* 18 (1974): 370–76.
Camm, Thomas. "Testimony Concerning our Dear and Honoured Friend Margaret Fox." In Fell, *Works*, A3–6.
Capp, Bernard S. *The Fifth Monarchy Men: A Study in Seventeenth-Century English Millenarianism*. London: Macmillan, 1972.
Carlson, Eric Josef, ed. *Religion and the English People, 1500–1640: New Voices, New Perspectives*. Kirksville, Mo.: Thomas Jefferson University Press, 1998.
Caton, William. *A Journal of the Life of Will. Caton*. London, 1689.
Christianson, Paul. *Reformers and Babylon: English Apocalyptic Visions from the Reformation to the Eve of the Civil War*. Toronto: University of Toronto Press, 1978.
Clement, C. J. *Religious Radicalism in England, 1535–1565*. Carlisle, UK: Paternoster Press, 1997.
Cobb, Ronald Lee. "George Fox and Quaker-Baptist Controversy." *Foundations: A Baptist Journal of History and Theology* 14 (1971): 236–39.
Cole, W. Alan. "The Quakers and the English Revolution." *Past and Present* 10 (1956): 39–54.
Cope, Esther. *Handmaid of the Holy Spirit: Dame Eleanor Davies*. Ann Arbor: University of Michigan Press, 1992.
Crawford, Patricia. *Women and Religion in England, 1500–1720*. London: Routledge, 1993.
Cressy, David. *Literacy and the Social Order: Reading and Writing in Tudor and Stuart England*. Cambridge: Cambridge University Press, 1980.
Crosfield, Helen G. *Margaret Fox of Swarthmoor Hall*. London: Headley Brothers, 1913.

Daiches, David. *The King James Version of the English Bible*. Chicago: University of Chicago Press, 1941.

Damrosch, Leopold. *The Sorrows of the Quaker Jesus: James Nayler and the Puritan Crackdown on the Free Spirit*. Cambridge, Mass.: Harvard University Press, 1996.

Dandelion, Ben Pink. *A Sociological Analysis of the Theology of Quakers: The Silent Revolution*. Lewiston, N.Y.: Edwin Mellen, 1996.

———. *The Creation of Quaker Theory: Insider Perspectives*. Aldershot, UK: Ashgate, 2004.

———. *An Introduction to Quakerism*. Cambridge: Cambridge University Press, 2007.

Dandelion, Ben Pink, Douglas Gwyn, and Timothy Peat. *Heaven on Earth: Quakers and the Second Coming*. Birmingham, UK: Woodbrooke College, 1998.

Davies, Adrian. *The Quakers in English Society, 1655–1725*. Oxford: Oxford University Press, 2000.

Davies, Lady Eleanor. *The rophetic Writings of Lady Eleanor Davies*. Edited by Esther Cope. Oxford: Oxford University Press, 1995.

Davies, Stevie. *Unbridled Spirits: Women of the English Revolution, 1640–1660*. London: Women's Press, 1998.

Despland, Michael. "Conscience." In *The Encyclopedia of Religion*. Edited by M. Eliade, 4:45–52. New York: Free Press, 1990.

Douglass, Jane Dempsey. *Women, Freedom, and Calvin*. Philadelphia: Westminster, 1985.

Douglass, Jane Dempsey, and E. Earle Cairns, eds. *The New International Dictionary of the Christian Church*. Grand Rapids: Zondervan, 1978.

Draxe, Thomas. *The Worldes Resurrection, Or the generall Calling of the Jews, A familiar Commentary upon the eleventh Chapter of Saint Paul to the Romaines, according to the sence of Scripture*. London, 1608.

Edwards, Thomas. *Gangraena*. 1646. Reprint of 3 parts in 1 vol. Exeter: University of Exeter Press, 1977.

Eeg-Olofsson, Leif. *The Conception of the Inner Light in Robert Barclay's Theology: A Study in Quakerism*. Lund: C. W. K. Gleerup, 1954.

Firth, Katherine R. *The Apocalyptic Tradition in Reformation Britain, 1530–1645*. Oxford: Oxford University Press, 1979.

Force, James E., and Richard H. Popkin, eds. *The Books of Nature and Scripture: Recent Essays on Natural Philosophy, Theology, and Biblical Criticism in the Netherlands of Spinoza's Time and the British Isles of Newton's Time*. Dordrecht: Kluwer, 1994.

Fox, George. *Gospel Truth Demonstrated in a Collection of Doctrinal Books*. London: T. Sowle, 1708.

———. *The Journal of George Fox*. Edited by John L. Nickalls. Cambridge: Cambridge University Press, 1952.

———. *The Journal of George Fox*. Edited by Norman Penney. 2 vols. Cambridge: Cambridge University Press, 1911.

———. *Newes coming up out of the North, Sounding towards the South*. London, 1654.

———. *The Works of George Fox*. 8 vols. Philadelphia: M. T. C. Gould, 1831.

Frank, J. *The Levellers: A History of the Writings of Three Seventeenth-Century Social Democrats: John Lilburne, Richard Overton, William Walwyn*. Cambridge, Mass.: Harvard University Press, 1955.

Freiday, Dean, ed. *The Day of the Lord: Eschatology in Quaker Perspective*. Newberg, Ore.: Barclay Press, 1981.

Garman, Mary, ed. *Hidden in Plain Sight: Quaker Women's Writings, 1650–1700*. Wallingford, Pa.: Pendle Hill, 1996.

Gentles, Ian. *The New Model Army in England, Ireland and Scotland, 1645–1653*. Oxford: Blackwell, 1992.

Gilsdorf, Joy. *The Puritan Apocalypse: New England Eschatology in the Seventeenth Century*. New York: Garland, 1989.

Gundry-Volf, J. M. "Conscience." In *Dictionary of Paul and His Letters*. Edited by G. F. Hawthorne and Ralph P. Martin, with associate editor Daniel G. Reid. Downers Grove, Ill.: InterVarsity, 1993.

Gwyn, Douglas. *Apocalypse of the Word: The Life and Message of George Fox (1624–1691)*. Richmond, Ind.: Friends United Press, 1984.

———. *Seekers Found: Atonement in Early Quaker Experience*. Wallingford, Pa.: Pendle Hill, 2000.

Haller, William. *The Elect Nation: The Meaning and Relevance of Foxe's Book of Martyrs*. New York: Harper & Row, 1963.

Headley, John M. *Luther's View of Church History*. New Haven: Yale University Press, 1963.

Hill, Christopher. *Antichrist in Seventeenth-Century England*. Oxford: Oxford University Press, 1971.

———. *The Experience of Defeat: Milton and Some Contemporaries*. New York: Viking, 1984.

———. *The World Turned Upside Down: Radical Ideas During the English Revolution*. New York: Penguin, 1972.

Hinds, Hilary. *God's Englishwomen: Seventeenth-Century Radical Sectarian Writing and Feminist Criticism*. Manchester, UK: Manchester University Press, 1996.

Hirst, Derek. *Authority and Conflict: England 1603–1658*. London: Edward Arnold, 1986.

Holorenshaw, Henry. *The Levellers and the English Revolution*. New York: H. Fertig, 1971.

Humpa, Bonnie Jo. "The Other Half's Story: Different But Equal in Importance. Margaret Fell Fox: Seventeenth-Century Religious, Social, and Political Influence." M.A. thesis, University of Texas at Arlington, 1996.

Ingle, H. Larry. *First Among Friends: George Fox and the Creation of Quakerism.* Oxford: Oxford University Press, 1994.

Irwin, Joyce L. *Womanhood in Radical Protestantism, 1527–1675.* Lewiston, N.Y.: Edwin Mellen, 1975.

Jones, Richard Foster. *The Seventeenth Century: Studies in the History of English Thought and Literature from Bacon to Pope.* With others writing in his honor. Stanford: Stanford University Press, 1951.

Jones, Rufus M. *Studies in Mystical Religion.* London: Macmillan, 1909.

———. *Mysticism and Democracy in the English Commonwealth.* Cambridge, Mass.: Harvard University Press, 1932.

Katz, David S. *The Jews in the History of England, 1485–1850.* Oxford: Clarendon, 1994.

———. *Philo-Semitism and the Readmission of the Jews to England, 1603–1655.* Oxford: Clarendon, 1982.

———. *Sabbath and Sectarianism in Seventeenth-Century England.* Leiden: E. J. Brill, 1988.

Katz, David S., and Jonathan I. Israel, eds. *Sceptics, Millenarians, and Jews.* Leiden: E. J. Brill, 1990.

Kelly, Kevin T. *Conscience: Dictator or Guide? A Study in Seventeenth-Century English Moral Theology.* London: G. Chapman, 1967.

Klaassen, Walter. *Living at the End of the Ages: Apocalyptic Expectation in the Radical Reformation.* Lanham, Md.: University Press of America, 1992.

Kunze, Bonnelyn Young. *Margaret Fell and the Rise of Quakerism.* Stanford: Stanford University Press, 1994.

Larson, Rebecca. *Daughters of Light: Quaker Women Preaching and Prophesying in the Colonies and Abroad, 1700–1775.* New York: Alfred A. Knopf, 1999.

Liechty, Daniel. *Sabbatarianism in the Sixteenth Century: A Page in the History of the Radical Reformers.* Berrien Springs, Mich.: Andrews University Press, 1993.

Loades, David, ed. *John Foxe and the English Reformation.* Hants, UK: Scholar Press, 1997.

Luther, Martin. *Luther's Works: American Edition.* 55 vols. Edited by J. Pelikan, et al. St. Louis: Concordia Publishing House, and Philadelphia: Fortress, 1955–1986.

McClendon, Muriel, Joseph P. Ward, and Michael McDonald, eds. *Protestant Identities: Religion, Society and Self-Fashioning in Post-Reformation England.* Stanford: Stanford University Press, 1999.

McGinn, Bernard, ed. *The Encyclopedia of Apocalypticism.* Vol. 2, *Apocalypticism in Western History and Culture.* New York: Continuum, 1998.

McGregor, J. F., and B. Reay, eds. *Radical Religion in the English Revolution.* Oxford: Oxford University Press, 1984.

Mack, Phyllis. *Visionary Women: Ecstatic Prophecy in Seventeenth-Century England.* Berkeley: University of California Press, 1992.

Manners, Emily. *Elizabeth Hooton: First Quaker Woman Preacher (1600–1672)*. London: Headley Brothers, 1914.

Manuel, F. *The Religion of Issac Newton*. Oxford: Oxford University Press, 1974.

Mendelson, Sara H., and Patricia Crawford. *Women in Early Modern England, 1550–1720*. Oxford: Oxford University Press, 1998.

Moore, Rosemary. *The Light in Their Consciences: The Early Quakers in Britain, 1646–1666*. University Park: Pennsylvania State University Press, 2000.

Morgan, Kenneth, ed. *The Oxford Illustrated History of Britain*. Oxford: Oxford University Press, 1984.

Morgan, Nicholas. *Lancashire Quakers and the Establishment, 1760–1830*. Halifax, UK: Ryburn Academic, 1993.

Morton, A. L. *The World of the Ranters: Religious Radicalism in the English Reformation*. London: Lawrence & Wishart, 1970.

Mullett, Michael. "George Fox and the Origins of Quakerism." *History Today* 41 (1991): 26–31.

———, ed. *New Light on George Fox, 1624–1691*. York: Ebor Press, 1993.

Newton, Isaac. *Isaac Newton's Observations on the Prophecies of Daniel and the Apocalypse of St. John*. Edited by S. J. Barnett. Introduction by Mary E. Mills. 2 vols. Lewiston, N.Y.: Edwin Mellen, 1999.

Oberman, Heiko A. *The Roots of Anti-Semitism in the Age of Renaissance and Reformation*. Translated by J. I. Porter. Philadelphia: Fortress, 1984.

Oliver, W. H. *Prophets and Millennialists: The Uses of Biblical Prophecy in England from the 1790s to the 1840s*. Auckland: Auckland University Press, 1978.

Olsen, V. Norskov. *John Foxe and the Elizabethan Church*. Berkeley: University of California Press, 1973.

Parkes, James W. *The Jew in the Medieval Community: A Study of His Political and Economic Situation*. New York: Hermon, 1976.

Penney, Norman. "George Fell and the Story of Swarthmoor Hall." 3 parts. *Journal of the Friends' Historical Society* 29 (1932): 51–61; 30 (1933): 28–39; and 31 (1934): 27–35.

Popkin, Richard H. "Jewish Christians and Christian Jews in Spain, 1492 and After." *Judaism* 41 (1992): 248–67.

———. "The Lost Tribes, the Caraites and the English Millenarians." *Journal of Jewish Studies* 37 (1986): 213–27.

———, ed. *Millenarianism and Messianism in English Literature and Thought, 1650–1800*. Leiden: E. J. Brill, 1988.

Rawlinson, Thomas. *[A book to] goe abroad onely amon all Friends in the Truth [in answer] to seuerall papers of Margaret Foxe*. London, 1667.

Reay, Barry. *The Quakers and the English Revolution*. New York: St. Martin's Press, 1985.

Robertson, D. B. *The Religious Foundations of Leveller Democracy*. New York: King's Crown Press, 1951.

Rogers, P. G. *The Fifth Monarchy Men*. Oxford: Oxford University Press, 1966.

Ross, Isabel. *Margaret Fell: Mother of Quakerism*. London: Longmans, 1949.
Roth, Cecil. *A History of the Jews in England*. Oxford: Oxford University Press, 1941.
———. *A Life of Menasseh Ben Israel: Rabbi, Printer, and Diplomat*. New York: Arno, 1975.
Schultz, Joseph P. *Judaism and the Gentile Faiths: Comparative Studies in Religion*. Rutherford, N.J.: Fairleigh Dickinson University Press, 1981.
Sharman, C. W. "George Fox and His Family." 2 parts. *Quaker History* 74 (1985): 1–19 and 75 (1986): 1–11.
Shaw, Howard. *The Levellers*. New York: Harper & Row, 1968.
Smith, Nigel, ed. *A Collection of Ranter Writings from the Seventeenth Century*. London: Junction Books, 1983.
Smith, Robert Michael. "Christian Judaizers in Early Stuart England." *Historical Magazine of the Protestant Episcopal Church* 52 (1983): 125–33.
Society of Friends, The. *The Life of Margaret Fox, Wife of George Fox, Compiled From Her Own Narrative, and Other Sources, With A Selection From Her Epistles, Etc*. Philadelphia: Association of Friends for the Diffusion of Religion and Useful Knowledge, 1859.
St. Clair, Michael J. *Millenarian Movements in Historical Context*. New York: Garland, 1992.
Taylor, Ernest E. *The Valiant Sixty*. London: Bannisdale Press, 1947.
Taylor, Phillip A. M., ed. *The Origins of the English Civil War*. Englewood: D. C. Heath, 1960.
T. M. [Thomas Mounsey]. *A Brief Account of Thomas Fell, of Swarthmore Hall*. Manchester, UK: Wm. Irwin, 1846.
Toon, Peter, ed. *Puritans, the Millennium and the Future of Israel: Purtian Eschatology 1600 to 1660*. Cambridge: J. Clarke, 1970.
Trachtenberg, Joshua. *The Devil and the Jews: The Medieval Conception of the Jew and its Relation to Modern Anti-Semitism*. Philadelphia: Jewish Publication Society of America, 1961.
Traill, H. D., and J. S. Mann, eds. *Social England: A Record of the Progress of the People in Religion, Laws, Learning, Arts, Industry, Commerce, Science, Literature and Manners, From the Earliest Times to the Present Day*. London: Cassell, 1953.
Trevelyan, G. M. *History of England*. 2 vols. New York: Longmans, 1956.
Trevett, Christine. *Quaker Women Prophets in England and Wales, 1650–1700*. Lewiston, N.Y.: Edwin Mellen, 2000.
———. *Women and Quakerism in the Seventeenth Century*. York: Ebor Press, 1991.
Tucker, Ruth A., and Walter Liefeld. *Daughters of the Church: Women and Ministry from New Testament Times to the Present*. Grand Rapids: Zondervan, 1987.
Tuveson, E. L. *Millennium and Utopia: A Study in the Background of the Idea of Progress*. New York: Harper & Row, 1964.

Ullmann, Richard K. *Between God and History: The Human Situation Exemplified in Quaker Thought and Practice*. London: George Allen and Unwin, 1959.

Van den Berg, J., and Ernestine G. E. van der Wall, eds. *Jewish-Christian Relations in the Seventeenth Century: Studies and Documents*. Dordrecht: Kluwer, 1988.

Vipont, Elfrida. *George Fox and the Valiant Sixty*. London: Hamilton, 1975.

Wakefield, Robert. *On the Three Languages [1524]*. Edited and translated by G. Lloyd Jones. Binghamton, N.Y.: Renaissance Society of America, 1989.

Warnicke, Retha M. *Women of the English Renaissance and Reformation*. Westport, Conn.: Greenwood Press, 1983.

Webb, Maria. *The Fells of Swarthmoor Hall and their Friends*. 2nd ed. Philadelphia: H. Longstreth, 1884.

Webster, Charles, ed. *Samuel Hartlib and the Advancement of Learning*. Cambridge: Cambridge University Press, 1970.

———. *The Intellectual Revolution of the Seventeenth Century*. London: Routledge and Kegan Paul, 1974.

Weddle, Meredith Baldwin. *Walking in the Way of Peace: Quaker Pacifism in the Seventeenth Century*. Oxford: Oxford University Press, 2001.

Wilcox, Catherine M. *Theology and Women's Ministry in Seventeenth-Century English Quakerism: Handmaids of the Lord*. Lewiston, N.Y.: Edwin Mellen, 1995.

Williams, George H. "Protestants in the Ukraine During the Period of the Polish-Lithuanian Commonwealth." *Harvard Ukrainian Studies* 2 (1978): 41–72.

Wilson, Katharina, ed. *Women Writers of the Renaissance and Reformation*. Athens: University of Georgia Press, 1987.

Zachman, Randall C. *The Assurance of Faith: Conscience in the Theology of Martin Luther and John Calvin*. Minneapolis: Fortress, 1993.

# Scripture Index

## Old Testament

| | |
|---|---|
| Genesis | 47, 149 |
| 1 | 149 |
| 3:13 | 149 |
| 3:14 | 36 |
| Exodus | 49 |
| Deuteronomy | 151 |
| 4:25-28 | 137, 192n80 |
| 4:42-31 | 131 |
| 28:64-68 | 131 |
| Psalms | 47 |
| 37 | 99 |
| Isaiah | 47, 135, 137–39, 149 |
| 51:17 | 139 |
| 53:1 | 135 |
| 53:3 | 136 |
| 53:12 | 192n77 |
| 54:13 | 149 |
| 56 | 136 |
| 61 | 136 |
| 61:1 | 192n75 |
| 65:1-12 | 135–36, 192n78 |
| Daniel | 60, 69, 105, 124, 144, 156 |
| 12:7 | 131 |
| Joel | |
| 2 | 153 |
| 2:28 | 149 |
| 2:28-29 | 48, 152 |

## New Testament

| | |
|---|---|
| Luke | |
| 24:23 | 74 |
| John | 47, 139 |
| 1 | 83–84 |
| 1:9 | 153, 184n64 |
| Acts | |
| 2 | 153 |
| 2:17 | 48 |
| 2:16-21 | 152 |
| 1 Corinthians | 151 |
| 14 | 149 |
| Galatians | 11, 86 |
| Ephesians | |
| 5 | 153 |
| 1 Timothy | 151 |
| 2 | 149 |
| 2:8-16 | 152 |
| James | |
| 2:16 | 107 |
| 1, 2, 3 John | 139 |
| Revelation | 47, 72, 62, 152, 156 |
| 12 | 15 |

# Index of Names

*Historical Figures and Authors*

Abraham, Daniel, 54, 175n102
Ames, William, 33
Andrew, Edward, 182n4
Archer, John, 158, 197n74
Askew, John, 34, 173n59

Bacon, Francis, 123
Bailey, Richard, 171nn11, 12
Bainton, Roland, 196n62
Bale, John, 15, 60–62, 177n13
Ball, Bryan, 178nn25, 26, 179nn28, 35, 36, 43, 47, 180nn47, 51, 52, 54
Ball, T. F., 176n135
Barbour, Hugh, 156, 171n14, 181nn87, 88, 96, 100, 103, 106, 194n25, 195n57, 196nn64, 65, 67, 197nn71, 72
Barclay, Robert, 58, 132, 183n14
Baylor, Michael, 182nn4, 7
Beck, William, 176n135
Blackwood, Bruce, 172n26
Bock, Gisela, 193n4
Brabourne, Theopilus, 64–65
Brailsford, H. N., 180nn68, 72
Braithwaite, William, 12, 170n9, 175n100, 176nn123, 129, 133, 135, 177nn150, 151, 182n108, 196n68

Bridenbaugh, Carl, 178n23
Brightman, Thomas, 179n26
Brinton, Howard, 191n45
Brockway, Fenner, 68, 180n71
Brown, Elisabeth, 146, 194n23
Bunyan, John, 16
Busher, Leonard, 189n22

Cadbury, Henry J., 128, 132, 134, 145, 177n52, 191nn45, 48, 62, 64–66, 70, 194n16
Calvin, John, 80, 182n7
Camm, Thomas, 14, 29–30, 170n10, 173nn 36, 37, 40
Capp, Bernard, 175n98, 181nn77, 78, 83, 101
Caton, William, 28, 57, 98, 132, 159, 172n28, 177n2
Cecil, Robert, 25
Charles I, 1, 67, 70, 144, 171n13
Charles II, 12, 28, 41–42, 45, 47, 54–55, 67, 73, 80, 158–59, 182n2
Christianson, Paul, 178nn13–15, 24, 179nn29, 33, 180nn56, 70
Clement VII (Pope), 59
Clement, C. J., 179n41
Clouse, R., 179n27

210

Cole, W. Alan, 157, 197n73
Cope, Esther, 193n11
Cranmer, Thomas, 59
Crawford, Patricia, 193n3
Cressy, David, 171n6
Cromwell, Oliver, Lord Protector, 1, 27, 31, 38–39, 41, 63, 68–80, 86, 101, 124, 126, 131, 133, 156, 173n44, 182n2, 190nn30, 35, 197n74
Cromwell, Thomas, 59
Crosfield, Helen, 7–10, 169n4

Daiches, David, 189n11
Damrosch, Leopold, 196n68
Dandelion, Ben Pink, xi, 162, 171n8, 187n180, 193n1, 195n56, 196n57, 197n89
Davies, Eleanor, 19, 144–45, 193n11
Davies, Stephen, 193n9
Dent, Arthur, 179n26
Dentière, Marie, 18, 143–44, 193n6
Despland, Michael, 182n4
Douglass, Jane, 193nn5, 6
Draxe, Thomas, 125, 189n22

Edward I, 18, 122
Edwards, Thomas, 31, 170n11
Eeg-Olofsson, L., 183n14
Elizabeth I, 18, 61, 64, 142

Farnsworth, Richard, 148, 174n61, 195n35
Fell, George, 51–52, 176n127
Fell, Margaret, *passim*
Fell, Rachel (Rachel Abraham), 49, 52–54
Fell, Sarah (Sarah Meade), 8, 53, 54, 132
Fell, Susannah, 54
Fell, Thomas, 3, 5, 13–14, 22–28, 30, 33, 41, 51, 171nn11, 13, 172n28, 196n69
Field, John, 178n18

Fiore, Joachim de, 189n18
Fox, George, 1–10, 13–14, 17, 22–39, 44–45, 49–57, 71–74, 77–79, 98, 101, 132–33, 136, 144–49, 156–59, 172nn24, 28, 174nn60, 67, 181n93, 194nn18, 20, 195nn35, 55, 197n74
Frank, J., 180n75, 181n76
Frost, J. W., 196n64, 65, 67

Garman, Mary, 181n106
Gentles, Ian, 180nn59, 60, 62, 63
Gilsdorf, Joy, 177n11
Gundry-Volf, Judy, 79, 182n6
Gwyn, Douglas, xi, 6, 33–35, 72, 173nn44, 47–49, 51, 54, 174n62, 176n126, 180n64, 181nn91, 93, 183n14, 187n180, 193n1, 195nn55, 56, 197n89

Haller, William, 177n9, 178n21
Head, Thomas, 193n6
Headley, John, 177n10
Henry VIII, 14–15, 58–59, 164
Hill, Christopher, 175n115, 177n2, 178nn18, 19, 179n37, 180n55, 181n80
Hinds, Hilary, 193n8
Holorenshaw, H., 180nn66, 74
Hooton, Elizabeth, 19, 144, 145, 193n13
Hunter, Cuthbert, 24

Ingle, H., 26, 70, 76, 171nn19, 20, 174nn86, 89, 176n137, 181nn85, 107
Ireton, Henry, 68
Irwin, Joyce, 193n8
Israel, Jonathan, 190n33
Israel, Menasseh ben, 18, 41, 104, 119–21, 125–37, 140, 165, 191nn55–60, 192n74

James II, 28, 55

Jessey, Henry, 125–26
Jones, Richard, 177n9
Jones, Rufus, 69, 173n47, 180n73

Katz, David, 129, 179n42, 180n50, 189nn10, 12–14, 21, 26, 190nn33, 35, 191nn49, 53
Kelly, Kevin, 182n4
Kirkby, Roger, 54
Kirkby, William, 54
Klaassen, W., 59, 177n8
Kunze, Bonnelyn, 5, 9–11, 25, 28, 30, 52, 82, 145, 170nn4, 6–8, 171nn11, 17, 172nn30, 31, 173n38, 175n100, 176nn127, 128, 130–32, 136, 137, 183n20, 190n38, 191nn60, 71–73, 194nn20, 21, 195nn29, 35

Lampitt, William, 26, 32, 35, 171n19
Larson, Rebecca, 9
Liechty, Daniel, 180n49
Liefeld, Walter, 193n3, 195n28, 197n88
Lightfoot, John, 124
Lilburne, John, 68–70, 180n70
Loades, David, 178n22
Luther, Martin, 59–60, 64, 80, 143, 179n44, 182nn7–9

Mack, Phyllis, 5, 12, 31, 144, 154–55, 173n43, 193nn3, 9, 10, 15, 196nn58–60
Mann, J., 190n34
Manners, Emily, 193n12
Manning, Brian, 68, 180nn67, 69
Manuel, F., 178n17
Marguerite of Navarre, 18, 142–43
McGinn, B., 59, 60, 177n7
McGregor, J. F., 177n4, 180n67, 181nn77, 86, 95
Meade, William, 54
Mede, Joseph, 16, 62–63, 179n26
Mendelson, Sarah, 193n3

Montezinos, Antonio de, 129
Moore, Rosemary, 156, 196n68, 197n70
Moore, Thomas, 38
More, Thomas, 25
Morgan, Nicholas, 22, 29, 38, 41, 49, 170n1, 171n7, 172nn26, 32, 174nn69, 70, 87, 89, 175nn95, 99, 116, 176nn125, 148, 177nn154–56
Morton, A., 177n6, 181n84
Mounsey, Thomas (T. M.), 171n11

Napier, John, 179n26
Nayler, James, 2, 9, 71–75, 133, 146, 156–57, 161, 174n61, 194n27, 196nn68, 69
Newton, Isaac, 61, 178n16

Oberman, Heiko, 179n44, 189n5, 192n93
Olsen, V., 179nn30, 38–40
Overton, Richard, 180n70

Parkes, James, 188n2, 189n8
Peat, Timothy, 187n180, 193n1, 195n56, 197n89
Penn, William, 10, 53, 55, 58, 195n30, 196n66
Penney, Norman, 176n129
Pococke, Edward, 124
Popkin, Richard, 128, 188n1, 189nn18, 27, 190n43, 191nn57, 61, 67, 69, 195n27
Porter, Henry, 44
Punshon, John, 24, 171n8

Rawlinson, Thomas, 10
Reay, B., 177n4, 180n67, 181nn77, 86, 95
Rijn, Rembrandt van, 128
Roberts, Arthur, 181n87, 88, 96, 100, 103, 106, 196n67, 197nn71, 72
Robertson, D., 180n70

Rogers, P., 179n32, 181nn81, 82
Ross, Isabel, 4, 8–10, 26, 30, 53, 170nn4, 5, 171nn11, 13, 22, 172nn25, 29, 173n39, 174nn83, 84, 175nn100, 106, 114, 118, 176nn122, 127, 137–39, 143–46, 177nn149, 152, 191nn68, 71, 73, 194nn14, 22, 24, 26, 195nn30–32
Roth, Cecil, 124, 128, 129, 189nn15–17, 19, 190nn30, 32, 36, 39–42, 44, 191nn46–47, 50, 52–56, 58–59

Sawrey, John, 26, 39–40, 171n23
Sevi, Shabtai, 124, 189n20
Shakespeare, William, 122
Shaw, Howard, 59, 177n5
Smith, C., 179n45
Spinoza, Baruch, 120
St. Clair, Michael, 175n97
Story, John, 51, 147
Stuard, Susan, 194n23
Stubbs, John, 191n63

Taylor, Ernest, 174n66
Toon, Peter, 179n27, 180n48, 189nn20, 23–25, 190nn29, 31, 191n51
Trachtenberg, Joshua, 121, 188nn3, 4, 189n6
Traill, H., 190n34
Traske, Dorothy, 64–65
Traske, John, 64–65, 123
Trevett, Christine, 5, 25, 37, 145, 155, 171n16, 172n35, 174n68, 176n140, 193n13, 194n17, 196nn60, 61

Tucker, Ruth, 146, 193n3, 195n28, 197n88

Van den Berg, J., 190n28
Van der Wall, E., 190nn28, 33
Venner, Richard, 44
Vipont, Elfrida, 174n66

Wakefield, Robert, 122, 189n10
Wakefield, Thomas, 122
Walwyn, William, 192nn70, 75
Ward, Mary, 143, 193n7
Warnicke, Retha, 193nn3, 7
Webb, Maria, 7, 169n3, 171n11
Weddle, Meredith, 156, 196n63, 65, 66
West, Colonel, 72
Wilcox, Catherine, 75, 145, 153, 154, 181n102, 194n17, 195nn39, 52, 53, 55, 196n60
Wildman, John, 180n70
Wilkenson, John, 51, 147
William and Mary of Orange, 55; *see also* William III
William III, 55–56, 81
Williams, George, 179n43
Wilson, Katharina, 193n6
Winstanley, Gerrard, 70
Wycliffe, John, 63, 178n19
Wyndham, Hugh, 24

Ximines de Cisneros, Francisco, 189n18

Yeamans, Isabel Fell, 53

Zachman, Randall, 182n7

# Index of Doctrine

*Key terms in Christian doctrine as they are used in the theology of Margaret Fell*

Adam, Adamic, 85, 96, 100, 102, 149
Antichrist, 40, 99, 152
Apocalyptic, 1, 2, 39, 40, 46, 47, 71–76, 99, 119, 150, 161, 164, 165

Baptism: *see* forms, outward
Bible: *see* Scripture

Children of [the] Light, 24, 75, 85, 90, 99–101, 109, 113, 116, 136, 150, 152, 158
chiliastic, chiliasm: *see* millennium
Christ (Light of Christ, Light that is Christ, Messiah), 3, 6, 16, 17, 20, 21, 39–48, 80–117, 120, 124, 133–40, 148–54, 160–62, 164–67
Church (Body of Christ, Bride of Christ), 16, 40, 41, 54, 107–16, 150–52
conscience, 3, 16–17, 21, 79–81, 87–96, 107, 138, 161
conversion: *see* convincement
convincement, 3, 90–91, 164
covenant, spiritual (new), 86–87, 91–92, 102, 110, 115, 133, 138–39
creation, 73, 84, 97

darkness, kingdom or powers of (devil's kingdom, domain of Satan, Babylon), 72, 75, 93, 99–102, 105–6, 111, 152
Day of the Lord: *see* Last Day
devil: *see* Satan

elect, election, 96–97
End Times: *see* Last Days
eschatology, 6–7, 17–19, 87, 99–106, 110, 141, 149–57, 161–67
Eve, 46, 149–51

faith, 43, 95–96
Fall, 93, 99–101
forms, outward (dead forms, empty forms), 21, 40, 91–93, 102, 107–8, 111, 115, 165
Friends (Society of Friends), 34–56, 77–117, 131–34, 141–67

God: *see* Trinity; Light, Inward
God the Father (the Creator), 20, 82–86, 90, 100
God the Son (Son of God), 82–87

holiness: *see* sanctification
Holy City: *see* New Jerusalem

Holy Seed: *see* Seed of God
Holy Spirit (Holy Ghost, Comforter), 20, 81–92, 114, 154

idolatry, 100, 111, 116
Inward Light: *see* Light, Inward

Jesus Christ: *see* Christ
Jews (Jewish People, Hebrew People, Jewry), 17–18, 131–40, 165–66

kingdom of God (reign of Christ, kingdom of Christ), 100–104, 133

Lamb's War, 19, 157, 161
Last Days (Day of Judgment, Second Coming, Day of the Lord), 17, 40–41, 46, 87–88, 99–107, 124–25, 133, 149–52, 161–62
law, Mosaic (outward law), 84–91, 102, 123, 133, 137–39
Light, Inward (The Light, Light that is Christ), 16–21, 77–116, 133–40, 153–54, 164–66; *see also* conscience
Lord's Supper: *see* forms, outward

Messiah: *see* Christ
millennium, millennialism (chiliastic, millenarian), 15, 41–42, 74, 76, 124, 140

New Jerusalem, 54, 101, 104–5

outward forms: *see* forms, outward

pacifism: *see* peace testimony
peace testimony (pacifism), 19, 73–74, 155–62
perfection, perfecting, 97–99, 106
prophesy, prophesying, 48, 147–52

Quakers: *see* Friends

resurrection, 84–85, 93, 97, 116, 151
righteousness, 94–95, 99–100

sacrament: *see* forms, outward
salvation (soteriology), 16–17, 90–100, 106, 133, 139, 165
sanctification (holiness), 95–98, 107
Satan (serpent), 72, 75, 92, 99–101, 150, 152, 160–61
Scripture, 47–48, 78, 82, 88–90, 101–3, 110, 132, 140, 147–48, 153
Second Coming of Christ: *see* Last Days
Seed of God (Holy Seed), 46, 88, 90, 149–50
sin: *see* Fall
Spirit of Christ: *see* Holy Spirit

That of God: *see* conscience
thousand-year reign of Christ: *see* millennium
Trinity (Godhead), 16–17, 20, 81–83, 87, 154, 164–65

women's ministry, 19, 48, 145–55